ARCHBISHOP FISHER, 1945–1961

The Archbishops of Canterbury Series

Series Editor: Andrew Chandler, University of Chichester UK

Series Advisory Board: Professor Katy Cubitt (University of York); Professor Anne Duggan (King's College, London); Professor Sally Vaughn (University of Houston); Dr Julia Barrow (University of Nottingham); Professor Robert Swanson (University of Birmingham); Professor Diarmaid McCulloch (University of Oxford); Professor Alexandra Walsham (University of Cambridge); Dr Judith Maltby (University of Oxford); Professor Jeremy Gregory (University of Manchester); Professor Stephen Taylor (University of Reading); Professor Arthur Burns (King's College, London); Professor David Hein (Hood College)

Developed in association with Lambeth Palace Library archives, this series presents authoritative studies on the Archbishops of Canterbury. Each book combines biographical, historical, theological, social and political analysis within each archiepiscopacy, with original source material drawn from the Archbishop's correspondence, speeches and published and unpublished writings. The *Archbishops of Canterbury* series offers a vital source of reference, of lasting importance to scholars, students and all readers interested in the history of the international Church.

Other titles in this series:

Archbishop Anselm 1093–1109
Bec Missionary, Canterbury Primate, Patriarch of Another World
Sally N. Vaughn

Archbishops Ralph d'Escures, William of Corbeil and Theobald of Bec
Heirs of Anselm and Ancestors of Becket
Jean Truax

Archbishop Fisher, 1945–1961

Church, State and World

ANDREW CHANDLER

and

DAVID HEIN

ASHGATE

Published by
Ashgate Publishing Limited
Wey Court East
Union Road
Farnham
Surrey, GU9 7PT
England

Ashgate Publishing Company
Suite 420
101 Cherry Street
Burlington
VT 05401-4405
USA

www.ashgate.com

British Library Cataloguing in Publication Data
Hein, David, Prof.
  Archbishop Fisher, 1945-1961 : church, state and world
  -- (The Archbishops of Canterbury series)
  1. Fisher of Lambeth, Geoffrey Francis Fisher, Baron, 1887-1972.
  2. Fisher of Lambeth, Geoffrey Francis Fisher, Baron, 1887-1972--Political and social views.
  3. Church of   England. Province of Canterbury. Archbishop (1945-1961 : Fisher)
  4. Bishops--England--Biography.
  I. Title II. Series III. Chandler, Andrew.
  283'.092-dc23

Library of Congress Cataloging-in-Publication Data
Chandler, Andrew.
  Archbishop Fisher, 1945-1961 : church, state and world / Andrew Chandler
and David Hein.
      p. cm. -- (The archbishops of Canterbury series)
  Includes bibliographical references (p.   ) and index.
   ISBN 978-1-4094-1232-8 (hardcover) -- ISBN 978-1-4094-1233-5 (pbk.)
  -- ISBN 978-1-4094-4748-1 (ebook) 1. Fisher of Lambeth, Geoffrey Francis Fisher, Baron, 1887-1972.
  2. Church of England--Bishops--Biography. 3. Anglican Communion--Bishops--Biography.
  4.Religion and politics--Great Britain. 5. Ecumenical movement. I. Hein,
David, Prof. II. Title.
  BX5199.F57C43 2011
  283.092--dc23
  [B]

                                                                              2011050814

ISBN 9781409412328 (hbk)
ISBN 9781409412335 (pbk)
ISBN 9781409447481 (ebk)

Printed and bound in Great Britain by the
MPG Books Group, UK

Contents

Foreword and Acknowledgements

The origins of this book lie in the early days of the Ashgate Archbishops of Canterbury series. David Hein's earlier study for the Princeton Theological monographs, *Geoffrey Fisher: Archbishop of Canterbury, 1945–1961*, here provides a foundation for a substantially new, collaborative study. Work on the present volume has also offered both authors a timely opportunity to incorporate a variety of new material, not least Alan Webster's authoritative entry on Fisher in the new *Oxford Dictionary of National Biography*. It has also reinforced our sense of how much is owed to the great labors of Edward Carpenter, a fine and generous scholar who became Fisher's 'standard' biographer.

We are grateful to The Trustees of Lambeth Palace Library for permission to present material from the papers of Archbishop Fisher and to all staff there for their kindness in assisting enquiries. We are also indebted to the librarians at Hood College and at the University of Chichester for their help at every turn.

Special thanks are owed to the Historical Society of the Episcopal Church for a research grant in support of the project.

We are particularly grateful to our editor at Ashgate, Sarah Lloyd, for the support, confidence, and patience that she has shown throughout the writing of this book, and also, Caroline Spender of Ashgate Publishing.

PART I
Life

Introduction:
Out of the Ruins ...

The 98th Primate of All England, William Temple, died in 1944, and the following year Winston Churchill named Geoffrey Fisher as his successor in the Chair of St Augustine of Canterbury. The prime minister's choice proved controversial, however, because another man, Bishop George Bell of Chichester, looked to many the wiser appointment. What was indisputable was the severity of the challenges that the new archbishop would face. The Second World War would soon be over, and then the mammoth project of rebuilding would commence in earnest. For both the church and the nation, this effort of reconstruction would be spiritual as well as material.

The facts of the situation were bald enough. The country was heavily in debt and dependent on a large, though not indulgent, American loan. Many cities had been bombed, some of them severely. More than a million houses in London had been damaged or destroyed outright. At least one city, Coventry, had seen its cathedral razed to the ground. Much of the population was displaced. The infrastructure was hard-driven, if not worn out. The churches, too, were battered but hopeful. The Church of England was ostensibly led by bishops who by and large had little clear idea of what they were supposed to be doing, though some of them did whatever they decided upon well. Some were industrious, others were simply enigmatic.

Few if any historians could evoke the postwar mood or depict the moral and physical ruins of civilization as effectively as the English novelist Rose Macaulay in her 1950 novel, *The World My Wilderness*, set in the years just following the Second World War.[1] In this book the author expresses in a clear and moving way her fears about the future of British society. This novel, she said, 'is about the ruins of the City [the business center of London], and the general wreckage of the world that they seem to stand for. And about a rather lost and strayed and derelict girl who made them her spiritual home'.[2] Although only 17 (and the daughter of a King's Counsel), this central figure, Barbary, is already barbarous:

---

[1]   Rose Macaulay, *The World My Wilderness* (1950; reprint, London: Virago, 1983). Hereinafter cited within the text.

[2]   Rose Macaulay, *Letters to a Friend, 1950–1952*, ed. Constance Babington-Smith (New York: Atheneum, 1962), p. 27.

wild, intractable, given to acts of defiance and petty theft. "'Civilised ...'" Barbary
seemed to examine civilisation, balancing it gravely, perhaps wistfully, against
something else, and to reject it, as if it were mentioned too late' (33). The child
of a broken home, during the war she had lived in the South of France with her
beautiful, intelligent, idle, pleasure-loving mother, whose notion of parental love
did not entail a heavy investment in adult supervision.

As a member of a band of boys and girls assisting the Maquis during the
Occupation, Barbary was brutally and far too rapidly transformed from a child
of innocence into a child of experience. After the war, living in London, she
remains somewhat of an anarchist, preferring to live amid 'the ruined waste
lands ... the broken walls and foundations ... the roofless, gaping churches,
the stone flights of stairs climbing high into emptiness' (61). These places, she
feels, are where she belongs: at 'the waste margins of civilisation ..., where other
outcasts lurked, and questions were not asked' (110).

In this novel, Rose Macaulay was shining the light of her torch on the
spiritual wreckage of postwar Britain – on the desolate areas of both cities and
souls which leaders such as Geoffrey Fisher would have to search out and tend
to. In a violent and treacherous world, one that bears a growing resemblance
to a moral wasteland, Macaulay was asking: how many Barbarys might we be
producing? How many children may be growing up too fast, lacking adequate
care and security, and hence rootless, sullen, suspicious and defiant? This novel
is full of compassion toward all of its characters, but especially toward Barbary,
who, as one literary scholar wrote in summarizing the author's attitude toward
her creation, 'is thoroughly lost, thoroughly pathetic, and very much worth
saving'.[3]

Toward the end of *The World My Wilderness*, Macaulay appears to raise a
final question: Does the church have a role to play in this work of rebuilding?
While Barbary's only religious belief is 'in hell' (174), her half-brother Richie –
who fought in the war, endured three years in a German prisoner of war camp,
escaped, and now desires only the beauty and refinement of 'aristocratic culture'
(150) – is drawn to the church. But the lure appears to be largely aesthetic and
nostalgic: 'In this pursuit he was impelled sometimes beyond his reasoning self,
to grasp at the rich ... panoplies, the swinging censors, of churches from whose
creeds and uses he was alien, because at least they embodied some continuance,
some tradition' (150). In the last pages of the novel, however, Richie literally
takes steps toward the church, possibly reflecting a deeper quest for order and
meaning in his life and in the lives of others. Fully conscious of the barbarian

---

[3]   Harvey Curtis Webster, *After the Trauma: Representative British Novelists since 1920*
(Lexington: University Press of Kentucky, 1970), p. 27.

threat ('the primeval chaos and old night'), he murmurs to himself T.S. Eliot's words from *The Wasteland*: 'We are in rats' alleys, where the dead men lost their bones' (253). Then, '[s]huddering a little, he took the track across the wilderness and towards St. Paul's [Cathedral]. Behind him, the questionable chaos of broken courts and inns lay sprawled under the October mist, and the shells of churches gaped like lost myths, and the jungle pressed in on them, seeking to cover them up' (253–4).

What the church received with the appointment of Geoffrey Fisher to the see of Canterbury was, at the very least, a man of strength, discipline and tenacity – indeed, a former headmaster – who would not readily submit either to primeval or to ecclesiastical chaos. Everything that he did was connected to the service of one overriding goal: building up the church, and thereby enlarging the clearing in the wilderness. Overshadowed both by his famous predecessor, the philosopher and ecumenist William Temple, and by his widely loved successor, the theologian and spiritual guide Michael Ramsey, Geoffrey Francis Fisher (1887–1972), 99th archbishop of Canterbury, has tended to be ignored by professional historians. But in fact his was a pivotal archiepiscopate, one that cries out for fresh examination. Not least was it the case that so many of the problems and initiatives of his tenure anticipated the major events in Anglican church history and theology in the decades that followed.

Fisher's period in office began and ended with the bridge-building work of ecumenism. Preaching at Cambridge in 1946, he urged the Church of England and the Free Churches to work toward establishing 'full communion': sharing the sacraments with one another but stopping short of complete union. And in 1960, at the end of his tenure in office, Fisher embarked on a tour that included stops in Jerusalem, Istanbul, and Rome. His meeting with Pope John XXIII marked the first time that an archbishop of Canterbury had visited the Holy See since Archbishop Thomas Arundel undertook the journey in 1397. Fisher was also the key person in building up the modern Anglican Communion. In the 1950s his trips to West Africa, Central Africa and East Africa were major parts of his successful effort to establish new provinces within the Communion. Indeed, his work anticipated the transformation of the British Empire from a far-flung imperial domain into a commonwealth of sovereign states. His frequent visits to Canada and the United States, coupled with his efforts to include the American bishops and others in the deliberations of the Lambeth Conference, helped to make the Anglican Communion an experienced reality for many Anglicans and Episcopalians outside Britain.

Of particular interest, too, is the relationship between the Church of England and the nation. The senior prelate whom millions of people around the world watched as he conducted the coronation ceremony for Queen Elizabeth II in

June 1953, Fisher has been referred to as the last archbishop of Canterbury to oversee the workings of a great Establishment church. After him, British society and the churches were forced to change, responding to increased immigration, religious pluralism and secularization. It was solidly in the context of the Establishment, too, that Fisher intervened in political affairs: in the Suez Crisis of 1956, in debates on the use of atomic weapons, and in his strong sense of the pervasive responsibility of the Established Church within national society. All of this offers an important opportunity to discern the positive as well as the negative aspects of that Establishment. This commitment influenced not only his responses (sometimes supportive, often critical) to government initiatives but also his understanding of the place of the Church of England in relation to the other churches.

Fisher's time in London, first as bishop of London (1939–45) and then as archbishop of Canterbury, was a period of war, devastation and rebuilding in the capital city and the nation. How well did Fisher prepare the Church of England for what followed? What were the strengths and weaknesses of his approach to the task of fortifying the church – and the Anglican Communion – for the future? What were his personal strengths and weaknesses as a leader for this crucial time in the history of Christian institutions? What kind of an ecclesiastical statesman was he? This time of both reconstruction and fresh initiatives was a bridge period for the church. One aspect of his work that should attract our attention is not only what an archbishop of Canterbury can do during such a time but also what he chooses not to do. It is fundamentally important to see what an administrator of Fisher's ability was actually able to accomplish, both in his own distinctive right and in working hard to bring about conditions within which diverse men and women could flourish. Fisher's tenure represents a distinctive approach to the office. His was not only a particularly significant archiepiscopate, one in which the central issues of his time and place are reflected. It was also a tenure that emphasized the archbishop as chief executive of a large and complex organization. Fisher personified one major way of inhabiting his role: the archbishop as administrator.

Through his example, then, we can gain some perspective on both the positive and the negative features of this archiepiscopal modus operandi, both in his own day and for succeeding generations. Being a highly competent administrator means more than being an efficient manager. It requires thoughtful strategic planning as well as day-to-day administration. But this style of leadership may result in a loss of personal stature, influence, and memorability if the archbishop's focus is largely on structure rather than on qualities of mind and spirit: if, in other words, the archbishop is not also known – and effective – as an intellectual force, a social prophet, or a wise spiritual teacher. The subject of this biography does suggest an irony: Geoffrey Fisher may well have been a more competent archbishop than either his successor or his predecessor, but somehow they are the ones whom later generations of church commentators, theologians, or aficionados of spirituality are more likely to remember. Perhaps this does something to justify the distinctive role of the historian in seeking to influence the ongoing reflections which inform the diverse perspectives and priorities of church life.

For most people in the United Kingdom, life at the end of the Fisher era at Lambeth looked very different from the way it did at the inception of his archiepiscopate. Probably to many outside observers the Church of England did not seem to change very much in the traditionalist 1950s, but no one could fail to remark that society as a whole was undergoing a significant transformation. In financial terms alone, the British people by 1961 were significantly better off than they had been in 1946, and they had reason to hope for continued gains. Greater purchasing power brought with it widespread access to labour-saving appliances as well as to automobiles and television sets. It was the beginning of a new, more prosperous era, with fewer restrictions and more freedom in all areas of life. But it was also an age that generated a fresh wave of anxieties about meaning, order and security.

In all of this the writer Rose Macaulay, a figure altogether very unlike Fisher, remains a striking guide. While *The World My Wilderness*, published in 1950, was very much a postwar novel, her last book, *The Towers of Trebizond*, published six years later, already anticipates the mood of the 1960s. Despite the seriousness of its leading themes, this later novel offers a much jauntier tone than the earlier work, which is unremittingly bleak. And *Trebizond* presents the religious questions even more squarely. Indeed, its main subject is the relation of faith and doubt in this exciting but rather frightening new era, when new possibilities were beginning to open up and old patterns of life were breaking apart. The central character in the novel is a young woman named Laurie, who likens the Church of England to 'a great empire on its way out, that holds its subjects by poetic force ... [T]hough for ever reeling, the towers [representing the church] do not fall ...'.[4]

Upon leaving office and going into retirement, Geoffrey Fisher did not see the church as being 'on its way out'. He said, 'I leave the Church of England in good heart'.[5] But the historian and theologian Adrian Hastings raises an intriguing

---

[4]   Rose Macaulay, *The Towers of Trebizond* (1956; reprint, New York: New York Review Books, 2003), p. 234. See David Hein, 'Rose Macaulay: A Voice from the Edge', in David Hein and Edward Henderson (eds.), *C.S. Lewis and Friends* (London, 2011), pp. 93–115.

[5]   Quoted in Adrian Hastings, *A History of English Christianity, 1920–2000* (London: SCM Press, 2001), p. 452.

point when he observes that several women writers of this period – not only Rose Macaulay but also Barbara Pym (in *A Glass of Blessings*), Iris Murdoch (in *The Bell*), and Pamela Hansford Johnson (in *The Humbler Creation*) – were producing novels with a different (and more accurate?) take on contemporary Anglican life and the future of the Church of England. The 1950s, Hastings writes, were a 'rather Anglican decade, and Anglican of a benignly conservative hue'. That was the Fisher era, reflected in each of these novels, where 'the Church appears on the surface as a relatively prospering institution with a decidedly traditionalist orientation'.[6] But in the view of all four of these novelists, 'A Church apparently very much in business turns out in each case to be ... worm-eaten .... [T]he impression given is one of a nice, rather ineffectual, socially respectable but bewildered rump not far off its last legs'.[7]

Hastings intimates little by way of appraisal of these writers' impressions. At this point in his narrative, his contribution to ecclesiastical history is neither to endorse nor to oppose their views but simply to ferret out and to highlight these fictional accounts, giving his readers the opportunity to consider what truth might be contained therein. Within the limited terms of the present study – and even though it might be to scrutinize his primacy from a perspective which Geoffrey Fisher would have struggled to imagine for himself – we might keep these novels in mind.

---

6   Hastings, *History*, pp. 451–2.
7   Ibid., p. 452.

Chapter 1
Formation, 1887–1932

Geoffrey Francis Fisher was, by and large, an uncomplicated man. Neither enticed by rebellion nor drawn by doubt, he was conservative and consistent, a loyal and devoted churchman. His considerable powers, both intellectual and physical, were steadily and happily employed in the service of established institutions. Self-aware without being self-absorbed, he would have recognized the applicability to his own case of the Romantic poet William Wordsworth's famous dictum that 'The Child is father of the Man', for such a dictum evoked the trajectory of his life from birth: the clerical forebears, the village rectory, the parish church, the intelligent and contented child, the purposeful young clergyman – and then steady advancement, largely unsought. Prepared over generations and seasoned beyond his years, Fisher already possessed, at the age of 27, sufficient gravitas to convince others that he had the necessary equipment to rule with authority. Years later, as archbishop of Canterbury, he remained, observers noted, very much the headmaster: a good, effective head, but still the lawgiving administrator.

A consistency of character and outlook marks his life, then, just as a certain consistency or conservatism marks this era in the history of the Church of England – and especially the Fisher years at Lambeth – before the tumultuous 1960s. Thus the first chapter of this book, perhaps to an unusual degree for a biographical study, delineates the contours of what follows in succeeding chapters. In a sense, there are no surprises after this first chapter, for all that Fisher did was rooted in the core convictions that he acquired in his formative years. At the same time, however, a career path is not a cross-country course; the vagaries of even a conservative human nature and the play of chance wreak havoc with predictions. In the case of Geoffrey Fisher, intelligence and initiative, yoked with determination and drive, were essential ingredients of his makeup, developments of the personal and social capital acquired during his youth. At the start of his public career, therefore, no one could say for certain either what challenges time and circumstance would confront him with or what use he would make of the opportunities that providence or fortune set before him. But the early years provide strong clues.

Higham-on-the-Hill, Leicestershire

A remarkable consistency marks Geoffrey Fisher's family background. In 1772 his great-grandfather, a clergyman by the name of John Fisher, was appointed to the benefice (an endowed church office providing a living) of Higham-on-the-Hill. Three miles from the market town of Nuneaton, Higham was then a small agricultural village of some three or four hundred people in Leicestershire, a county in central England that lies east of Birmingham and northeast of Coventry. He held this benefice until his death 60 years later. As the living was in the gift of the family, it could be handed down from one generation to the next. Eventually John Fisher's son and his grandson – as well as his great-grandson, Legh, one of Geoffrey's elder brothers – would hold the same position, ministering to this small Midlands community.[1] In the temporal lot he drew, Geoffrey Fisher's father, Henry, who served the church of Higham-on-the-Hill for more than 40 years, was perhaps the most fortunate, because, as Edward Carpenter has observed, 'the rise in status of the rural parson [reached] its peak in the eighties when the rectory often became the centre of a revived village life'.[2]

Geoffrey Fisher was born at Higham on 5 May 1887, the youngest of 10 children. His mother, Katherine Richmond Fisher, he later recalled, was 'a very lovely, very handsome woman with a great presence'.[3] With her, Fisher enjoyed a special bond. She had a good sense of humour, enjoyed playing games with her children, and ran the rectory effectively, becoming its emotional centre.[4] Her youngest child called her 'the presiding genius' of his childhood home, 'a great stronghold in the whole life of the house'.[5] Born at Higham-on-the-Hill in 1837 and educated at Jesus College, Cambridge University, Fisher's father in middle age was a spare, shy, industrious man. On behalf of the denizens of both the village and the countryside, he was comfortable and conscientious in carrying out his duties. As a preacher, however, he tended to be long-winded and uninspiring, except on those occasions when he became too excited in the pulpit.[6] Undoubtedly, his parishioners, like sermon auditors everywhere, would have preferred to listen to better preaching. But it is important to remember that the Anglicanism of the Victorian rural village was a distinctive form of Christianity, whose centre was not necessarily the Sunday-morning sermon.

---

[1] Bernard Palmer, *A Class of Their Own: Six Public School Headmasters Who Became Archbishop of Canterbury* (Lewes, 1997), p. 153.

[2] Edward Carpenter, *Archbishop Fisher: His Life and Times* (Norwich, 1991), p. 4.

[3] Quoted in William Purcell, *Fisher of Lambeth: A Portrait from Life* (London, 1969), p. 30.

[4] Carpenter, *Archbishop Fisher*, p. 5.

[5] Quoted in Carpenter, *Archbishop Fisher*, p. 5.

[6] Ibid.

It was a far cry, for example, from today's neo-evangelical megachurch, for whom the minister is, first and foremost, an engaging preacher: everything in that style of worship leads up to and follows from the proclamation of the message. Although he may have been more Protestant than Catholic in his Anglican sensibilities, Geoffrey Fisher never viewed the role of the clergyman in such restrictive terms. In his father's practice in the environs of Higham, he would have seen the priest as a minister who spreads the evangel by living a particular kind of life within the community. Ideally, the clergyman would instantiate in his own person the truths of his faith and the virtues of daily living, teaching by example as much as by precept. This approach to ministry was part of a characteristically Anglican understanding of the duties of a priest. It stressed personal engagement, pastoral care and prayer: the clergyman as mediator and exemplar.[7] An Anglican priest could best be depicted, then, not primarily as a preacher but as a *parson*, whose value depended upon the quality of his person. As the eighteenth-century legal scholar William Blackstone wrote in his famous *Commentaries*, a priest 'is called parson, *persona*, because by his person the church, which is an invisible body, is represented'.[8]

Typically in this era the parish church was the centre of the community, and this was the case at Higham.[9] As A.N. Wilson notes, the local church was the 'place where communities gathered – partly for worship, partly for music, ribaldry, and gossip, partly for nebulous reasons which did not need to be defined'; and this habitual use of the church went on long 'after the box pews were removed'.[10] Of course, far too often the village parson did not match the ideal but instead was ill trained, indolent, focused more on cricket than on theology, and therefore roundly ineffectual. In many instances if parishioners went to church for a religious reason it was not to hear good preaching but rather, as Adrian Hastings says, 'to draw some spark of inspiration from the Cranmerian vocabulary of a sung matins, from pillars and vaults and monuments, but seldom from the clergy'.[11]

---

[7] David Hein, *Noble Powell and the Episcopal Establishment in the Twentieth Century* (Urbana, 2001), p. 4.

[8] William Blackstone, *Commentaries on the Laws of England* (1765; reprint, New York: Oceana, 1966), p. 1: 372.

[9] '[T]he parish church of Higham on the Hill and its local school exercised an influence which the two Methodist chapels could not rival'. Carpenter, *Archbishop Fisher*, p. 344.

[10] A.N. Wilson, *After the Victorians: The Decline of Britain in the World* (New York, 2005), p. 305.

[11] Adrian Hastings, *A History of English Christianity, 1920–2000* (London: SCM Press, 2001), p. 71.

In fine, the Fishers were a family well integrated into this little community of Higham-on-the-Hill, which was, as Geoffrey Fisher later said, 'the background and the life-blood of everything'.[12] That is, the quality of community itself was the vital element that coursed through the overlapping social spheres in which young Fisher found himself. As sources of meaning and identity, these circles of association were formative of the future archbishop. To use his phrases, there were 'the community and my family in the rectory', 'the community of the village and all its doings' and 'the community of the church in which all of us had our place'.[13] Throughout his life and professional career, Geoffrey Fisher would find fulfillment – and seek fulfillment for others – in appropriate structures. Like a good Burkean, he carried deep in his bones the belief that order is the only environment within which true freedom can thrive and human beings can flourish. By both nature and nurture, he was bred to believe in arrangements in which everyone could find his or her place.

Education

After a brief stay in the Higham village school, Geoffrey Fisher – aged eight – went to Lindley Lodge, a local preparatory school of 40 boys. Located within walking distance of the rectory, this school was his academic home for six years. His record during his first term was poor, but he worked hard to shore up areas in which he was initially weak. He eventually rose to the top of the school in Latin, Greek, French, English, and mathematics. At Lindley Lodge, he received a good preparatory education, he learned how to take responsibility for boys placed in his charge, and he worked hard at sports even when he had little natural aptitude for them.[14] In September 1901, at the age of 14, he entered Marlborough College, in Wiltshire (a county in southern England), on a foundation scholarship. Established to provide an education for the sons of clergymen, this public school had opened in 1843. Here Geoffrey Fisher excelled – as scholar, as student leader (he made a brave and resolute senior prefect), and even as young Christian. He apparently never experienced a spiritual crisis; the religion of his youth and young adulthood was in important respects continuous with the faith in which he was raised. 'I learned', he later said of these years, 'how to tackle everything that came along in what I now recognize was an intelligent Christian way, not borrowing from Christ, but translating into my daily duties

---

[12]   Quoted in Purcell, *Fisher of Lambeth*, p. 29.

[13]   Quoted in Carpenter, *Archbishop Fisher*, p. 7.

[14]   Carpenter, *Archbishop Fisher*, pp. 6–7.

and occupations and pleasures the spirit which flowed from His revelation of the Kingdom of God'.[15]

From Marlborough, Geoffrey went up to Oxford on a scholarship in October 1906. His college, Exeter, had been founded in 1314 by Walter de Stapeldon, bishop of Exeter (who, 12 years later, was murdered by a London mob). By Geoffrey Fisher's time, Exeter College had 182 students and eight Fellows. Anglican tradition still predominated there. The rector of Exeter College was a priest, W.W. Jackson, and students were required to attend one Sunday service in the chapel and four weekday services.[16] Fisher acquitted himself well at Oxford, becoming president of the junior common room, a fine athlete (he was captain of his college boat club and was given his colours for rugby), and an outstanding student. He went down with a 'triple first', having gained first classes in Mods (Classical Moderations: Greek and Latin literature) in 1908, in Greats (*Literae Humaniores*: philosophy and ancient history) in 1910, and in theology in 1911. Fisher always had a good, clear head, but he seems never to have had a particularly adventurous or curious mind – which is itself rather curious in someone so bright.[17] He was simply not attracted by intellectual questions, such as current debates in biblical criticism, or prone to challenge received opinion, at least past a certain point. He had, one might say, the right sort of intelligence for the practical problems of administration. He would not have made a first-rate scholar, however, for scholars must be intellectually imaginative and also persistently dissatisfied, even skeptical, in a way that Fisher never was.

But Geoffrey Fisher did have an imagination for friendship. While at Oxford he became a good friend of the eccentric Anglo-Catholic theologian N.P. Williams, Fellow and Chaplain of Exeter (and, from 1927, Lady Margaret Professor of Divinity and Canon of Christ Church). Fisher later recalled this man who was intellectually, theologically, and temperamentally so different from himself: Williams 'was a very great scholar'. But he was also 'a very shy, frightened man who crept about the College, and when you talked to him he kept his eyes almost shut. He had a queer way of speaking as though he was saying prunes and prisms all the time'.[18] Theologically, Fisher was more drawn to the evangelicals, although he did not share their enthusiasm for emotional conversion experiences. As a budding ecumenist, he was attracted to the efforts of those men – especially John R. Mott (1865–1955) and Joseph Oldham

---

[15]   Quoted in Carpenter, *Archbishop Fisher*, p. 10.

[16]   Carpenter, *Archbishop Fisher*, p. 11.

[17]   Ibid., p. 12.

[18]   Quoted in Carpenter, *Archbishop Fisher*, p. 13. The quotation refers to the admonitions of Mrs General, a risible character in Charles Dickens' mature novel, *Little Dorrit* (1857).

(1874–1969) – who were working to draw the world's churches closer together in faith and mission.[19]

By the time Fisher left Oxford in the summer of 1911, he had observed the full range of church parties within Anglicanism. In churchmanship, he was then what he would be for the rest of his ecclesiastical days: a centrist, leaning slightly toward the Low Church Protestant wing, but – both by deep-seated personal inclination and on principle – averse to party affiliation. A prayer-book Anglican, he respected the best features of both the Protestant and the Catholic emphases within the church, but he disliked the problems that extremists on either wing could cause by their exclusivist notions that they had special keys to the truth. His own judgment was that the evangelicals and the Anglo-Catholics represented positions that were not contradictory but complementary – 'provided that', in his words, 'the holders of these views never allow themselves to become militant or political. That destroys everything'.[20]

Marlborough College (1911–1914)

Upon graduating, Geoffrey Fisher turned down offers from two colleges to begin his professional career in the University of Oxford. He knew that this sort of life was not the right one for him. He did not care to spend his time, as he put it, 'correcting somebody else's answers'; and he did not want to pursue a subject – academic theology – that would mean having 'to go on asking questions to which there was no answer'.[21] And so he accepted an offer from Frank Fletcher, the head of Marlborough College, to return to the school as a member of its teaching staff. Fletcher had been a significant influence on Geoffrey when he was a student there. A first-rate instructor, Fletcher encouraged his students to learn to think for themselves.[22]

Fisher spent three happy years at his *alma mater*, proving to be a successful teacher, an effective disciplinarian, and an eager participant in all aspects of school life. He had no thought of leaving or of doing anything else, no burning ambition to rise higher. But then something happened that, *mutatis mutandis*, would happen again 30 years later: William Temple's old job became available and Geoffrey Fisher emerged as a leading candidate to fill it. In 1914 the post was the headmastership of Repton, a top-tier British public school located in

---

[19]   Carpenter, *Archbishop Fisher*, p. 14.

[20]   Ibid., p. 14; Purcell, *Fisher of Lambeth*, p. 67 (quotation); Michael De-la-Noy, *Michael Ramsey: A Portrait* (London, 1990), p. 52.

[21]   Quoted in Carpenter, *Archbishop Fisher*, p. 15.

[22]   *DNB 1971–1980*, s.v. 'Fisher, Geoffrey Francis, Baron Fisher of Lambeth'.

Derbyshire, in central England. Founded as a charity school in 1557, by the middle of the nineteenth century it had become, in the words of one educational historian, 'a fee-paying school catering to the needs of a burgeoning, *arriviste* middle class'.[23]

William Temple had accepted a call to be rector of St. James's, Piccadilly, a prominent parish in London. When consulted by Geoffrey Fisher, both he and Frank Fletcher – now headmaster of Charterhouse – advised him to proceed with an application for the vacancy at Repton. In fact, both men had already discussed Fisher's potential as a headmaster and were keen on his appointment. After a fairly relaxed session with the school's governors, Fisher was offered the post. He accepted, and remained at the school for the next 18 years. Having been ordained deacon in 1912 and presbyter in 1913 after a short period of study (one term in the long vacation of 1911) at Wells Theological College, he was able to serve Repton as a priest-headmaster, a dual capacity that he believed essential to his ability to superintend all aspects of the school's life.[24]

Repton (1914–1932)

Only two months after his appointment as headmaster in June 1914, Geoffrey Fisher had to confront problems caused by the outbreak of the First World War: a diminished teaching staff, incompetent replacements, and anxiety and restlessness among the boys. Sixty of the older students had already left to join the army, and six masters had also volunteered for war service.[25] Fisher would have had enough to do merely finding his feet and taking on these special wartime challenges. But he also had to deal with the situation left behind by his predecessor, whose four years as headmaster were not an unalloyed success. William Temple had been a vital presence at Repton – religiously inspiring and intellectually stimulating – but he left the school with some serious deficiencies, particularly in the areas of organization and discipline. 'I doubt if headmastering is really my line', he admitted to his brother.[26]

---

[23]   Peter C. Gronn, 'An Experiment in Political Education: "V.G.", "Slimy" and the Repton Sixth, 1916–1918', *History of Education* 19 (1990), p. 2.

[24]   Carpenter, *Archbishop Fisher*, pp. 16–17, 26; Purcell, *Fisher of Lambeth*, p. 49; F.A. Iremonger, *William Temple, Archbishop of Canterbury: His Life and Letters* (Oxford, 1948), p. 154.

[25]   Palmer, *A Class of Their Own*, p. 157.

[26]   William Temple, letter to his brother, October 1910, quoted in Iremonger, *William Temple*, p. 128.

Relishing the mundane details of administrative tasks, Fisher plunged into the work of structural renovation. More so than most institutions, boarding schools live by their daily and weekly schedules. Like his predecessor, the new headmaster knew next to nothing about the natural sciences, but he recognized that science courses require not only reasonably up-to-date equipment but also sufficient time for laboratory experiments. Thus, he made sure that the labs were properly outfitted, and from the ground up he constructed a new timetable, one that incorporated double periods for lab exercises. He also moved quickly, by expulsions and by the promulgation and enforcement of carefully spelled-out rules, to restore order among the boys.[27] His own assured demeanour helped, for a headmaster could not be seen as wishy-washy. Just as Fisher made it clear to the boys who was on the right side in the world war ('[W]e are fighting for God's cause against the devil's'), so he had no difficulty making it clear who possessed sole authority to write and apply the rules.[28] In particular, during his first year, he moved ruthlessly to stamp out homosexual practices.[29] His actions, he believed, quickly transformed the school: 'Very soon', he said, 'so far as one could tell, the thing was gone; and years afterwards, after I had left, a parent who was a boy under me said to someone else, and it reached me, that in his day while there was dirty talk still, nobody would have dreamt of going any further than that'.[30]

An Old Reptonian, Roald Dahl, the author of *Charlie and the Chocolate Factory*, caused a Fisher-related sensation when he claimed in his 1984 memoir, *Boy: Tales of Childhood*, that Geoffrey Fisher had been a sadistic flogger while headmaster of Repton. In *Boy* Dahl remembers that '[t]he Headmaster ... struck me as being a rather shoddy bandy-legged little fellow with a big bald head and lots of energy but not much charm'. Probably many of the boys would have offered a similar description, but then Dahl goes on to say that Fisher 'used to deliver the most vicious beatings to the boys under his care'.[31] Dahl provided an example of one of these terrible incidents. His best friend, Michael, told him about a merciless beating he was subjected to by Fisher, who paused every now and then to fill and light his pipe and 'to lecture the kneeling boy about sin and wrongdoing'.[32] After the flogging, the story goes, Fisher handed 'the victim' a sponge, a basin, and a clean towel, and told him 'to wash away the blood before

27   Palmer, *A Class of Their Own*, p. 163; Carpenter, *Archbishop Fisher*, pp. 17–19; Purcell, *Fisher of Lambeth*, p. 54.

28   Carpenter, *Archbishop Fisher*, p. 18 (quotation), p. 19.

29   Palmer, *A Class of Their Own*, p. 158.

30   GF Papers, MS. 3467, fol. 37.

31   Roald Dahl, *Boy: Tales of Childhood* (New York, 1984), p. 130.

32   Ibid., p. 131.

pulling up his trousers'.[33] Dahl wrote that this brutal treatment caused him to 'begin to have doubts about religion and even about God. If this person, I kept telling myself, was one of God's chosen salesmen on earth, then there must be something very wrong about the whole business'. He could scarcely reconcile the Christian preacher of love with the ruthless headmaster: 'I would sit in the dim light of the school chapel and listen to him preaching about the Lamb of God and about Mercy and Forgiveness ... and my young mind would become totally confused', for he knew (or thought he knew) 'that only the night before this preacher had shown neither Forgiveness nor Mercy in flogging some small boy who had broken the rules'.[34]

Dahl's biographer, Jeremy Treglown, has pointed out, however, that the incident Dahl describes took place in May 1933, one year after Fisher left Repton. The headmaster that administered this beating was John T. Christie, Fisher's successor. 'If Dahl got his sadists mixed up', Treglown adds, 'he also gives the impression that the beating was purely arbitrary .... In fact, the offender, who was almost eighteen and a house prefect, had been caught in bed with a younger boy'.[35] Treglown notes that when Dahl's memoir came out, Archbishop Fisher was dead, but members of his family as well as many Old Reptonians were still alive, and they complained about the way in which Dahl had portrayed Fisher.[36] Treglown acknowledges, however, that Dahl may have had a point regarding the customary harshness of Fisher's methods: 'While some of [Dahl's] contemporaries remember Fisher as a great and good man', who was liked by all the boys, 'others say that even by the standards of the day he was a severe head'.[37] Treglown cites his interview with Stuart Hampshire, for example: 'Fisher was very strict, Hampshire says, if not abnormally so, judged by the standards of the time. "He was very unfeeling and illiberal", and he certainly beat boys excessively – "by which I don't mean too often but too hard"'.[38] The next headmaster, Christie, is remembered as having been much worse than Fisher. Following

---

[33]   Ibid., p. 132.

[34]   Ibid.

[35]   Jeremy Treglown, *Roald Dahl: A Biography* (New York, 1994), pp. 24–5.

[36]   In a book published in 1997, Palmer notes that '[t]he incorrect [i.e., Dahl's] version of the story had caused a minor sensation on its appearance ten years earlier [than the publication of Treglown's biography of Dahl]. Members of the Archbishop's family had been justifiably outraged at this slur on his memory, and they and a number of Old Reptonians complained to Dahl – who was, apparently, unrepentant'. Palmer, *A Class of Their Own*, p. 165.

[37]   Treglown, *Roald Dahl*, p. 25.

[38]   Ibid., p. 25. Treglown is quoting from a telephone interview that he conducted with Sir Stuart Hampshire. See also Victor Gollancz, *More for Timothy: Being the Second Installment of an Autobiographical Letter to His Grandson* (London, 1953), pp. 148–9.

his move to Westminster in 1937, he became known, Treglown says, 'for his learning, his piety, and his savagery'.[39] Dahl's biographer also mentions that the boys, not the masters, administered most of the violence at Repton and at other public schools, and that as a student Roald Dahl himself could sometimes be sadistic and bullying.[40]

The Victor Gollancz Controversy

In the history of this period at Repton, Dahl's story of Fisher the brutal flogger has its counterpart in the story of Fisher the narrow-minded educator. This account also involves someone who later became particularly famous through book publishing: the charismatic Victor Gollancz (1893–1967). Fisher's principal biographer refers to 'the Gollancz–Somervell row' as a 'remarkable' story.[41] Given its historical context, however, this little episode instead seems rather unremarkable, even drab and inconclusive. The story begins with one of the problems mentioned at the outset of this chapter: the shortage of teachers owing to so many young men volunteering for the armed forces. In early 1916, needing to fill a vacancy in classics, Fisher turned to an employment agency for help and came up with Gollancz, a 22-year-old subaltern in the army who, because of poor eyesight, had been rejected for combat duty and assigned to Home Service with the Northumberland Fusiliers. Nine years older than Gollancz, David C. Somervell was the senior history master at Repton. Together they developed an idea for a new elective in the curriculum, a course that they believed would help students to understand the roots of the present conflict. With their headmaster's consent, they began in 1917 to teach a civics class – not a boring one on how the various units of government function but an exciting one that tackled contemporary political and social issues: imperialism, militarism, capitalism compared to socialism, and so on. This course was to be an early experiment in relevance.[42] As a teacher, Gollancz was intellectually dazzling; Somervell was more reserved but also possessed of a remarkable mind. In some ways they made, in the words of a chronicler of their educational partnership, 'a curious alliance: the young, vibrant and pulsating Gollancz; the

---

[39]   Treglown, *Roald Dahl*, p. 25.

[40]   Ibid., pp. 26, 27. See Palmer, *A Class of Their Own*, pp. 160–61, 163; and De-la-Noy, *Michael Ramsey*, p. 51.

[41]   Carpenter, *Archbishop Fisher*, p. 20.

[42]   Victor Gollancz and David Somervell, *Political Education at a Public School* (London, 1918), chaps. 1–4; Gollancz, *More for Timothy*, pp. 239–40; Ruth Dudley Edwards, Victor Gollancz: A Biography (London, 1987), pp. 95–109.

measured, sober and circumspect Somervell. But the mercurial Gollancz and the rigorous Somervell were to prove a formidable combination'.[43] Their civics class, launched in January 1917, grew increasingly popular with the students of the Upper Sixth Form. The following June, they published the first issue of a course-related newspaper, *A Public School Looks at the World*, which Fisher had also given his approval for. Although it ran for only five issues over nine months (until March 1918), this newspaper, which the students called the *Pubber*, proved to be more of a problem than the class.[44]

Eventually outsiders caught wind of what was going on at Repton and asked pointed questions about the school's apparent pacifism. Not only senior masters at the school but also residents of Repton village began to voice their opposition to academic policies and practices that might undermine morale even as Reptonians were dying in the trenches. The headmaster received indications that the War Office was also concerned about what was happening at the school and indeed might decide to withdraw the government's recognition and funding of the Repton Officer Training Corps. Years after her husband's death, Lady Fisher recalled that if the War Office had terminated the school's OTC programme, then 'of course [this action] would have finished Repton because nobody would have sent a boy there in those days who couldn't get into an O.T.C'.[45] Perhaps worst of all from the point of view of a headmaster, Gollancz and his allies provoked not only dissent but also factional divisions and animosities within the school: master versus master, student versus student. In front of the boys, Gollancz, who in July 1916 had been warned by Fisher not to become too familiar with the lads, openly ridiculed and taunted faculty colleagues. Also, apparently with Gollancz's approval, one of his student protégés, an editor of the *Pubber*, had the paper sold at a radical bookseller's, Henderson & Sons, in Charing Cross Road, London, an establishment familiarly known as 'the Bomb Shop'. This incident exacerbated tensions by making the Repton situation more widely known outside the school. It probably increased the War Office's suspicions of Victor Gollancz's pacifist leanings. The last issue of the paper even listed Henderson's as a co-publisher. Finally, the headmaster, who had gone along with the experiments in liberal education and even praised these ventures at a number of points, decided that Gollancz had to go. Fisher could not risk further damage to his school's reputation, particularly during such a fraught

[43]   Gronn, 'An Experiment', p. 6.

[44]   Edwards, *Victor Gollancz*, pp. 112–15; Carpenter, *Archbishop Fisher*, pp. 20–21; Purcell, *Fisher of Lambeth*, pp. 55–6; Gronn, 'An Experiment', pp. 5–9; Gollancz, *More for Timothy*, pp. 264–5.

[45]   Letter from Lady Fisher to Gronn, 27 October 1983, in Gronn, 'An Experiment', p. 17. See Palmer, *A Class of Their Own*, p. 177.

period. Between the outbreak of war in 1914 and December 1917, the names of 247 Old Reptonians had been read out in chapel as among the fallen – roughly the equivalent of two-thirds of the total student body in any one year.[46]

Decades after they had squared off against one another, each of the principals in this conflict could speak well of one other. Fisher called Gollancz brilliant and idealistic – though 'not yet at all aware as to how to be a respectable idealist in such a community as a school'.[47] And the publisher gratefully acknowledged that his old boss had given him an opportunity – to launch the civics class and the newspaper – that few other headmasters in that era would have provided.[48] In July 1940, James R. Darling, who had been a student editor of the *Pubber* and was now headmaster of Geelong Grammar School in Australia, told his brother-in-law, 'It isn't easy running a school in war time. I have much more sympathy for Fisher than I ever had before and have meditated writing him an apology ... for my failure to understand when I was at school'.[49]

Accomplishments

Fisher's achievements during his years at Repton were many, but surely his most important accomplishment was his marriage in 1917 to Rosamond Chevallier Forman; together they would build a happy and close-knit family. Her father, the Reverend Arthur Francis Emilius Forman, had been a Repton housemaster until his premature death in 1905. Her grandfather was Steuart Adolphus Pears, who as headmaster of Repton between 1854 and 1874 did so much to transform it into one of Britain's leading public schools that he became known to history as the second founder.[50] Eventually Geoffrey and Rosamond Fisher had six sons, all born while the family was at Repton; each son went on to a career of noteworthy achievement. Rosamond enthusiastically entered into the life of the school and

---

[46]   Edwards, *Victor Gollancz*, pp. 121–2; Carpenter, *Archbishop Fisher*, pp. 21–2; Gronn, 'An Experiment', pp. 13–18; Palmer, *A Class of Their Own*, p. 177; Gollancz, *More for Timothy*, chaps. 4–5.

[47]   GF Papers, MS. 3467, fol. 40. In the same statement, Fisher says of himself: 'Gollancz was 24. I was 30. I was still, as a matter of fact, as flexible in outlook as Gollancz was ... but rather more sober'.

[48]   Gollancz, *More for Timothy*, p. 309.

[49]   J.R. Darling to R. LeFleming, 17 July 1940, quoted in Gronn, 'An Experiment', p. 21. Revived after the war, the civics class was guided between 1920 and 1932 by a steadier hand: that of the Reverend Henry Balmforth, a High Church Anglican whose encouragement and influence proved important to a Repton student named Michael Ramsey, who succeeded his old headmaster in the Chair of St. Augustine of Canterbury. De-la-Noy, *Michael Ramsey*, p. 50.

[50]   See Bernard Thomas (ed.), *Repton, 1557–1957* (London, 1957), chap. 2.

of the community. A gracious, devout, and attractive young woman, Rosamond was a prop and a mainstay to Geoffrey Fisher, and so she would remain wherever they went.[51] Any difficulty Fisher might have had in understanding intuitively the *angst* of unhappy private lives must surely have been enhanced by the robust security and solidity of his own. Besides this, Fisher successfully carried on the work of the school: restoring old buildings (most notably the medieval priory), hiring a superior faculty, doing some teaching and advising, and generally in both academics and athletics helping Repton to thrive, which it did in the 1920s, prospering in the postwar boom that benefited other public schools as well.[52] Repton produced a commendable number of scholarship winners at Oxford and Cambridge. In 1921 the curriculum underwent a significant modification to allow more time for specialized study by boys of superior ability.[53] Throughout this period, Fisher proved his mettle as a headmaster: he 'remained in the background', a biographer has written, 'the efficient administrator waving his organizational wand to ensure the smooth functioning of the school'.[54]

Fisher regularly spoke in chapel, preaching basic Christian doctrine and ethics to his young charges. His sermons were, if not brilliant like his predecessor's, at least meet for the occasion; they tended to stress aspects of practical morality for daily living, such as the Christian use of money.[55] In his talks with individual students, Fisher knew how to say the right word to buoy up the diffident or frightened boy. And, years after his service at Repton was over, he made a comment which revealed that he also understood how to talk with the brighter and more-confident lads: 'They were a joy because they were so easy to talk to if you were prepared to discuss anything with them without ... embarrassment .... It meant argument, endless argument, and all the fun of the chase'.[56] Besides the ecclesiastic Arthur Michael Ramsey, the outstanding graduates of Repton during Fisher's headmastership included the writer Christopher Isherwood and the church historian Charles Smyth, among many others. Ramsey's biographer, Owen Chadwick, has written of his subject's admiration for Fisher as a teacher of classical languages: 'Fisher had zest. He rushed them along. He did not delay boringly on points of scholarship. He bubbled along with enthusiasm and humour. He made the dead languages into living literature'.[57] In his last school report on Michael Ramsey, the headmaster wrote perceptively of the future

---

[51] Purcell, *Fisher of Lambeth*, pp. 57–9.
[52] Thomas, *Repton*, p. 109.
[53] Ibid., pp. 109–10.
[54] Palmer, *A Class of Their Own*, p. 181.
[55] Ibid., p. 167.
[56] GF Papers, MS. 3467, fol. 55.
[57] Owen Chadwick, *Michael Ramsey: A Life* (Oxford, 1990), p. 11.

archbishop: 'A boy with plenty of force of character who, in spite of certain uncouthnesses, has done good service on his own lines'.[58] Charles Smyth recalled the influence that Fisher could have through his informal comments – remarks that helped to train up a boy in the Anglican way: 'I constantly remember things that he said in casual conversation which cumulatively taught me to understand, as nothing else outside of parochial experience has done, the nature and ethos of the Church of England'.[59]

Fisher was an effective head of school and it would almost be held against him for the rest of his life by commentators who could not forget it. Possessing the essential ability to balance the near and the distant, he could handle a welter of details in an efficient manner while holding in mind the larger strategic plan. When Fisher stepped down as headmaster of Repton, William Temple said of him: 'His skill and efficiency was subordinated to clear educational principles and high idealism'.[60] No doubt Fisher was aided by the fact that he did not have to revitalize a financially struggling institution or spend endless hours on fundraising. The school's reputation when he arrived was so strong that, after the war, he had little trouble attracting good students and first-rate instructors.[61] Clearly Repton thought well of him. After his 18 years of service, he continued to influence the school first as a member of the board of governors and then as its chairman.[62]

---

[58] Ibid., p. 15.

[59] Smyth, 'G.F.F.: An Appreciation', in Thomas, *Repton*, p. 114.

[60] Quoted in Thomas, *Repton*, p. 112.

[61] Charles Smyth has noted that a headmaster's choice of faculty members is crucial to the success of a school: 'Part of the explanation of the Archbishop's success as a headmaster, and of the fact that these were vintage years in the history of Repton, is the self-evident truth that he possessed this flair [for choosing masters] in an exceptional degree. The scholarship lists ... reflect the wisdom of his [choices]'. Smyth, 'G.F.F.: An Appreciation', in Thomas, *Repton*, p. 113.

[62] Thomas, *Repton*, p. 104.

Chapter 2
Chester and London, 1932–1945

Bishop of Chester (1932–1939)

By 1932 Geoffrey Fisher had been at Repton for 18 years, and, with his characteristically good sense of timing, he knew he was ready for a change. He felt that parochial ministry – preferably, a rural benefice – would provide the best occupation for his personality and strengths. But those who were familiar with his work at Repton, particularly with his outstanding administrative skills, believed that he was well suited to be a bishop.

William Temple, who had become archbishop of York in 1929, considered the diocese of Chester (more or less equivalent to the county of Cheshire) to be the right one – both in churchmanship and in its varied town-and-country ministry – to engage the talents and interests of his successor at Repton. Therefore he urged Fisher upon Cosmo Gordon Lang, the archbishop of Canterbury. Lang wrote to the premier, Ramsay MacDonald, providing the names of the men he thought best qualified for the Chester bishopric. He had two names bracketed in the first spot on his list: Fisher's and that of Nugent Hicks, the bishop of Gibraltar (responsible for southern Europe). In due course the prime minister selected Fisher for the post (Hicks would shortly be appointed bishop of Lincoln), and in early May he notified Fisher that he intended to submit his name to the Crown to succeed Luke Paget. The king approved Fisher's appointment, and on 14 May it was made public.[1] Frank Fletcher, Fisher's old boss at Marlborough College and now headmaster of Charterhouse, wrote to him to say that he thought that this 'promotion' was the right move: it would 'involve *harder* work, something that would really extend' his former protégé.[2] On 21 September 1932, at York Minster, Geoffrey Fisher was consecrated bishop of Chester.

When he became a bishop, Geoffrey Fisher had never been a parish priest. Moreover, as headmaster of Repton, he largely confined his activities to the work of the school and therefore did not attract much attention outside it. His appointment to the bishopric of Chester came as a surprise to many. He was

---

[1]   Edward Carpenter, *Archbishop Fisher: His Life and Times* (Norwich, 1991), pp. 29–30; Bernard Palmer, *A Class of Their Own: Six Public School Headmasters Who Became Archbishop of Canterbury* (Lewes, 1997), p. 182.

[2]   Quoted in Carpenter, *Archbishop Fisher*, p. 30.

going into a diocese that was unfamiliar to him and where he was unknown by the people. It comprised 300 priests, some of whom resented their new bishop for his lack of parochial experience. But Fisher's administrative work as a schoolmaster served him in good stead. He always felt that the tasks of a headmaster and those of a diocesan bishop were similar.[3] His greatly admired predecessor had not been a notably effective administrator, and so Fisher set out to put diocesan organization and finances to rights. He enjoyed excellent relations with the cathedral dean (Frank Selwyn Macaulay Bennett, who had done so much to make the cathedral an active, welcoming centre of religious life[4]), with the archdeacons of Chester and Macclesfield, and with the rural deans, who were the vital links between the parish clergy in the various localities and the diocese.

Fisher's good humour and his intelligent commitment to duty carried him far. Early in his episcopate, in the autumn of 1933, he lent his support to an evangelistic crusade sponsored by the Industrial Christian Fellowship Mission, preaching in the evenings in the slums of Birkenhead. To increase the financial support of inadequately funded congregations and their clergy, he labored to establish the Bishop's Appeal Fund. In a debate in the Church Assembly, he successfully argued on behalf of the maintenance of a diocesan institution threatened with closure: the Church Training College in Chester, which also served the dioceses of Manchester, Liverpool, and Blackburn. And he warmly embraced his official visitations: at confirmations and institutions he spent time with the people, talking easily with all sorts and conditions of men, women, and children. In a short while, both the clergy and the laypeople grew to like their friendly and capable, if occasionally rather authoritarian, bishop, and this response was reciprocated by Geoffrey and Rosamond Fisher. Indeed, the latter became diocesan president of the Mothers' Union (and later its central president), and she used her own motor car to visit parishes all over Cheshire.[5]

Fisher's work in Chester and his characteristic manner of carrying it out revealed another essential component of his leadership besides intelligence and industry. Someone who knew him well, Ian White-Thomson, a former dean of Canterbury who also served as Fisher's chaplain at Lambeth, stresses his sheer resilience. As bishop of Chester, Fisher seemed incapable of ever letting intractable problems or fractious individuals get him down. 'Among his chief qualities were his sense of humour, his imperturbability, his resilience, and his astonishing physical stamina. Short and sturdy in build, he seemed to

---

3   William Purcell, *Fisher of Lambeth: A Portrait from Life* (London, 1969), pp. 65–6.

4   See Roger Lloyd, *The Church of England, 1900–1965* (London, 1966), pp. 392–9, 401–2.

5   Carpenter, *Archbishop Fisher*, pp. 32–52; Purcell, *Fisher of Lambeth*, pp. 69–78; *DNB 1971–1980*, s.v. 'Fisher, Geoffrey Francis, Baron Fisher of Lambeth'.

exude energy and strength'.[6] Betokening a balanced blend of humility and self-confidence, this ability to bounce back and persevere no matter what suggests both a healthy ego and a bulldog determination that any would-be antagonists would have to take into account. In the event, his opponents in the Chester diocese were few. The parish clergy, including those who had questioned the fitness of a man who had never been an incumbent, were grateful not only for Fisher's mastery of episcopal administration but also for the warm personal concern he consistently displayed on their behalf.

Bishop of London (1939–1945)

His outstanding performance as bishop of Chester made Geoffrey Fisher someone to be thought of as soon as one of the most senior ecclesiastical posts became available. In the Church of England, the sees of Durham, London, and Winchester enjoyed a special prominence. They ranked higher than all others except for the two archiepiscopal sees, Canterbury in the southern province and York in the northern. Regardless of his seniority of consecration, a bishop of one of these three dioceses was entitled to sit in the House of Lords as soon as he took possession of his see. Among these three dioceses, London ranked first (followed by Durham). The two archbishops in England and the bishop of London always became members of the Privy Council. Moreover, this ancient see city was the capital of the British Empire, the centre of finance and culture, and the hub of the Anglican Communion: Lambeth Palace, Church House, various church party and voluntary society headquarters, the major church publishing houses, the most famous churches – all were in London.

When Arthur Foley Winnington-Ingram, who had been bishop of London since 1901, finally stepped down in 1939, he left behind an important but also troubled diocese, one that for many years had been allowed to come perilously close to disintegration. Indeed, the diocese was in quite the sort of neglected state that Geoffrey Fisher was known among church leaders to be capable of putting right. Once again a jurisdiction cried out for someone who would bring order, and who better than this longtime headmaster and adroit diocesan to exercise the necessary discipline? Fisher and Bishop Cyril Garbett of Winchester – who, at 63, was 12 years Fisher's senior – quickly became the leading candidates for the London bishopric, although two other bishops – Kirk of Oxford and Rawlinson of Derby – were also under consideration. Winnington-Ingram thought that

---

[6]   *DNB 1971–1980*, s.v. 'Fisher, Geoffrey Francis, Baron Fisher of Lambeth'.

Fisher was the best man to succeed him – an opinion undoubtedly influenced by the fact that both men were Old Marlburians.[7]

The story of how the bishop of Chester eventually received this appointment has two interesting features: the initial hesitancy of the prime minister in backing Fisher, and the hesitancy of the candidate in accepting the offer when it did come. Archbishop Lang was in favour of Fisher, but the prime minister, Neville Chamberlain, had no decided preference. His concerns centred not on the quality of Fisher's intellect or administrative ability but on his spiritual character. Lang took up this matter with a friend, a canon missioner in the diocese of Chester, who offered reassuring testimony on behalf of his bishop. With this information in hand, Lang told the premier that he need not have any worries about Fisher's spiritual depth: 'The Bishop is undoubtedly a man of genuine deep personal religion. His piety is that of the best type of English layman ... rather than that of "religious"'. Fisher's spirituality, the archbishop pointed out, is not readily apparent for two reasons: 'he is very shy and humble about it (very English)', and 'his other gifts of intellect and administration are vastly more obvious to the world'.[8] Satisfied with this appraisal, Chamberlain moved forward with Fisher's nomination.[9] Upon receiving the prime minister's letter offering the bishopric and Lang's letter urging him to take it, Fisher was overcome by an uncustomary spell of doubt and indecision. 'I knelt down and wept like a child', he wrote in his diary.[10] It was not that the offer had come as any kind of surprise. Rather, he was not certain in his own mind and heart that he could fulfill the requirements of this position. Various churchmen, including the dean of St. Paul's, assured him that he could. After much prayer during Good Friday and Holy Saturday of 1939, Fisher, too, was sufficiently convinced.[11]

It is not hard to see why he hesitated before the jump. To him London was unfamiliar territory, and what he knew of the ecclesiastical situation there was more than enough to give him pause. Comprising 600 parishes, the London diocese seemed unwieldy in size and unrestrained in its diversity. For the contentious extremism of its church parties, this diocese was notorious. A biographer of Fisher has written that many clergy and laypeople in London 'complained that there was a lack of order and general discipline in the parishes; ... the Prayer Book was being ignored and ... many a church was becoming an

---

[7]   Charles Smyth, *Cyril Forster Garbett: Archbishop of York* (London, 1959), p. 237.

[8]   CGL Papers 169, fols. 241–2.

[9]   Bernard Palmer, *High and Mitred: A Study of Prime Ministers as Bishop-Makers, 1837–1977* (London, 1992), pp. 210–11.

[10]   Quoted in Palmer, *High and Mitred*, p. 211; Carpenter, *Archbishop Fisher*, pp. 55–8.

[11]   Carpenter, *Archbishop Fisher*, pp. 57–8; W.R. Matthews, *Memories and Meanings* (London, 1969), p. 17.

"island refuge" for a bewildering variety of liturgical exiles'.[12] Among the church societies that had their headquarters in the capital, one stood out as the most problematic: the Church Union, formed in 1934 by the amalgamation of the English Church Union and the Anglo-Catholic Congress. The Protestant wing of the Established Church also had its extremist section.[13] Writing to Archbishop Temple while still trying to make up his mind, Fisher acknowledged his fears: yes, he had powers sufficient to the demands of a friendly diocese such as Chester was, but London was a mare's-nest. When called to speak on religious subjects, he could do well, but he was an amateur in spirituality and his resources in that line were quickly depleted. He was no intellectual and no statesman: he was uncomfortable with abstractions, and he disliked making the kinds of public pronouncements that people expected to hear from a bishop of London. In reply, Temple did not challenge this self-assessment, but he made clear his conviction that Fisher was the right man for London – he had the skills that were wanted – and that he had to accept this offer. By Easter Sunday, Fisher was largely of the same mind. God, he considered, had been good to him. 'Lovest thou me?' he remembered the Risen Lord saying to Simon Peter (John 21). If Geoffrey Fisher was truly grateful for what God had done in his life, and if he trusted in God's mercy, then, he asked himself, how could he now turn aside from a clear call to feed God's sheep?[14]

London in Wartime

Fisher took up his new post on 1 September 1939. Two days later, Britain was at war with Germany. The long, quiet period known as the 'phoney war' ended in mid-August 1940, when France fell and the German air attacks on London and other British cities began. The Blitz – a British colloquialism derived from *Blitzkrieg*, the German word for lightning war – fell on London every night but one between mid-September and mid-November. Other cities involved in war production – including Manchester, Sheffield, Coventry, Belfast, and Glasgow – also suffered. During 1940–1941, this aerial bombardment killed 42,000 men, women, and children in the United Kingdom. More than 139,000 were injured and approximately 1,000,000 houses destroyed. The effects of the Blitz took their toll on morale, but for many Londoners the attacks steeled their resolve and strengthened their sense of solidarity.

---

[12]   Carpenter, *Archbishop Fisher*, p. 60.
[13]   Purcell, *Fisher of Lambeth*, pp. 79–81.
[14]   Carpenter, *Archbishop Fisher*, pp. 56–8.

For the Fishers, life in Fulham Palace, the home of the bishops of London (until 1973), brought its own stresses. Even before it was bombed, the palace was in a shabby state, forcing its occupants to confine themselves to one wing. After the Blitz began, Rosamond Fisher felt compelled to abandon the episcopal residence, removing herself and her youngest boys to Minehead, in Somerset, where her mother lived.[15] At the palace, the bishop of London experienced the air raids like everyone else in the capital. All were vulnerable. Fisher had a certain toughness of spirit that enabled him to soldier on, consistently, no matter what the circumstances. Residents of the palace slept in the house in improvised shelters, made as secure as possible by the placement of large beams and sandbags. In early September they could see the glow in the sky from the fires caused by incendiary bombs dropped on the London docks and on neighbourhoods in east London along the bank. During the day Fisher worked according to an ad hoc schedule, trying to meet demands as they arose. He visited the East End, saw the demolished houses, and tried to bolster the confidence of the people and their clergy. Sometimes, following a bomb hit, he would help with the rescue work.[16] He told his wife how impressed he was by the 'quiet heroism' and the 'persistent humour' of ordinary Londoners.[17] For one night during the Blitz – 11 September – the bishop's residence accommodated 200 evacuees, babies to pensioners, bombed out of their houses in surrounding neighbourhoods; the next night they were moved to a nearby school.[18] During the nights of 25 and 26 September, Fulham Palace, which occupied a vulnerable spot along the river Thames (just west and north of Putney Bridge), was damaged by *Luftwaffe* raids, which had expanded beyond the East End to include other parts of London. Rosamond Fisher badly wanted to return home, but her husband, realizing the risk involved if both parents and their youngest children should be together in one place, would not let her leave the country. Finally, at the end of September, her youngest boys having returned to school, Mrs. Fisher rejoined her husband. The couple's anxiety continued, however, as four of their sons were to serve in the army during the war, and one of them would be a prisoner of war in Italy for 18 months before escaping.[19]

Life at Fulham Palace would continue to be extraordinarily trying. Whenever part of the residence was seriously damaged by bomb blast, the area had to be closed off. If living quarters were damaged, then the occupants had to move to a portion of the house that had so far been spared. The bishop's secretary during

---

[15] Ibid., p. 63.
[16] Ibid., p. 64; Purcell, Fisher of Lambeth, pp. 85–6, 90.
[17] Quoted in Carpenter, *Archbishop Fisher*, p. 65.
[18] Carpenter, *Archbishop Fisher*, pp. 65–6; Purcell, *Fisher of Lambeth*, p. 84.
[19] Carpenter, *Archbishop Fisher*, pp. 66–8.

this period later recalled that her boss 'slept in an underground shelter beneath the Porteous Library, while Mrs. Fisher was in another part of the Palace. That was planned so that, if a direct hit were received, the risk of both parents being killed was at least halved'.[20] The one exception to the palace sleeping arrangements was the customary practice of F.C. Synge, the bishop's chaplain, who slept on the lawn. Better to chance being hit by flying shrapnel, he mused (while lying outside on his camp bed?), than to risk being buried alive under a pile of palace rubble.[21] It was Synge – who not only survived the war but also went on to become principal of Christchurch College, New Zealand – who insightfully explained the source of the deep satisfaction that Fisher derived from completing each day, after lunch, *The Times* crossword puzzle. Through this activity, which was his 'supreme recreation', Fisher for the moment could be both blissfully focused on a challenge and unusually carefree – because, unlike what awaited him, the daily puzzle was 'an artificial problem'. Exercising his faculties was 'his delight and his calling'; being able to do so 'without responsibility' was a peculiar joy. And indulging his penchant for the crossword prepared the bishop for what lay ahead: 'throwing light upon dark confusion, organising, rearranging, making machinery work smoothly, solving problems of manpower or finances'. These tasks he could apply himself to, 'confident that (like the crossword puzzle) the solution was there to be found'.[22]

One of the most important of these tasks concerned postwar reconstruction: not only the rebuilding but also the reorganization of church life in the many areas severely damaged by war. To this crucial matter the Church Assembly turned its attention. Officially called the National Assembly of the Church of England, the Church Assembly was – until its replacement by the General Synod in 1970 – the chief deliberative and legislative body of the Church of England. It consisted of the House of Bishops and the House of Clergy, who were the members of the two Upper and the two Lower Houses of Convocation of the Provinces of Canterbury and York, and of the House of Laity, who were laymen elected by the diocesan laity. Under the Enabling Act of 1919, the Legislative Committee of the Church Assembly had the authority to submit church-related measures to the Ecclesiastical Committee of Parliament. This committee comprised 15 members of the House of Lords nominated by the Lord Chancellor and 15 members of the House of Commons nominated by the Speaker of the House of Commons. If the Ecclesiastical Committee cleared the proposed legislation, then it went to Parliament, which could either accept

---

[20] Marjorie Harry Salmon, quoted in Purcell, *Fisher of Lambeth*, p. 85.

[21] Purcell, *Fisher of Lambeth*, p. 82.

[22] Synge, quoted in Purcell, *Fisher of Lambeth*, p. 87.

or reject – but not amend – the proposal. If accepted, then the measure received the Royal Assent and became law.[23] Which is what happened to both the Diocesan Reorganisation Committee Measure 1941 and the Reorganisation Areas Measure 1943, although the route leading to their final approval was long and full of challenges. Having been appointed by the Church Assembly to chair the Archbishops' War Damage Committee, which initiated this legislation, Fisher played the leading role throughout this process. Set up in late 1940, this committee comprised, in addition to its chairman, eight clergy and four laymen. It was, in particular, an ecclesiastical response to the War Damage Act of 1940, which recognized that the Nazis' serial bombing of British cities had caused such extensive devastation that local authorities and private institutions alone could not be expected to take on the massive work of reconstruction. This situation called for a much wider view and for a truly comprehensive effort of planning and rebuilding.[24]

The War Damage Act spurred the various church bodies – the Roman Catholics, the Anglicans, and the Free Churches – to plan in a correspondingly thoughtful and all-encompassing fashion. They needed to take into account the fact that not everything that had been lost could – or should – be replaced. It might make little sense, for example, to rebuild a huge edifice in a neighbourhood that already had more churches than it could support. Thus the disaster of war presented a horrendous problem but also an opportunity for the restructuring of ministry. In the House of Lords, Fisher made exactly this point: 'In London and other great cities there are whole districts in which hardly a church remains untouched. It is neither possible nor desirable that a very large destroyed church should be rebuilt as it was and where it was'. The reason was that '[c]onditions have changed, old needs have disappeared, new needs have been created and in many parts of our great cities there were before the war too many separate parishes and too many churches'.[25]

The reorganization measures for which Fisher and his committee eventually won approval helped the dioceses of the church to negotiate claims for compensation, to strategize with greater freedom, to deploy resources appropriately, and, if necessary, to reconfigure the shape of ministry in damaged areas, even if that meant adjusting parish boundaries, reallocating endowments,

---

[23]   The Enabling Act is officially known as the Church of England Assembly (Powers) Act 1919. 'The Enabling Act, 1919', in R.P. Flindall (ed.), *The Church of England, 1815–1948: A Documentary History* (London, 1972), pp. 342–3; *ODCC*, 3rd edn., s.v. 'Church Assembly'; Cyril Garbett, *Church and State in England* (London, 1950), p. 115; Cyril Garbett, *The Claims of the Church of England* (London, 1947), p. 193.

[24]   Carpenter, *Archbishop Fisher*, p. 69.

[25]   Quoted in Carpenter, *Archbishop Fisher*, p. 69.

or holding benefices in plurality.[26] Fisher's committee carved out a path for the future: showing how parishes could be yoked together, ministries teamed, and incomes redirected, with monies channeled by the Ecclesiastical Commissioners through diocesan funds to parishes as needed.[27]

At the end of the one and one-quarter hours that it took Fisher to unfold the Reorganisation Areas Measure before the Church Assembly, William Temple, who presided over this meeting, told him how well he had succeeded not only in clearly presenting the complex material but also in holding everyone's attention throughout his lengthy explanation.[28] The work of the Archbishops' War Damage Committee – difficult and painstaking, but successfully completed – brought the bishop of London, with his top-flight administrative skills and fair and equable manner, increased recognition in the Church of England. It was really his first turn in the spotlight of the national church, although he was still not widely known when he became archbishop of Canterbury in 1945. His committee service was arduous, then, but useful. From this complex work he learned a great deal about the customs – not only the procedures but also the folkways – of the Church Assembly. As Edward Carpenter has written, chairing this important committee was undoubtedly a constructive learning experience for someone who was soon to preside at the sessions of the Church Assembly – 'a role which, though it irritated Cosmo Lang and bored William Temple, delighted Geoffrey Fisher'.[29] This legislative achievement was also beneficial to the Church of England and to the bishop of London as a harbinger of things to come, for Fisher was to be an active leader of the postwar effort to modernize the Church of England.[30]

Fisher chaired other important, war-related committees as well. In December 1940 he established his own committee to look out for the architectural treasures of the City of London. This committee established procedures for churches to follow if they were damaged by bomb attacks, it instituted measures to salvage valuable artifacts, and it made decisions regarding plans for individual churches that had been bombed.[31] He also chaired the Churches' Main War Damage Committee, which reached across ecclesiastical boundaries to include representatives of other church bodies – from Roman Catholics on the right

---

[26]   Carpenter, *Archbishop Fisher*, pp. 70–77.

[27]   Purcell, *Fisher of Lambeth*, pp. 101–2; see Cyril Garbett, *Church and State in England*, pp. 283–8. The Church Commissioners were formed in 1948 by an amalgamation of the Ecclesiastical Commissioners and Queen Anne's Bounty.

[28]   Purcell, *Fisher of Lambeth*, pp. 101–2.

[29]   Carpenter, *Archbishop Fisher*, p. 77.

[30]   Purcell, *Fisher of Lambeth*, p. 104.

[31]   Carpenter, *Archbishop Fisher*, pp. 78–83.

wing of the liturgical spectrum to Baptists on the left. By coordinating and presenting churches' claims for compensation under the War Damage Act, this committee provided assistance to the War Damage Commission.[32]

Upon becoming bishop of London, Fisher had been asked by Archbishop Lang to chair the Archbishops' War Committee. This committee had a rather vague but nonetheless important charge. Modern war generated its own peculiar questions and problems; this committee was to consider those matters that directly affected the church. Its members included the bishops with sees in or near London. One regular topic involved the Home Guard. Their commanding officers tended to schedule their training on Sunday mornings, making it impossible for those who wanted to attend divine worship to do so. Might not the 11 o'clock training be rescheduled, if at all possible? The director-general of the Home Guard issued instructions along the lines proposed by Bishop Fisher.[33] Another example of the sort of question that came up: May the military use church towers as lookout posts or even as places to mount anti-aircraft guns? Yes to the former, replied Anthony Eden, the Secretary of War: with invasion by the Nazis a real threat, church towers might be especially useful in this period (the summer of 1940) for spotting enemy parachutists or troop-carrying aircraft. But no to the latter: the church officials need not worry about the towers being used for machine guns or other weapons. Not all questions were decisively answered: What if the observer carried a rifle into the tower?[34]

Complicated issues arose which were often hard to resolve: troubling matters, for example, having to do with the occupation of consecrated ground by local units of the Home Guard. Because these units' actions were not always in strict compliance with the regulations issued by the Home Office, the same sorts of problems tended to recur. Parish priests were naturally distressed to find military forces using churchyards for gun emplacements and digging up hallowed ground for defense works. Fisher strongly protested against the use of holy ground for profane purposes, sent Eden a set of safeguards designed to prevent future problems, and received a reply that only partially met his demands: Eden could not order procedures to be followed (such as obtaining the prior consent of both the incumbent and the diocesan registrar) which might cause dangerous delays.[35]

Many other matters – from bishops' petrol rationing, to coupons required for vestments, to blackout regulations for early-morning Christmas services – came before the Archbishops' War Committee. One particularly interesting

---

[32]   Purcell, *Fisher of Lambeth*, pp. 102–4.
[33]   Carpenter, *Archbishop Fisher*, pp. 85–6.
[34]   Carpenter, *Archbishop Fisher*, pp. 87–9.
[35]   Ibid., pp. 89–90.

question concerned the extent to which clergy might actively participate in war-related duties. Some Anglican clergy wanted to join the Home Guard. Fisher said that the Bench of Bishops did not wish to encourage clergy to do this but could not forbid them either, as long as they fulfilled their pastoral duties.[36]

Disorder in the Diocese

The Second World War presented uniquely exigent demands, but, year in and year out, being a father in God to his clergy was every bishop's chief pastoral concern. Before Fisher took over the diocese from his predecessor, Winnington-Ingram invited him to Fulham Palace and indicated that he would like to tell him everything he needed to know about his new post. It was a short lesson, Fisher later recalled: 'We are just one gloriously happy family', the bishop of London assured him. 'Of course you and I are both Marlburians, and we are used to meeting unusual situations. But that will be all right, my boy; just carry on and all will be well'.[37]

The actual ecclesiastical situation was more complicated – and more worrisome – than Winnington-Ingram revealed to anyone, including himself. He 'had retired in a rosy glow of sentiment', writes William Purcell. 'But in terms of the true condition of his diocese, he had by then long parted company with reality'.[38] Because of the concentration in London of the leadership of the more extreme church parties, this bishopric, in the words of another observer, was 'certainly no sinecure', even in peacetime.[39] Under Fisher's mild-mannered predecessor, discipline – normally imposed through episcopal oversight – had been weak for years, with clergy openly dissenting from the provisions of the prayer book. Upon Fisher's arrival, the diocese was divided, confused, and unhappy.[40]

The new bishop attempted to improve discipline by issuing a series of pronouncements on acceptable liturgical practice. The principal concerns centered on the extreme Anglo-Catholics' unauthorized departures from the prayer book, especially in relation to the service of Holy Communion, which

---

[36] Ibid., pp. 92–3.

[37] Quoted in Purcell, *Fisher of Lambeth*, p. 81.

[38] Purcell, *Fisher of Lambeth*, p. 81. Winnington-Ingram attempted to forbid benediction with a monstrance, but many Anglo-Catholic clergy simply refused to accept his regulations. See Nigel Yates, *Anglican Ritualism in Victorian Britain, 1830–1910* (Oxford, 1999), pp. 350–51.

[39] Peter Staples, "Archbishop Geoffrey Francis Fisher: An Appraisal," *Nederlands Theologisch Tijdschrift* 28 (1974), p. 242.

[40] Purcell, *Fisher of Lambeth*, p. 94.

they would have called the Mass. From the beginning of the twentieth century, controversy revolved around a particular Anglo-Catholic ritual known as Benediction. Following the practice of the ancient church, Anglicans have often (though not always) said that the consecrated bread and wine could be 'reserved' for the communion of the sick and for similar weighty causes. Disputes arose over the appropriateness and therefore the permissibility of private devotions and public rituals centered on this consecrated bread and wine, which was typically held in a tabernacle on the altar or in an aumbry in the wall of the sanctuary.

A service of public devotion to the Reserved Sacrament, Benediction (or Adoration) was not provided for in the prayer book. Understood by those who practiced it as a ritual means of expressing their faith in and their devotion to the sacramental presence of Christ in the Mass, this service involved the veneration of the Host exposed outside the service of Holy Communion. The reserved Host was removed from the tabernacle or aumbry, placed in a monstrance (a frame or vessel of gold or silver with a round window for displaying the consecrated bread), and censed. The service included prayers and hymns stressing Christ's real presence in the eucharistic elements. The culmination of the service was the blessing of the people with the Host: the priest held the Host in the monstrance and made the sign of the cross over the people. He then returned the Host to the tabernacle.

Through his Bishops' Regulations, Fisher made it clear where the church's bishops authorized deviations from the 1662 Book of Common Prayer (for example: in the Communion service, allowing the exhortation to be omitted or permitting a gradual hymn to be sung between readings from the Bible) and where the bishops did not authorize deviations (such as Benediction). In addition, through careful appointments to vacant livings he hoped gradually to gain a greater degree of obedience and conformity in the diocese, especially in those parishes which were liturgically the farthest out of line. Change came slowly, but by the time his tenure of office ended in 1945, he had made a bit of headway. At least all the clergy in the diocese of London were aware of what the official standards were.[41]

Fisher was disappointed, however, that he had not been more successful in bringing about a fuller measure of discipline and respect for authority in the disordered diocese he had inherited. For the most part, the extreme Anglo-Catholic clergy continued to do as they liked, and securing agreement on proper liturgical boundaries was as elusive a goal as ever. For several reasons, however, this reality soon ceased to be quite as irksome as it had been. After the

---

41   Ibid., p. 95.

war, the liturgical movement brought about major changes in the worship lives of both Protestants and Roman Catholics, stimulating interest in the practices of the early church and making the decades-long battles between high and low Anglicans seem outdated. Many changes that now occurred were ones long advocated by Anglo-Catholic liturgical scholars. In addition, London churches increasingly drew on a self-selected clientele who were less likely to be confused or offended by what they found there. They attended a particular church not because it was their local parish church but because they liked its clergy and its distinctive style of worship. And the church as a whole largely moved on to fresh concerns – in theology, in social ethics, and in ecumenical relations with other church bodies.[42]

Ecumenism in Wartime

In the decades before the Second Vatican Council (1962–5), relations between the Roman Catholic church and other ecclesial communities were typically difficult and often strained. Pope Leo XIII's bull *Apostolicae Curae* (1896) had declared Anglican orders invalid. Rome did not believe that the Anglican church was in the true apostolic succession; and of course Anglicans rejected key doctrines of the Roman Catholic church, such as papal infallibility. As one church historian has written, 'For Rome, the *Via Media Anglicana* was the worst of abominations. Not only had schismatics and heretics broken away with impunity – indeed, with triumphant success: here was also an uncomfortable rival, affirming itself to be both Catholic and Reformed'.[43] This estrangement between the Church of Rome and the Church of England was one reason why Archbishop Geoffrey Fisher's visit to Pope John XXIII in 1960 would be both a decidedly low-key affair and a momentous event: a quiet meeting remarkable for having occurred at all. It is also why the ecumenical engagement with the Sword

---

[42]   Carpenter, *Archbishop Fisher*, pp. 116–25. 'The liturgical changes of the 1960s and 1970s resulted in an overall leveling-up of Anglican worship in general, though a leveling-down in those Anglo-Catholic churches that felt they ought to be more in line with mainstream developments, not just in their own church but in Western Christendom as a whole'. Wearing eucharistic vestments and reserving the Blessed Sacrament no longer distinguished Anglo-Catholic parishes. See Yates, *Anglican Ritualism*, pp. 368–71, 383 (quotation, pp. 370–71).

   Unauthorized departures from the Book of Common Prayer, particularly in Anglo-Catholic parishes in London, continued to be a concern for GF in the 1950s. Officially prohibited, Benediction was nonetheless still practiced. Fisher hoped that new canons and ecclesiastical courts would help remedy the problem. See GF Papers, 73, fol. 387; 79, fols. 259–64; 93, fols. 308–14; 113, fols. 77–9.

[43]   Peter Nichols, *The Politics of the Vatican* (New York, 1968), p. 314.

of the Spirit was significant: at least as noteworthy for what it attempted as for what it accomplished.

Launched by the cardinal archbishop of Westminster, Arthur Hinsley (1865–1943), on 1 August 1940, the Sword of the Spirit was a large-scale campaign of the Church of Rome, although in its first year it also encouraged non-Roman Catholics to participate. It grew out of the recognition that the problems of society and of international relations were spiritual problems that the church must confront.[44] Through study, prayer, and action, this movement sought to promote international efforts on behalf of justice and concord among nations and peoples, thereby establishing the conditions for a lasting peace. The Sword of the Spirit derived its ethical marching orders both from traditional natural-law principles and from the five peace points of Pope Pius XII. Laid down in his Christmas Allocution of 1939, the pope's conditions for a just peace were founded on the right of every nation, no matter how small or weak, to life and independence, and on the right of every minority population within a nation to exist, with their basic freedoms intact. To advance these ends, Pius XII called for progressive disarmament – a disarming of the bellicose spirit as well as of war materiel – and the establishment of an international court.

As conceived by Cardinal Hinsley, the Sword of the Spirit was a weapon to be used to fight for justice both in the present conflict and in the peace that followed. The Sword's program declared a simple and stark contrast between the principles of Christianity and the values of all forms of totalitarianism, including Nazism. In the face of this totalitarian threat, the Sword sought to make clear what was at stake in the war. Totalitarian regimes struggle to impose an alternative way of life, one that opposes, as the Sword's executive committee put it, 'all the natural rights that Christianity upholds – the rights of God, of man, of the family, of minorities, of dependent peoples'. Therefore Christians must fight both for victory against this oppressor and for a 'reconstruction of Europe ... based upon these same natural and Christian principles'.[45]

Proponents of the Sword understood the Second World War to be not merely a battle between competing national interests but also – in the words of Cardinal Hinsley's biographer, writing during the Second World War – 'a battle for the possession of the human soul'.[46] For this reason, they said, the armaments of war must include what the New Testament refers to as 'the sword which the Spirit gives you, the word of God', for the enemies are 'cosmic powers ... the authorities and potentates of this dark age'. These words are from the sixth

---

[44]   Adrian Hastings, *A History of English Christianity, 1920–2000* (London, 2001), pp. 393–4.

[45]   Quoted in John C. Heenan, *Cardinal Hinsley* (London, 1944), p. 183.

[46]   Heenan, *Cardinal Hinsley*, p. 184.

chapter of Ephesians, the key text for Cardinal Hinsley's interpretation of the underlying nature of this fight.[47] 'We can never compromise', he said, 'with any form of idolatrous absolutism, whatever be its name, communism, nazism or fascism'.[48] Leading British ecumenists such as Bishop George Bell of Chichester found this new cause thoroughly appealing. They recognized its potential for good and relished the ecumenical scope and possibilities of such a venture. The horrors of war and the hopes of such churchmen as Archbishop William Temple had brought Christians closer together, at least in spirit. Perhaps now was the time, for the sake of the future, to cooperate in a shared programme for international peace and justice.[49]

The basic principles of the Sword of the Spirit were affirmed in a letter published in *The Times* on 21 December 1940 – a letter signed not only by Cardinal Hinsley but also by the Moderator of the Free Church Federal Council (Walter H. Armstrong) and by the archbishops of Canterbury (Lang) and York (Temple). As guiding principles for national life and international relations, this statement cited and supported both the pope's peace points and the five standards of the Oxford Conference, an ecumenical meeting held in 1937 which had addressed social and political problems.[50] The specific content of this published letter mattered less than the fact of its production: 'Such a letter was ... wholly unprecedented', one church historian has noted. It was tangible evidence that 'in face of the national emergency the ecumenical fraternity had widened ... to include the cardinal archbishop of Westminster'.[51]

These principles also received attention on 10 and 11 May 1941, when two well-attended public meetings were held: the first, on 'A Christian International Order', chaired by Cardinal Hinsley, and the second, on 'A Christian Order in Britain', chaired by Archbishop Lang. The speakers – from the Church of England, the Roman Catholic church, and the Free Churches – composed a strong bench. They included such well-known names as George Bell, Dorothy L. Sayers, and Father Martin d'Arcy, S.J. Cardinal Hinsley was the major force behind this unusual inclusiveness. At the end of the first meeting, the cardinal

---

[47]   See the long quotation from Hinsley in Heenan, *Cardinal Hinsley*, p. 187. Hinsley called Eph. 6:10–20 'the charter of the Movement'. Quoted in Heenan, *Cardinal Hinsley*, p. 194.

[48]   Quoted in Heenan, *Cardinal Hinsley*, p. 195.

[49]   Ronald C.D. Jasper, *George Bell: Bishop of Chichester* (London, 1967), p. 250; Heenan, *Cardinal Hinsley*, p. 189.

[50]   The five standards were (1) the abolition of extreme inequality, (2) the right of every child to an education, (3) the defense of the family, (4) the restoration of a sense of divine vocation in each person's daily work, and (5) the careful use of the earth's resources as God's gifts to all human beings. Heenan, *Cardinal Hinsley*, p. 181.

[51]   Hastings, *History*, pp. 393–4.

archbishop, at Bell's suggestion, led the assembly in saying together the Lord's Prayer. But after this meeting he was taken to task by his fellow bishops for praying with non-Roman Catholics, who, when the organization's new constitution was adopted three months later, were excluded from full membership in the Sword of the Spirit.[52]

The Roman Catholic position was that a total merging of efforts with non-Roman Catholics would be dangerous and misleading. Many Roman Catholic bishops had been worried about the Sword from its inception. To them the character of its makeup was, Hastings writes, suspiciously 'lay, ecumenical, intellectually progressive, decidedly English and fairly upper class'.[53] Their fear derived in part from the possibility that large numbers of enthusiastic Sword members from outside the Church of Rome – for whom the ecumenical thrust of the new movement was its most attractive feature – would overwhelm the Roman Catholic members. Such an influx could cause the Sword to lose its original identity and focus, which was not ecumenism.[54] It could also lead to confusion when, under the auspices of the Sword, Protestant members made speeches and published articles that contained material at variance with Roman Catholic teaching.[55] Cardinal Hinsley pointed out that 'we [Roman Catholics] cannot conceive the visible Church of Christ as merely a confederation of various Christian communities holding different and mutually exclusive doctrines. Such a union would not be a unity'.[56] A Roman Catholic bishop remarked that Anglicans and others might well ask how Roman Catholic clergy could be acting in concert with the local vicar while simultaneously 'trying to persuade members of [the vicar's] congregation to believe he had no valid orders, and to leave his church'.[57]

---

[52]   Purcell, *Fisher of Lambeth*, p. 106; Hastings, *History*, pp. 394–5; Jasper, *George Bell*, p. 249; Stuart Mews, 'The Sword of the Spirit: A Catholic Cultural Crusade of 1940', in W.J. Sheils (ed.), *The Church and War* (Oxford, 1983), p. 427; Michael J. Walsh, 'Ecumenism in War-Time Britain: The Sword of the Spirit and Religion and Life, 1940–1945 (1)', *Heythrop Journal* 23 (1982), p. 248.

[53]   Hastings, *History*, p. 394.

[54]   See Mews, 'The Sword of the Spirit', pp. 426–7. The Sword was not founded as an ecumenical venture. A chronicler of its early development writes that 'it is hardly accurate to suggest that what would now be called ecumenism was in the minds of the founders of the movement, or indeed that it ever constituted a major part of its activities – though that is how Fr. Heenan, when a Cardinal, remembered it as he wrote his autobiography'. Walsh, 'Ecumenism in War-Time Britain (1)', p. 250.

[55]   Heenan, *Cardinal Hinsley*, p. 194.

[56]   Quoted in Heenan, *Cardinal Hinsley*, p. 196.

[57]   William Francis Brown, 'Cardinal Hinsley', in *Through Windows of Memory* (London, 1946), p. 100. See the strongly critical response to the Roman Catholic policy in the *Church*

Although full membership in the Sword had to be restricted to Roman Catholics, sympathetic observers could set up a group that was parallel but distinct. Thus, the Anglican and Free Church communions established an organization called Religion and Life. These two movements were then connected via a joint standing committee, designed to foster cooperation among all the churches that endorsed the principles of the Sword. Ably chaired by Geoffrey Fisher, this joint committee, with representatives from both Religion and Life and the Sword of the Spirit, held 17 meetings between 1942 and 1944. The bishop of London called the cooperation envisioned by the leaders of the movement 'a measure of joint action such as has not happened in this country since the Reformation'.[58]

Possessing the skills of a diplomat, Fisher was able to keep the representatives of the different religious bodies working together more or less effectively. Building upon enhanced cooperation and understanding among the various Christian communions, the joint committee hoped to advance a spiritual and social reformation in the world at large. After issuing a widely remarked Statement on Religious Co-operation in May 1942, however, the committee made little progress. Roman Catholics and Free Church members found themselves at loggerheads over a request from the latter for joint prayer, an activity for which the Roman hierarchy was not yet ready. A larger controversy arose over a proposed joint statement on religious freedom, an ecumenical development that the Roman Catholic authorities also concluded was a bridge too far.

Fisher was both saddened and annoyed by their response. In a confidential memorandum sent on 14 September 1944, to A.C.F. Beales, a Roman Catholic layman who carried out most of the administrative work for the Sword, Fisher said that Rome's rejection of the statement on religious freedom was 'something worse than a disappointment'. It raised a 'fundamental question' concerning the Roman Catholic church's real reasons for refusing to go along.[59] At the 28 September 1944 meeting of the joint committee, Fisher asked whether Rome rejected the statement because it went beyond the proper work of the committee, because it improperly touched on matters of ecclesiastical doctrine, or because the statement's content was simply, from the Roman Catholic point of view, inexpedient, given the Church of Rome's desire to safeguard its position

---

Times lead article 'Not Excalibur', 15 August 1941, quoted at length in Heeney, *Cardinal Hinsley*, pp. 198–200.

[58] Quoted in F.A. Iremonger, *William Temple, Archbishop of Canterbury: His Life and Letters* (London, 1948), p. 423.

[59] Quoted in Michael J. Walsh, 'Ecumenism in War-Time Britain: The Sword of the Spirit and Religion and Life, 1940–1945 (2)', *Heythrop Journal* 23 (1982), p. 391.

in Roman Catholic countries.[60] In fact, the entire movement had been dealt a crippling blow in March 1943, when its leading light, Cardinal Hinsley, died.[61] He was succeeded at Westminster by Archbishop Bernard Griffin, who was, Hastings notes, 'a great deal more circumspect'. Under him, 'the Sword would shrink till it became little more than a penknife'.[62] Thus, Fisher later lamented, 'the whole thing sank, without any result. That was a great disappointment'.[63] For Fisher, however, chairing the joint committee was in important respects a valuable experience, a preparation for what lay ahead. For the first time he had undertaken a task that brought him into close and lively contact with outstanding Roman Catholic thinkers.[64] Like his efforts to bring about clerical discipline in the diocese of London, this work would end in disappointment – but not in disillusionment. As archbishop of Canterbury, he would have another chance – a larger opportunity – to effect change in the areas of both ecclesiastical order and ecumenical relations. As archbishop, he would also have to focus considerable attention on the role of the church in the nation and in the world community.

---

[60]   Ibid. Walsh writes: 'Fisher could not have been far from the truth when he wrote, in his memorandum for the meeting of 18 September 1944: "The Roman Catholic authorities may feel that while the document correctly expresses the principles of natural justice and does not directly conflict with their principles of ecclesiastical doctrine, yet, owing to the conditions of their own Church in various countries, its publication would be inexpedient and place them in difficulty" – which comes close to accusing Roman Catholics of having double standards' (p. 392).

[61]   Purcell, *Fisher of Lambeth*, pp. 106–7; *ODCC*, 3d edn., s.v. 'Sword of the Spirit'; Jasper, George Bell, pp. 251–53; Carpenter, *Archbishop Fisher*, pp. 104–9; Walsh, 'Ecumenism in War-Time (1)', pp. 255–8.

[62]   Hastings, History, p. 396.

[63]   Quoted in Purcell, *Fisher of Lambeth*, p. 107. R.C.D. Jasper provides a broader view and a more positive reading of the fruits of these joint endeavors in his George Bell, pp. 254–5. See also Carpenter, *Archbishop Fisher*, pp. 113–14.

[64]   Carpenter, Archbishop Fisher, p. 113.

Chapter 3
Archbishop of Canterbury, 1945–1961: The Church of England

The Death of Archbishop William Temple

On 26 October 1944, at the age of 63, William Temple died unexpectedly. The spiritual leader of the Anglican Communion for but a short time – a mere two and a half years – he has since been reckoned one of the greatest men to have occupied the Chair of St. Augustine of Canterbury. When someone asked the Conservative prime minister why he had appointed a socialist to this most important see, Winston Churchill famously replied that Temple was 'the only sixpenny article in a penny bazaar'.[1] Such had been Temple's immense, even superb, reputation that a successor might well have dreaded the responsibility of following in his footsteps.

The shock which Temple's death provoked across the Church of England was profound. Cosmo Gordon Lang, his predecessor, had retired at the age of 78 in order to make way for him. Now he found that he was outliving his successor. It was not simply that Temple had been so admired by church people. He was known as the people's archbishop, the archbishop whose public views matched those of the politicians of the progressive Left who were now busily at work in the departments of the wartime coalition government. Temple had represented a national church which was actually in tune with the mood of the democratic nation itself. His death suddenly disordered this happy harmony and left the Church of England with no clear path before it. Even Lang, whose faith was sober and steady enough, found himself to be brutally shaken. Geoffrey Fisher was in the Bishops' Robing Room of the House of Lords when he received the news of Temple's death. 'I knelt down at one of the chairs', he recalled, 'and ... I was there for about an hour not thinking about anything at all but just trying

---

[1] Quoted in David L. Edwards, *Leaders of the Church of England, 1828–1978* (London, 1978), p. 353. In his diary, Sir Alexander Cadogan, the secretary of the Cabinet during the war years, recorded Churchill's reaction to Temple's death: 'Thursday, 26 October 1944. News came of death of Archbishop of Canterbury. P.M. delighted'. Quoted in Trevor Beeson, *The Church of England in Crisis* (London, 1973), p. 101.

to assimilate myself to a completely changed world and a completely changed Church.[2]

It would be good to know what each of these figures thought of the other man. What distinguished them from one another would have been obvious to both, and from early on. As his immediate successor at Repton School, Fisher would have been deeply aware of Temple's strengths and weaknesses as a leader, a scholar, and a personality; and over the years Temple would have grown increasingly familiar with Fisher's skills and deficiencies. Their similarities would also have been apparent to both men: their educational and religious backgrounds, their support of ecumenism, and their reliability as high-ranking officials of the church. In the public realm the two represented different possibilities for an archbishop of Canterbury in a democratic society. Temple had been an intellectual; Fisher was not. Temple wrote voluminously and Fisher hardly at all. Temple was attracted by campaigns and rallies; Fisher was not much at home on a public platform. Temple was revered abroad; Fisher was barely known there. Temple was a capable administrator but nothing conspicuous; Fisher made a virtue of efficiency. In private virtues, in the choosing of men for positions, Temple was unreliable and Fisher possessed a surer eye. But, in their different ways, both men were ecclesiastical thoroughbreds, capable of meeting tough challenges without flinching. Each had an unwavering commitment to the good of the Church of England. They undoubtedly felt a large measure of affection and respect for one another.

Perhaps the relationship echoed that other connection which the political world observed in the work of Winston Churchill and the Labour Party leader, Clement Attlee. Churchill was a vivid public presence who could command the public and stir the imagination with a single phrase. Attlee concentrated on getting things done in the background. Six years younger than William Temple, Geoffrey Fisher was neither his predecessor's peer nor his protégé, still less his underling. And yet many times as bishop of London he helped out the archbishop in the Upper House of the Convocation of Canterbury by taking care of the business that Temple did not like to handle. Fisher provided some insights into their working relationship when he said that

> Lang had dominated [the House of Bishops] too much, and William Temple was a very different kind of person. He was perfectly clear on principles, but he was not really interested in the process of reducing principles to rules or regulations or clear direction. As it happened, I had always had an interest in this kind of process, and a

---

2   Quoted in Edward Carpenter, *Archbishop Fisher: His Life and Times* (Norwich, 1991), p. 129.

good deal of experience in it. I think William appreciated and valued that fact and it enabled me to take some things off him. As Bishop of London, under him, I made it my duty to keep an eye upon the details of many matters, to see how conflicting details might be brought to order, and irreconcilable views brought together. It was work which exactly suited me. William Temple, meanwhile, living on a higher level, spiritually and intellectually, could draw people together in seeking and finding sometimes a statement by a mere verbal alteration in a resolution which could be accepted as the right conclusion in accordance with the will of God.[3]

The relationship between these two churchmen was like that of elder to younger brother, where two gifted siblings acknowledge one another's differing skills and interests but each brother also recognizes – with appreciation undiluted by rivalry – the other's brilliance and utter devotion to the family firm. At the very least, Temple and Fisher must have seen their respective talents as strongly complementary.[4] A stray, private remark by Temple shows that he regarded Fisher as his successor. Not long before he died, William Temple, enjoying his last summer holiday with his wife and talking with her about retirement, indicated that he thought the choice an obvious one: 'I must give up in time to let Geoffrey have his whack'.[5]

Winston Churchill would take two months to decide which of the remaining pennies in the bazaar should now be the next archbishop of Canterbury. Among all the bishops and archbishops in the Anglican Communion, the archbishop of Canterbury had a uniquely complex role to play. Besides being bishop of the diocese of Canterbury (which consisted of the county of Kent east of the river Medway together with the rural deanery of Croydon), he had jurisdiction over all 29 dioceses in the southern province of the Church of England. Thus he presided over the Upper House of the Convocation of Canterbury, as well as over the Church Assembly. Like other senior bishops, the archbishop of Canterbury was a member of the House of Lords. He alone crowned the British monarch. Because the archbishop of Canterbury was also the spiritual leader of the worldwide Anglican Communion, he presided over the Lambeth Conference, the decennial gathering of Anglican bishops.

---

[3]   Quoted in William Purcell, *Fisher of Lambeth: A Portrait from Life* (London, 1969), p. 98.

[4]   In the late 1950s, Peter Kirk, the son of Bishop K.E. Kirk, commented that Fisher's 'basic virtue is his great business acumen, something in which Temple was completely lacking. They would have made a great team together, as in many ways they were complementary'. Peter Kirk, *One Army Strong?* (London, 1958), p. 71.

[5]   Quoted in F.A. Iremonger, *William Temple, Archbishop of Canterbury: His Life and Letters* (London, 1948), p. 620.

As early as 1942, following the retirement of Cosmo Lang, some members of the Conservative Party, impressed with Fisher's performance as bishop of London, recommended him to Churchill as an alternative to William Temple. These Conservatives were troubled by the prospect of a Temple primacy, for the archbishop of York was a highly engaging man of the Left.[6] On this occasion, the premier did not choose Fisher, presumably because he did not deem his worth to be appreciably superior to that of the other articles in the penny bazaar. But after Temple's death Fisher emerged as the leading candidate to succeed him, although two other English bishops were also in the running: Cyril Garbett, who had succeeded Temple at York, and George Bell, the longtime bishop of Chichester.[7]

An impressive man – diligent, commonsensical, and widely respected – Garbett had one drawback: his age. Before his translation to York he had been bishop of Southwark, where he oversaw the beginning of religious broadcasting, and then bishop of Winchester, where he also proved himself an able pastor and an effective teacher.[8] He believed, however, that he was too old to take up this new work: 'I should be at least 73 by the next Lambeth Conference and ought to resign at 75'. He also felt that he lacked 'the gifts for this post', although many would have disagreed with his assessment. In Garbett's view, Canterbury needed a dynamic presence for some years, not a caretaker, and Geoffrey Fisher fitted the bill: 'I should work with him with great happiness'.[9]

But there was another conspicuous contender. At 63, George Bell was young enough to be an effective archbishop, and he knew Lambeth Palace inside and out. While in his thirties he had served as secretary to Randall Davidson (archbishop of Canterbury from 1903 to 1928), and he had been assistant secretary to the 1920 Lambeth Conference. In 1935 he published a well-executed, two-volume biography of Davidson. As dean of Canterbury (1924–29), he abolished visitors' fees and arranged for the first performance of religious drama in an English cathedral in modern times (John Masefield's *The Coming of Christ*). As bishop of Chichester, he was both a thoughtful innovator in his own diocese, encouraging religious education and religious art, and an excellent

---

[6]   Palmer, *A Class of Their Own: Six Public School Headmasters Who Became Archbishop of Canterbury* (Lewes, 1997), p. 186; Charles Smyth, *Cyril Forster Garbett: Archbishop of York* (London, 1959), p. 274.

[7]   Another candidate seriously considered by Churchill was Mervyn Haigh, the bishop of Winchester. See Bernard Palmer, *High and Mitred: A Study of Prime Ministers as Bishop-Makers, 1837–1977* (London, 1992), p. 225; and F.R. Barry, *Mervyn Haigh* (London, 1964), p. 191. Palmer notes, however, that Haigh was unhealthy, highly strung, and indecisive.

[8]   Edwards, *Leaders*, p. 354.

[9]   Quoted in Smyth, *Cyril Forster Garbett*, p. 295.

pastor and administrator. He was also a major figure in the church at large. Indeed, after William Temple, Bell was the most highly regarded Anglican in the international religious community. For many years a leader of the ecumenical movement, he supported the Confessing Church in its opposition to the Nazi regime, and he established important contacts with German Christians, including the Lutheran pastor Dietrich Bonhoeffer, hanged by the Gestapo at Flossenbürg in 1945.[10]

Like Cyril Forster Garbett, Bell had an Achilles' heel, at least as far as Churchill was concerned. He had meddled with the government's war policy and even made speeches against it. On 9 February 1944, the bishop of Chichester delivered a widely remarked speech in the House of Lords questioning the morality of the strategic bombing offensive against German cities: 'I desire to challenge the Government on the policy which directs the bombing of enemy towns on the present scale, especially with reference to civilians who are non-combatants, and non-military and non-industrial objectives'. Bell's challenge was based on traditional just-war theory, which prohibits the intentional killing of noncombatants. He asked whether the government was aware of the moral implications of its actions or of the harm that its policies would do to future relations with the peoples of Europe. 'The policy', he declared, 'is obliteration, openly acknowledged. That is not a justifiable act of war'. And then he added this statement, which dared to suggest a moral equivalence in Allied and Axis war methods as well as in their justification: 'To justify attacks inhuman in themselves by arguments of expediency smacks of the Nazi philosophy that Might is Right'.[11]

This speech undoubtedly damaged Bell's chances to be archbishop, though it was not the only factor. A shy man who was uncomfortable with small talk, he had an unfortunate reputation – though no reader would guess it from the speech just quoted – as a dull speaker, given to lecturing his audience. And he could be a mulish opponent.[12] In any case, Churchill chose Fisher, and once again Bell suffered being passed over for higher preferment. As one twentieth-century church historian has observed, '[b]eing the senior clergyman in Sussex

---

[10]   Edwards, *Leaders*, pp. 354–5.

[11]   George Bell, *The Church and Humanity* (London, 1946), pp. 129–41; R.C.D. Jasper, *George Bell: Bishop of Chichester* (London, 1967), pp. 284–5; David Hein, 'George Bell, Bishop of Chichester, on the Morality of War', in *Anglican and Episcopal History* 58 (1989), pp. 498–509; Peter Staples, 'Archbishop Geoffrey Francis Fisher: An Appraisal', *Nederlands Theologisch Tijdschrift* 28 (1974), pp. 246–7; Edwards, *Leaders*, p. 357.

[12]   Edwards, *Leaders*, pp. 355–6; Jasper, *George Bell*, pp. 285–6; Palmer, *High and Mitred*, p. 226.

cannot be martyrdom'.[13] Yet, although he behaved impeccably, Bell was deeply wounded.

From Churchill's comment about 'the only sixpenny article', we have a good idea of what the premier thought of William Temple. But we know little about Churchill's assessment of Geoffrey Fisher, whose social and political outlook he would have found more congenial than either Temple's or Bell's. The premier must have been aware of Fisher's reputation as a skilled executive, and we can be sure that he would have heard from his advisors that what the Church of England needed in the postwar era was not a prophetic figure but a top-flight administrator who would modernize the church's organization and finances.[14]

What did Churchill and Fisher make of each other? When the bishop of London was invited to lunch with the prime minister at 10 Downing Street he was asked what he thought of a rationalistic exercise titled *Vie de Jésus*. Written by the French historian and philosopher Ernest Renan, this popular work – it sold 60,000 copies in its first six months – presents Jesus as an amiable Galilean preacher: a sublime human being but not a divine personage. The *Vie de Jésus* caused a sensation when it was published in 1863, and it led to Renan's removal from his appointment as a professor of Hebrew at the Collège de France.[15] Churchill would have been more in sympathy with the skeptical tenor of this book than Fisher would have been, for the prime minister did not care for either Christian theology or church officials.[16] Once, during an after-dinner speech when he was archbishop of Canterbury, Fisher referred to Churchill, who was present, as a source of great support in certain ecclesiastical matters. Churchill replied, 'I hope that, when you call me a supporter of the Church, you do not imply that I am a *pillar* of the Church. I am not. Though I might perhaps claim to be a buttress – a flying buttress, on the outside'.[17] On the occasion of his Downing Street interview, Fisher admitted to the prime minister that he had never read Renan's *Vie de Jésus*. 'What, you've never read it!' he later recalled Churchill exclaiming.[18] And there, presumably, the subject was dropped. Churchill no doubt relished a private victory; it is unlikely that Fisher saw it as such himself.

---

[13] Edwards, *Leaders*, p. 358.

[14] Trevor Beeson, *The Bishops* (London, 2002), p. 128.

[15] *ODCC*, 3rd edn., s.v. 'Renan, Joseph Ernest'.

[16] Edwards, *Leaders*, p. 353.

[17] *Church Times*, 29 January 1965, p. 15. The author of this *Church Times* article said that this story was 'supplied by the Rev. P.N.H. Coney, of Milverton, Taunton, ... [who] had it from Archbishop Garbett in 1952'. Another version of this story appears in Alistair Horne, *Harold Macmillan: 1957–1986* (London, 1989), p. 611.

[18] GF, quoted in Purcell, *Fisher of Lambeth*, p. 110.

After what some observers – including Archbishop Garbett – thought an indecent interval, Winston Churchill, busy with the Pacific campaign and frankly lacking either interest in or knowledge of ecclesiastical appointments, chose Geoffrey Fisher to be the 99th archbishop of Canterbury.[19] The appointment was announced on 2 January 1945. At the time of his selection, Fisher was known in his own diocese but not well known throughout the country. As one historian has said of him, 'he did not emerge at the end of the Second World War as a truly national figure'. Much better known were both Archbishop Garbett, 'a solid and ever-dependable national figure', and the 'controversial' George Bell. Also, of course, the new archbishop was not cast in the same mould as the sublimely charismatic Temple'.[20] He was simply Geoffrey Fisher: eager to modernize the functioning of the Church of England, to build up the Anglican Communion, and to reach out in ecumenical friendship to other Christian bodies. Which is not to say that he coveted the post of archbishop of Canterbury, for he had grown to like his London diocese very much. By the time he left, he had visited fully half of its 600 parishes. Feeling that he was especially capable in the role of committee chairman, moving disparate personalities toward a positive result, he knew that the one episcopal task he particularly disliked was a duty that he would have to perform over and over again as archbishop of Canterbury: 'The one thing I did not like', he recalled, 'was pronouncements, the sort of thing one has to say on one's own authority, as one's own final judgment .... I said [to Cyril Garbett] I couldn't face that ....'[21] But when he accepted the archbishopric it was without the perturbation that accompanied his decision to go to London. And, in time, his reluctance to issue public pronouncements gave way to a far greater willingness to make himself heard on the day's controversies. Indeed, '[d]uring his Canterbury years', writes one episcopal commentator, 'he could not keep quiet'.[22]

How did those who knew him well regard his selection? Archbishop Garbett's diary comment may be fairly representative: Fisher 'has not Temple's genius, but he has great ability, especially on the administrative side, combined with charm and humility'.[23] But those who thought that the postwar church needed a prophet were undoubtedly disappointed.[24] At the same time, Fisher's broad virtues ensured that his appointment did not throw any of the parties in

[19]   Smyth, *Cyril Forster Garbett*, p. 296.
[20]   Staples, 'Archbishop Geoffrey Francis Fisher', pp. 242–3.
[21]   Quoted in Purcell, *Fisher of Lambeth*, p. 108.
[22]   Beeson, *The Bishops*, p. 131.
[23]   Quoted in Smyth, *Cyril Forster Garbett*, p. 295.
[24]   Palmer, *High and Mitred*, p. 225.

the Church of England into outright dismay. He was neither Evangelical nor Anglo-Catholic. He could be claimed by neither wing.

The Church of England in 1945

On 19 April 1945, as the Second World War was entering its final months, Geoffrey Fisher was enthroned in Canterbury Cathedral as Primate of All England. Less than three weeks later, on 9 May, the Allies celebrated V-E (Victory-in-Europe) Day. On 14 August, following the devastation of Hiroshima and Nagasaki by atomic blasts, Imperial Japan surrendered. Fisher's primacy began with the commencement of the atomic age, the beginning of the Cold War, and the continuation of deprivation and anxiety. In July 1945 the new Labour government of Clement Attlee swept into government with a landslide majority of 147 seats in the House of Commons. Those who were not appalled were jubilant. The phrase 'We are the masters now', however unjustly quoted (and attributed), spoke of a new mood of public purpose. In the general elections of 1918 David Lloyd George had promised a new age, and the broad public had been disappointed. This would not happen again: the new politicians of the Labour Party were utterly in earnest and they had the power that they needed. The next six years would see the creation of a welfare state and the nationalization of industries. This was a government with a task to modernize society and anchor its arrangements on a planned economy.

Fisher knew that his task mirrored that of the new Labour government: he must not merely rebuild what had gone before, but build anew. This postwar world would be quite different from what they had known before. British society was about to change fundamentally. The question which dominated Fisher's horizon was how to reform the national church so that it could meet the needs presented by this new landscape?

It was as well that the public mood was so buoyant. The condition of the country was dismal. The economy was almost exhausted, large swathes of the cities were in ruins; necessities were available but luxuries were few. A visitor in the early 1950s found Britain to be 'a cold, bleak, bombed-out, seedy, unpainted, half-lit place, a country of rationing and austerity that appeared to be recovering much more slowly from the traumas of the war than … Italy and France…'.[25]

---

[25]   Dan Jacobson, "'If England Was What England Seems": Safety in Spelling Things Out: The Changes of the Last Fifty Years', in *Times Literary Supplement*, 11 March 2005, p. 11. See Tony Judt, *Postwar: A History of Europe since 1945* (New York, 2005), pp. 162–3; Dominic Sandbrook, *Never Had It So Good: A History of Britain from Suez to the Beatles* (London, 2005), pp. 44–5; and A.N. Wilson, *After the Victorians: The Decline of Britain in the World* (London, 2005), p. 518.

The Fishers' own home in London, Lambeth Palace, substantially rebuilt around 1830, had been heavily damaged by bombing. In 1945, at the end of the war, the thirteenth-century chapel stood completely gutted, and the Great Hall was still partly roofless. Restoration of the palace proved to be an extensive and prolonged operation, lasting from 1945 to 1955.[26]

The new archbishop would have to face both the material wreckage and the spiritual unease so ably depicted by Rose Macaulay in *The World My Wilderness*. Confronting the desolate areas of cities and souls, he would have to do what he could to fix, in her words, 'the roofless, gaping churches', the bombed-out shells that 'gaped like lost myths'.[27] He would not only have to carry out routine maintenance but also build for the future, and for that he would need a vision.

Fisher's broad plan encompassed two major goals: first, to improve the administration, finances, and laws of the church so that the pastoral ministry could do its work more effectively; second, to fortify the Church Universal by strengthening the ties both among worldwide Anglicans and among the various Christian communions – Protestant, Roman Catholic, and Orthodox.[28] 'Strengthen', in this case, did not usually mean 'tighten'. Better relations grew out of open communication, mutual respect, and in some cases a loosening of bonds. Evidently, Fisher's goals did not include any remaking of theology, deepening spirituality, or altering the church–state relationship. Because he accepted the underlying structures of church and society as givens, he may best be characterized as a conservative reformer.

---

[26]   Purcell, *Fisher of Lambeth*, pp. 129–35. Charles Smyth writes that GF, 'as Archbishop of Canterbury, amid all the labours of preparing for the Lambeth Conference of 1948, ... enjoyed chatting naturally, as man to man, with the workmen who were restoring Lambeth Palace ...', and one of his former Chaplains writes: 'I think he knew more about their families by the time their work was finished than ... their employers did'. ... Nor was it necessary for Geoffrey Fisher, as it was for William Temple, to try to come down to their level, because, from his broader experience of life, he had a genius for getting quickly and effortlessly onto easy terms with anyone that he met, simply by being his natural, friendly self'. Smyth, 'In Duty's Path: Fisher of Lambeth', in *Theology* 73 (1970), p. 68.

[27]   Rose Macaulay, *The World My Wilderness* (London, 1950), pp. 61, 254.

[28]   Roger Lloyd, *The Church of England, 1900–1965* (London, 1966), p. 466.

Reforming Canon Law

It was widely felt that that the machinery by which the Church of England was governed had grown archaic. In 1945 the archbishop of York, Cyril Forster Garbett, had written a book with the title *Physician, Heal Thyself: A Call for Church Reform*, which made the anxiety palpably clear and showed that it emanated from the top of the hierarchy itself. Yet reform of this kind was not a task for the campaigning idealist. Canon law was not merely dull, except to the mind of the enthusiast. It was a minefield of explosive intricacies. To overhaul it would condemn an archbishop and the Church Assembly to years of painstaking, unglamorous attrition. There was a danger that a church which expended its powers on healing itself might end up looking self-absorbed and indifferent to the world at large.

Fisher inherited this challenge and was, in any case, in no mood to perpetuate what had obviously worn out. He regarded the internal administration of the church as his primary responsibility as archbishop of Canterbury. And, although it may have appeared curious to his critics, in looking back on his career it was that revision of the canons – the laws by which the church governs itself – which struck him as his greatest achievement.

The canons in effect when Fisher took office were still those of 1603, which were issued just after the death of Queen Elizabeth I. Some of these laws – for example, rules about clergy nightcaps and the wearing of yellow stockings – did not seem merely out of date, but looked positively ludicrous.[29] Some of them – such as proper vestments for morning prayer – were still obeyed.[30] Others were openly flouted. Too often the lack of a modern code had caused not tolerance and harmony but dissension, as the various church parties took advantage of the dearth of clear guidelines. 'Many of the conflicts which engaged the Victorian and post-Victorian bishops', David L. Edwards points out, 'arose because the Church of England had ceased to have an acceptable and enforceable code of regulations'.[31] In the absence of up-to-date rules, each bishop had tried to act as the legal authority in his diocese, with the archbishop of Canterbury playing an appellate role. But, as Edwards notes, 'the situation was a nightmare to anyone with an orderly mind'.[32] To some extent, the movement for reform of the canons was driven by laypeople. 'The later developments of the Oxford Movement had plunged the Church of England into a condition approaching liturgical anarchy', another historian, Charles Smyth, has noted, 'and for nearly a century

---

[29]   Owen Chadwick, *Michael Ramsey: A Life* (Oxford, 1990), p. 101.
[30]   Ibid.
[31]   Edwards, *Leaders*, p. 360.
[32]   Ibid.

the laity had been indignantly demanding that the bishops should put their house in order'.[33]

Fisher was not, of course, the first person to recognize the need to resolve this problem. Archbishops Lang and William Temple had set up the Canon Law Commission in 1939. Chaired by Archbishop Garbett, who succeeded Temple at York, this commission issued a report in 1947, *The Canon Law of the Church of England*, which made it clear that canon-law revision was required. This report provided an historical introduction to canon law and proposed a set of 134 canons.[34] Reform was necessary, but whether the canons had to come up in the way they did under Fisher, year after year, like the Chancery case in *Bleak House*, is another question. Not until 1969 was the new body of canon law finally approved. Not least in the 1960s some younger church people found this tortuous. What use could it be to set one's own house in order while the world at large raged and burned?

In a larger sense, however, canon-law reform may be taken as but a part for the whole. What Fisher was really after was a transformation of the Church of England so that it could meet the demands of a changed and rapidly changing world. He sought to rebuild the church in order to render it capable of ministering to a modern, postwar society. And updating the canons was a necessary though clearly not a sufficient step in this effort of reconstruction.

To Fisher canon-law revision did lie at the heart of what was needed. He later referred to this work as 'the most absorbing and all-embracing topic of my archiepiscopate'.[35] This former headmaster had a high view of the law. '[T]he clergy', he said, 'ought to be bound by canons; that [is] what canonical obedience means'. When canons are breached, '[c]onsistory courts ought to be able to impose penalties, even deprivation'.[36] In this strict attitude toward canon law he differed from his predecessor, for William Temple distinguished between obeying a canon 'with mechanical uniformity' and observing it 'with reverent regard'. A canon, Temple said, ought to be 'followed with that freedom of spontaneity which belongs to the spiritual life' that the canon itself was designed to regulate. 'Nothing could more conduce to the true welfare of our Church than a recovery of the original sense of canonical authority as something which claims not detailed conformity but reverent loyalty'.[37] Temple's approach – focusing on

---

[33]   Smyth, 'In Duty's Path', p. 70.

[34]   John R.H. Moorman, *A History of the Church in England*, 3rd edn. (Harrisburg, 1994), p. 440.

[35]   Quoted in Edwards, *Leaders*, p. 360.

[36]   Quoted in Carpenter, *Archbishop Fisher*, p. 209.

[37]   William Temple, foreword in J.V. Bullard (ed.), *Standing Orders of the Church of England: An Attempt to State What Canon Law Is Now in Force* (London, 1934), p. vi.

'loyalty' – allowed greater freedom of interpretation than Fisher's more black-or-white, legalistic understanding.[38] In his strict attitude toward canon law Fisher also differed from his successor, Michael Ramsey, an Anglo-Catholic. While not in favour of anarchy, Ramsey disliked the idea of using law to impose conformity on worship.[39] At all events, the business made a great mountain of work for a veritable army of industrious canon lawyers, clergy and lay, lavishing time and effort on intricacies which many barely knew existed. The process was often unwieldy. One aspect of canon-law revision – overhauling the ecclesiastical courts – meant repealing or amending 200 acts of Parliament. Transforming this system of church courts proved so large and complex a task that it had to be spun off from the work of canon revision and handed to another commission to take on. In a debate in the Church Assembly, Fisher argued for retaining the judicial committee of the Privy Council as the final court of appeal in ecclesiastical cases. But his opinion flew directly in the face of the expressed views of most members of the Church Assembly. Why, they asked, should the judicial committee of the Privy Council, which is a court of laymen appointed by the state, decide questions of worship and doctrine?[40] It was during this debate that members of the Assembly shouted 'No!' at the archbishop of Canterbury.[41]

Many were unhappy with either the process or the results of canon-law revision. W.R. Matthews, the former dean of St. Paul's Cathedral in London, may be representative of those who held an alternative – perhaps more Temple-like – view of how canon-law reform should have been carried out. Matthews thought that taking the 'detailed legislation of 1604 ... as a model for 1950' was 'a fatal mistake'. He believed that the only discipline needed was 'a set of principles laying down in a broad way the purposes and ideals of the pastoral office, as understood in the Anglican branch of the Catholic Church'. The bishops should be fathers in God to their clergy, encouraging and helping them. Instead, the revised canons made the bishops too much the authority figures. Matthews noted that the language of the canons reflected this stress on hierarchy: 'Reading through them, one constantly comes upon "with the consent of the bishop" or

---

[38]   Timothy Dudley-Smith, *John Stott: The Making of a Leader* (Downers Grove, Ill., 1999), p. 310.

[39]   Chadwick, *Michael Ramsey*, p. 101.

[40]   Paul A. Welsby, *A History of the Church of England, 1945–1980* (Oxford, 1986), p. 43.

[41]   Eric Kemp, 'Chairmanly Cantuar', *Times Literary Supplement*, 10 April 1992, p. 23. See also Kemp's comments on the impetus that canon-law revision gave to other important matters that had to be dealt with separately, including the role of the laity in church government and the revision of liturgical rites. The situation related to church courts was more complicated than indicated here; on the problems and inutility of the judicial committee, see Welsby, *History of the Church of England*, p. 43.

"shall be referred to the bishop", all expressions tending to restrict the initiative of the parish priest'.[42]

Others viewed the amount of work involved as effort that would have been better expended elsewhere. After describing the tortuous path that each canon had to take before winning final approval, one observer wryly noted that when the process was finally completed, members of the Church of England learned that a man was not allowed to marry his daughter, that the clergy should prepare for confirmation persons who wished to be confirmed, that every church should have a copy of the prayer book, and that clergy should wear suitable attire.[43]

It was hardly surprising that both Anglo-Catholics and evangelical Anglicans were apprehensive about the possible results of canon-law revision. In 1957, for example, a small group of evangelical leaders, including John Stott, the rector of All Souls, Langham Place, London, called on Geoffrey Fisher at Lambeth Palace to let him know what concerned them about the revisions. By this time, as Stott's biographer writes, revision was 'dragging its slow length along on the floor of the Church Assembly'.[44] The process was now in its eleventh year. Doubting that the new canons would effect any positive change in what the evangelicals cared most about – evangelism, personal holiness, and vital worship – these evangelical leaders worried that the result might be to impose on them liturgical requirements that were, in their eyes, theologically unacceptable. If – to cite a principal concern – the revised canon law required them to wear eucharistic vestments, such as chasubles, then this apparel might imply their endorsement of the Roman view of the Mass – of priesthood, sacrifice, even transubstantiation. These understandings of the Lord's Supper were inconsistent with the reformed interpretation not only of the Holy Communion but also of the life of faith in response to the work of Christ. Or again, if the canons said that only communicant members of the Anglican church could receive Holy Communion, then evangelical Anglican clergy would be required to drop their practice of the 'open table', according to which communicant members of other denominations were admitted to the Lord's Supper. At All Souls, for example, John Stott always invited, as he put it, 'any baptized and communicant member of another church who loves and trusts the Lord Jesus' to receive the consecrated bread and wine.[45]

At the same time, Anglo-Catholics feared the imposition of restrictions on liturgical customs that they had long practiced. Ritualists, Fisher's eventual obituarist in *The Times* recalled, worried that hiss aim was to allow, 'under the

---

[42] W.R. Matthews, *Memories and Meanings* (London, 1969), p. 306.
[43] Beeson, *Church of England in Crisis*, p. 124.
[44] Dudley-Smith, *John Stott*, p. 309.
[45] Ibid., p. 310.

guise of liberalism, certain modest deviations from the Book of Common Prayer merely in order to get an excuse for enforcing conformity more vigorously than before'. They feared that in 'the name of the middle way … he was plotting the destruction of the Anglo-Catholic movement as a prelude to the creation of an unequivocally Protestant National Church', which would then be absorbed 'in a loose federation of Churches without even the common bond of episcopacy'.[46] Meanwhile, Anglican liberals, most anxious about how the laws would be enforced, trembled that there might be an outbreak of wholesale prosecutions for disobedience.[47]

For all this the revision of canon law went forward, with Fisher providing generally effective guidance of the Convocations as well as of the House of Laity in the Church Assembly. As the legislation took place, the different church parties could see that when the process was completed the church would be both comprehensive and more prescriptive. In the matter of clerical vestments, for example, the canons would not prescribe only one mode of attire but rather an acceptable range of options.[48] Fisher later said that the debates over canon-law revision led to 'major clashes' and to 'dismay and discouragement' caused by the expenditure of so much time and energy on a 'seemingly endless task'. He sometimes had to exert himself to keep his teams in harness: 'More than once, to the bishops or in Church Assembly, I had to hold forth at length about the central place of canon law for the renewal of the Church'.[49] Those small numbers who were concerned with the administration of the Church of England would continue to feel that great debt was owed. But to the greater number who knew little of such things, and perhaps cared less for them, this vast legalistic campaign remained shrouded in ecclesiastical obscurity.

Three Controversies: Two Bishops and a Dean

Fisher took an unsentimental view of the clergy at large. He was sure that he must support them in their work at every level. He did more for their working conditions than any other archbishop of Canterbury in the twentieth century. He was generally popular with them. Yet he also knew they could be notoriously awkward when it came to reforms, and he suspected the clergy as a breed of a kind of trades-union mentality which was not immune from confusing

---

[46] 'Lord Fisher of Lambeth, Former Archbishop of Canterbury', *The Times*, 16 September 1972.

[47] Ibid.

[48] Edwards, *Leaders*, pp. 360–61.

[49] Quoted in Edwards, *Leaders*, p. 361.

professional advantage with the general good.[50] Edward Courtman, the bigwig of the Parochial Clergy Association, was a predictable and regular antagonist. Fisher also knew clerical vanity, or egoism, when he saw it and he disliked being in such company.[51]

It was a widely heard justification of episcopacy that bishops created and ensured order in the church. But some bishops became the focus for argument and disorder. What to do in such a situation? The canons aimed at the discipline of the whole church. In the Bishop Barnes affair, Archbishop Fisher faced a situation involving the discipline of one person, and no laws could tell him precisely how to handle this problem. In retrospect, it can be seen that the most interesting aspects of this case had to do not so much with Bishop Barnes and his controversial book, which was not in itself a particularly significant scholarly achievement, as with other aspects of the problem: The conundrum presented by Bishop Barnes was both an administrator's nightmare and a harbinger of things to come.

Ernest William Barnes had become bishop of Birmingham in 1924 – the single episcopal appointment made during the brief first Labour government of that year. Barnes was a mathematician in training and a modernist in theology. He knew how to restrain his more controversial opinions (as he did, for example, as a pacifist during the Second World War). But he could also indulge them provocatively – and could even seem to his junior clergy to belittle matters of faith which were not his own. He took great care to prove scientifically that transubstantiation was nonsense.

For many years a virtual state of war existed between the bishop and a handful of stout Anglo-Catholic churches in the diocese. Although he was not primarily a biblical scholar, Barnes undertook to write a book about the origins of the Christian religion. Published in 1947, *The Rise of Christianity* caused a stir because it was so frankly dismissive of traditional Christian dogma, especially the miraculous. In this book, for example, Barnes called the birth stories 'edifying legend'.[52] He observed that the roots of the story of the Virgin Birth were 'pagan'.[53] He questioned the doctrine of the Logos – the eternal Word

[50] See, for example, the dispute over differentials in the clergy stipend, in Andrew Chandler, *The Church of England in the Twentieth Century: The Church Commissioners and the Politics of Reform, 1948–1998* (Woodbridge, 2006), pp. 83–7.

[51] Canon Eric James once recalled to Andrew Chandler how Fisher avoided the attention of his hosts at a deanery breakfast in London in the 1950s on the grounds that, far from creating a collaborative ministry, the priests there were simply out for themselves. See Eric James, [   ].

[52] Ernest William Barnes, *The Rise of Christianity* (London, 1947), p. 68.

[53] Ibid., p. 87.

incarnate in this man, Jesus – set forth in the first chapter of John's Gospel.[54] And he denied the bodily resurrection of Christ.[55] He admired Jesus' character and teaching.[56] If Barnes had been a university professor these claims might scarcely have raised an eyebrow. The difficulty was that a sitting Anglican bishop was making them, a person charged with teaching others the historic Christian faith. The book, whatever its merits, was widely noticed, and it caused a commotion.

Fisher did not care at all for this. He found that Barnes had strayed too far from orthodoxy in his statements touching on the Incarnation and the Resurrection. In a private letter to Barnes he did not equivocate: 'You make fundamental departures from the doctrines held by the communion to which you belong'. Furthermore, 'the holding of your opinions and the holding of your office are incompatible, and for myself I believe that you ought in conscience to feel the same'.[57] In reply, Barnes pointed out that his book was an attempt to depict the early history of Christianity, not to write Anglican theology; moreover, he did not believe that his views were incompatible with church teachings.[58]

Under increasing pressure to take action, Fisher had to choose one of three options: ignore the book, arraign its author on heresy charges, or do something in between these extremes (a public statement of condemnation or disavowal?). The case for ignoring the book was strong. The highly respected theologian Leonard Hodgson, Regius Professor of Divinity at Oxford, came up with what may have been the best alternative: to do nothing direct or active while offering a positive statement, a clear affirmation by the bishops of the central tenets of the Christian faith. This seemed to suit some bishops: Bishops William Wand of London and K.E. Kirk of Oxford also advocated a policy of benign neglect.[59] In practical terms, a quiet approach stood the best chance of curtailing additional publicity and sales for the book, which had not received glowing reviews. But many others, including Archbishop Garbett, urged Fisher to take a stand in opposition to Barnes. No one was pushing for a heresy trial.[60] Even a debate in Convocation, Fisher realized, would be impossible to keep within foreseeable bounds. It would be better to avoid one.[61]

Fisher decided that he had to say something publicly, and so he opted for a straightforward statement in the full synod of the Convocation of Canterbury.

---

[54]   Ibid., p. 97.

[55]   Ibid., pp. 166, 170.

[56]   Welsby, *History of the Church of England*, p. 54.

[57]   John Barnes, *Ahead of His Age: Bishop Barnes of Birmingham* (London, 1979), p. 405.

[58]   Ibid., p. 405.

[59]   Carpenter, *Archbishop Fisher*, p. 297.

[60]   Barnes, *Ahead of His Age*, p. 406.

[61]   Ibid., p. 408.

Dean Matthews recalled that '[t]he Archbishop was confronted by a majority of bishops who would have insisted on passing a vote of censure for heresy unless he spoke plainly condemning Barnes's theology and he chose the course which was least provocative'.[62]

In his President's Address, delivered at a joint meeting of both houses on 15 October 1947, Fisher noted that *The Rise of Christianity* had caused 'both distress and indignation among Church people'. In this book, Fisher declared, Bishop Barnes 'discards or omits ... much which holds a central place in generally accepted Christian doctrine and belief'. Indeed, his book 'so diminishes ... the content of the Christian Faith as to make the residue which is left inconsistent with the scriptural doctrine and beliefs of the Church in which [Barnes] holds office'. For example, the bishop of Birmingham 'reduces the resurrection of Our Lord to a subjective conviction on the part of His disciples'. A book containing such an inadequate expression of the church's doctrine 'cannot but disturb and shock us'. A bishop has 'stricter standards' applied to him. In his teaching he must 'adequately and faithfully' express 'the general doctrines of the Church and their scriptural basis which he is pledged by his office to defend and promote'. Barnes may be convinced that his book is in accord with church teaching, but 'I must say ... that I am not so satisfied. If his views were mine, I should not feel that I could still hold episcopal office in the Church'.[63]

Bishop Barnes defended his work and refused to resign.[64] No further official action was taken against him. On his subsequent visits to the diocese of Birmingham, however, Fisher shunned Barnes, turning down his offers of hospitality. He believed that to visit the bishop would imply some kind of endorsement and thereby undermine the point of his statement in Convocation. In his account of the archbishop's treatment of the bishop of Birmingham, John Barnes (the bishop's son) reminds his readers of Fisher's former career: 'As the headmaster could not sack his wayward housemaster, he preferred to ignore him and deal directly with the prefects'.[65]

Barnes's refusal to retract his controversial statements coupled with Fisher's disinclination to opt for more punitive measures against the bishop of Birmingham reflected and reinforced those features of the Anglican ethos which favoured breadth and toleration. As Laurie, the central character in Rose Macaulay's novel *The Towers of Trebizond*, observes, 'Anglicans have less

---

[62] Matthews, *Memories and Meanings*, p. 310.

[63] *The Chronicle of Convocation: Being a Record of the Proceedings of the Convocation of Canterbury in the Sessions of October 15, 16 and 17, 1947* (London, n.d.), pp. 187, 188, 190, 191.

[64] Barnes, *Ahead of His Age*, p. 412.

[65] Ibid., p. 418.

certainty but more scope, and can use their imaginations more'.[66] At all events, the outcome of the Barnes case tended to affirm Anglicans' (even bishops') freedom to accept radical biblical criticism and modernist interpretations of Christian doctrine.[67] Of course, the way that bishops made use of their freedom would continue to give headaches to the hierarchy of the Church of England.

Senior Anglicans had often to live with the unhappy sense that their various hierarchies could seem obscure to foreign observers as well as national ones. In the 1930s Archbishop Lang had found his views associated with those of Bishop Headlam of Gloucester because it was known that the bishop was chairman of the archbishop of Canterbury's Council of Foreign Relations. Did this make his opinion the view of the whole church? Did he frame the policy of the church itself? Had he even become, by accident, archbishop of Canterbury? As Lang and Headlam were at odds over the activities of the Nazi regime at the time, the confusion had become deeply awkward. Now Fisher had a Council on Foreign Relations in the safe hands of Herbert Waddams. But he had somehow ended up with a dean of Canterbury who was, if anything, far more voluble than Headlam ever had been. Canterbury Cathedral was, in Fisher's own words, 'the Mother Church of the Anglican communion'.[68] Who was to know that a dean of Canterbury was not junior only to the archbishop of Canterbury? Who could be sure that by a further accident of misunderstanding he might become known as the archbishop? These public confusions mattered because, while he was not a member of the Communist Party, Dean Hewlett Johnson was, in the eyes of his many critics, a brazen apologist for communism who in 1941 had published a best-selling book called *The Socialist Sixth of the World* and who in 1953 published another, *China's New Creative Age*. In 1953 Britain no longer viewed that socialist fraction of the world as its ally. The Cold War had made any such apologetics strangely out of tune with the time itself. The dean of Canterbury sailed on regardless. On Easter Day in 1956 Fisher bumped into the Soviet politburo chief, Georgi Malenkov, in the cathedral after evensong.[69]

The Lambeth postbag bulged with complaints. In 1951 T.S. Eliot withdrew from an engagement at Canterbury Cathedral. Yet somehow Fisher managed to take Hewlett Johnson in his stride. He irritated, indeed exasperated, him. But in public the archbishop acknowledged that the dean of Canterbury possessed courage and many other merits. He was, perhaps, wayward in politics,

[66]   Rose Macaulay, *The Towers of Trebizond* (1956; reprint, New York, 2003), p. 203.

[67]   Henry Currie Snape, 'A Dean and an Archbishop', in *The Modern Churchman*, n.s., 14 (1971), p. 289. See C.E. Raven, 'E.W.B.—The Man for the Moment', *The Modern Churchman* 45 (1955), pp. 11–24.

[68]   See Carpenter, *Archbishop Fisher*, pp. 144–5.

[69]   Ibid.

but his theology was entirely sound. He was also personable and kind. If he was inefficient as a dean then so were many others. If anything, he was more of a liability abroad – and he kept disappearing abroad a good deal. In 1947 Hewlett Johnson wanted to go to Bulgaria and Romania. Waddams asked Fisher if he could dissuade him. The Foreign Office was anxious. When he received the archbishop's letter, the dean appealed loftily to the principle of Christian reconciliation. After the dean had toured the United States, Fisher had to content himself with a public disclaimer. In 1956 Hewlett Johnson condemned the British government for invading Egypt but appeared to justify the Soviet occupation of Hungary. Fisher was still sure that he could do nothing to remove him from office. When a further visit to China produced an accusation by the dean that American forces had resorted to bacterial warfare on Chinese soil, there were ructions everywhere, and Fisher found himself having to justify himself in the House of Lords. Johnson was entirely unrepentant and suggested to Fisher that it was the political view of the archbishop of Canterbury which stood in the way of relations with Eastern churches. The press had an interest in stoking every controversy up. Fisher had every intention of throwing cold water on it. Hewlett Johnson simply used his pulpit to justify himself. Fisher was sure that he had no right to remove his dean. He must have known that Hewlett Johnson was safe because by canon law privileges of the clergy were sharply protected – and the clergy knew it.

A third controversy showed Fisher in a less indulgent light. He no doubt thought himself strong in defence of public morality but sexual controversies brought out the authoritarian in him. Even so, the solid ground which he sought to shore up around himself was all too clearly giving way everywhere else. In 1960 the suffragan bishop of Woolwich, John Robinson, appeared for the publishers Penguin Books in the obscenity trial concerning an unexpurgated version of D.H. Lawrence's *Lady Chatterley's Lover*. In his responses in court, Robinson went so far as to say that the novel 'portrays the life of a woman in an immoral relationship, in so far as adultery is an immoral relationship'. Asked if Lawrence's novel was a book that Christians ought to read, Robinson replied, 'Yes, I think it is'.[70]

---

[70]   GF Papers 246, fols. 158–9. Robinson's comments are from a newspaper cutting appended to a letter from the Reverend L.H. Cuckney, of Wimbledon, to Col. R.J.A. Hornby, Chief Information Officer, Church House, Westminster, 29 October 1960, in which Cuckney refers to the trial and to the effect it might have on parishioners. See G.I.T. Machin, *Churches and Social Issues in Twentieth-century Britain* (Oxford, 1998), p. 187; John A.T. Robinson, *Christian Freedom in a Permissive Society* (London: SCM Press, 1970), chap. 4, 'Obscenity and Maturity'; and Eric James, *A Life of Bishop John A.T. Robinson: Scholar, Pastor, Prophet* (Grand Rapids, Mich.,

A few days after the trial, Fisher sent Robinson a letter in which he reminded him that he had given the bishop 'a private hint which you did not welcome. I am now in the very embarrassing position of having to answer protests of distressed and indignant people at the evidence which you gave ...'. He told Robinson, 'I cannot defend you, of course, at all'. Moreover, because 'the distress which you have caused to very many Christian people is so great ... I think I must say something in public'. He enclosed a copy of the brief statement he proposed to make: 'I was preparing to say a good deal more, but in the end I made it as brief as I could without obscuring what I had to say'.[71]

Two days later, on 5 November 1960, Fisher publicly rebuked Robinson at the diocesan conference at Canterbury. He took Robinson to task for supposing that he could give testimony in this trial and not be 'a stumbling-block and a cause of offence to many ordinary Christians'. Fisher declared, 'The Christian fact is that adultery ... is always a sin, and ... at present a very prominent, even all pervasive, one. The good pastor will teach his people to avoid both the fact of and the desire for sex experience of an adulterous kind ...'.[72]

Towards the Conversion of England and Billy Graham's Greater London Crusade, 1954

In 1945 a firm purpose was evident across the British churches that a society which had been inclined to turn away from the Christianity of its forebears must be encouraged to return to it. In 1945 a report, significantly called *Towards the Conversion of England*, excited genuine enthusiasm in congregations of every denomination. Evangelical Anglicans looked to a new Commission on Evangelism, chaired by one of the very few self-consciously evangelical bishops, Chavasse of Rochester. Both reports found in the advance of a broadly sympathetic contemporary media a grand opportunity for mission.[73] Both aimed squarely at the increasingly absent laity. The upshot was a great deal of industrious activity in parishes up and down the land. Statisticians have observed

---

1988), pp. 93–6. James points out that most people in the court interpreted Robinson's words 'in so far as adultery is an immoral relationship' to mean 'inasmuch as adultery' is immoral (p. 95).

[71]   GF to Robinson, 3 November 1960, GF Papers 246, fol. 160.

[72]   GF Papers 246, fol. 162. See *The Times*, 7 November 1960; Machin, *Churches and Social Issues*, pp. 173, 188; William L. Sachs, *The Transformation of Anglicanism: From State Church to Global Communion* (Cambridge: Cambridge University Press, 1993), p. 324; Welsby, *History of the Church of England*, p. 111; Carpenter, *Archbishop Fisher*, pp. 304–5.

[73]   See Keith Robbins, *England, Ireland, Scotland, Wales: The Christian Church, 1900–2000* (Oxford, 2008), p. 326.

a growth in congregations between 1945 and 1947. Thereafter, the figures held firm – but not for long.[74]

Mission in any form was welcomed by most Christians in the British Isles. If it came from the United States, that was all very well. Perhaps it might bring a certain glamour to the cause? Perhaps there might even be a miracle? The British public mind was oddly caught between admiration for American popular culture, which it lapped up eagerly, and skepticism about American enthusiasm, which seemed brash if not discordant. But, as Keith Robbins has observed, the British churches saw clearly that the United States had two things which they increasingly appeared to lack: robust congregations and a great deal of money.[75] Fisher was not by character much enamored of campaigns or gimmicks, and, while he was adept at courting North American bishops, he was not a ready advocate of noisy transatlantic evangelists and mass rallies. However, Graham was a phenomenon: he was marvelously charismatic and flawlessly charming – and he also had dreamt that he must save Britain for Christ. There was soon a bustling lobby organizing a visit in Britain itself.

In short, Fisher soon became a supporter of Billy Graham's famous London Crusade of 1954. He said of it: 'The mission has beyond doubt brought new strength and hope in Christ to multitudes, and won many to Him; and for this God is to be praised'.[76] Moreover, he believed that the churches could learn something from Graham's methods. 'So often', he asserted, the churches 'do not begin far enough back. They expect people to understand whole sentences of church life and doctrine before they have been taught the letters of the Christian alphabet and the words of one syllable'. That was a natural mistake. But 'Dr. Graham has taught us all to begin again at the beginning of our evangelism and speak by the power of the Holy Spirit of sin and of righteousness and of judgment'.[77]

The Graham mission lasted three months and gobbled up vast public venues with an almost insatiable appetite. Fisher appeared with Graham on the platform of the final meeting at the Empire Stadium, in Wembley. One hundred and twenty thousand people crowded in. Moved by what he had seen and heard, Fisher turned to the evangelist Grady Wilson and said, 'We'll never see such a sight again until we get to heaven!' Enthusiastically putting his arm

---

[74] For the most recent, sustained treatment across the 1945–60 period, see S.J.D. Green, *The Passing of Protestant England: Secularization and Social Change, c. 1920–1960* (Cambridge, 2011), pp. 242–72.

[75] Ibid., p. 326.

[76] GF, 'A Remarkable Campaign', in Charles Cook, *London Hears Billy Graham: The Greater London Crusade* (London, 1954), p. viii.

[77] Ibid., pp. viii–ix.

around Fisher's shoulder, Wilson told him, 'That's right, Brother Archbishop, that's right!'[78] It was hardly surprising that a year later Graham was back again. A million heard him in Glasgow. In just two missions, as many as 36,000 people in England and 26,000 in Scotland stepped forward to accept the faith.[79] Evangelicals of all denominations were jubilant. Yet the historian now views the great moment as a spectacle of an age, not the breaking of a new dawn for the faith.

---

[78]   Dudley-Smith, *John Stott,* p. 299.
[79]   Robbins, *England, Ireland, Scotland, Wales*, p. 324.

Chapter 4
Church and Society, 1945–1961

The Church of England which Fisher inherited was not merely archaic in many of its internal structures. As a national body it could look incoherent. While it was in some terms rich – it owned vast tracts of land, much of it farming – in others it was poor – not least because the government had expropriated so much money through the Tithe and Coal Acts between the two wars and war damage and nationalization subsequently.[1] More than this, the church was perilously out of step with the society to which it sought to minister. That society was undergoing a revolution both demographically and socially.

The Age of Reform: The Church Commissioners

Fisher must have known that his appointment to become archbishop of Canterbury owed much to the reputation he had established for himself as the rebuilder of the diocese of London. Though rather far from a man of the socialist Left, he would have responded to the conviction that modernization was the order of the day and that modernization demanded a national strategy. He looked at the Church of England with a level, pragmatic eye and aimed to simplify what was complicated, abolish what was unnecessary or obscure, improve what was useful but dilapidated or parlous, and draw together divisions and irregularities within one new standard where it could be done. This was no mean feat. Fisher had only to look at Lambeth Palace to see that a mountain of work awaited an improving archbishop. There was reason to start at home: the library was a disaster. The hall was open to the skies. The outhouses were derelict.

It was one thing to rebuild Lambeth Palace. How might one rebuild the practical arrangements on which the whole Church of England rested? There was very little appearance of uniformity to start with. Forty-four dioceses did things in 44 different ways. There were at least as many ways of paying the clergy. The houses they inhabited came in all shapes and sizes. Some bishops lived in

---

[1]   For an assessment of profits and losses at this time, see Andrew Chandler, *The Church of England in the Twentieth Century: The Church Commissioners and the Politics of Reform, 1948–1998* (Woodbridge, 2006), pp. 39–42.

ancient piles which might soon fall down, others in houses that were modern but inadequate. At least one was perching in a hotel.

When Fisher was headmaster of Repton he could handle a welter of details in an efficient manner while holding in mind the larger plan. When he was bishop of London, he began work to reorganize the finances of the church. Often the fact that he was not a spiritual adept, or a theologian or an academic, proved to be just as well for the rank-and-file clergy. He had a practical common sense and empathy rooted in experience which could work to the advantage of the clerical soldiers in the field. At the end of the Second World War, his strategy for the Church of England incorporated, as one of its chief goals, improving the abysmal stipends of parish clergy.

In order to increase the remuneration of clergy, Fisher knew that the church had to raise revenues. The best chance of accomplishing this objective lay in consolidating the financial agencies of the church and focusing on greater, more productive, investment. To these ends he oversaw the amalgamation of the Ecclesiastical Commissioners and Queen Anne's Bounty to form a new agency called the Church Commissioners for England. Established as a permanent body in 1836, the Ecclesiastical Commissioners had been the main trustees of the church's endowments, the earnings from which were used to augment the endowment income of the poorer benefices. A smaller outfit, Queen Anne's Bounty, established in 1704, used its funds to help support underpaid clergy and to provide funds to repair clergy houses, but by 1945 the financial assistance that it was providing to parishes was meager.[2] It was in 1948, the year in which the new National Health Service came into effect, that the old Queen Anne's Bounty amalgamated with the Ecclesiastical Commissioners to form the new Church Commissioners. Fisher was soon coming to enjoy this organization. Its leading lights were men like James Brown, a quiet, purposeful administrator on a mission to reform what was archaic and indefensible, and Mortimer Warren, his sage chief financier. When Brown and Mortimer proposed that the Church Commissioners should invest their new general fund in stocks and shares, Fisher did not object. Indeed, he threw his weight behind them. When, in just a few years, it became clear that their value had risen several-fold, making a vast and growing fund to plough into reform, Fisher was delighted. Soon he also had his eye on Malcolm Trustram Eve as a new Secretary. Eve was a businessman, in charge of a large cement company. His financial acumen was formidable, and he knew it. He was also a man who could look down on a bishop and the bishops did not like him for it. All of this suited Fisher to a tee: he pressed for Eve to be First Church Estates Commissioner – and he got him.

---

2   Paul A. Welsby, *A History of the Church of England, 1945–1980* (Oxford, 1986), p. 30.

This alliance between the archbishop and the Commissioners would prove to be one of the most constructive and remarkable relationships in the history of the twentieth-century Church of England. In an age of austerity Fisher knew that the church needed to achieve successes of material kinds. Brown, Warren, and Eve were the men to provide him with something to celebrate. With the Church Commissioners busily at work investing money, making money, and spending money from their offices across the Thames at 1 Millbank, Fisher had a motor for reform the like of which no archbishop of Canterbury had known before. There was, indeed, very little in which the Commissioners had no hand: most parish matters came to concern them at some level or other; they supported the raising of stipends and pensions; and they looked to bring a just measure of uniformity to a church almost hopelessly divided by inheritances of different kinds and traditions of various characters.

Throughout his archiepiscopate, Geoffrey Fisher maintained a lively and direct involvement in the affairs of the Church Commissioners. Indeed, as the historian of the Commissioners has written, 'of all the archbishops of Canterbury [in the second half of the twentieth century], Fisher alone understood the fundamental significance of the Church Commissioners to the Church of England.' Participating in the work of the Commissioners more actively and more knowledgeably than any other archbishop in this 50-year period, Fisher gave the leaders of the Church Commissioners 'the assurance that they acted with authority and that their work did actually stand at the heart of the Church of England.'[3] The work of the Commissioners is easily underestimated. In truth, they became 'the great co-ordinating power in the Church, centralizing, reordering, integrating, standardising: stipends, pensions, bishoprics, properties'. The modernization of the Church of England was largely their achievement.[4] Even when the dioceses grew in confidence, organizational capacity, and independence, they drew from the example and resources provided by the Commissioners.

---

[3]   Chandler, *The Church of England in the Twentieth Century*, pp. 477–8. Moreover, Fisher worked well with the other key figures who oversaw the Church Commissioners (Sir Malcolm Trustram Eve, Sir James Brown, and Sir Mortimer Warren). Each of these four men, Chandler observes, 'appeared to possess what the others lacked. Fisher knew the politics of the Church thoroughly and pragmatically; he saw how new ideas might seem to the people who mattered and, sometimes, how to persuade those whose approval might be necessary in bringing new ventures to life' (p. 46).

[4]   Ibid., p. 478. Chandler places the work of the Church Commissioners in its historical setting: This body 'came to life in the context of the great Labour governments of 1945–51 and the new primacy' of Geoffrey Fisher; it 'was ... a pragmatic liberal bureaucracy which existed not merely to maintain arrangements but actively to reform them' (p. 4).

But it was, above all, in the matter of investments that the Commissioners proved successful. The time had come to move beyond a wasteful, overly cautious approach based on government bonds and on income from low-yielding agricultural lands. Working to establish a more diversified portfolio, the Church Commissioners bought industrial and commercial shares that promised much higher returns. Income from landowning had been depressed by the holding of long leases at rents that were typically below the market rate. The Church Commissioners addressed this problem either by raising these rents when the leases were renewed, by unloading farmland and investing the revenue in more-profitable ventures, or by selling valuable lands in or near urban areas for commercial or residential development. By no means, however, did the church sever its traditional ties to rural England, as it continued to own more than 1,000 farms.[5]

This new strategy succeeded. From a total income of £7.5 million in the first year of their existence as a combined entity, the Church Commissioners by 1961 – Geoffrey Fisher's last year in office – were raising twice that amount per annum.[6] Trevor Beeson likens the amalgamation to a prospering union of husband and wife: 'Although the parties to the marriage were somewhat elderly and prim, and although their marriage had been "arranged" by the Church Assembly, their new life together was vigorous and highly productive.'[7] As a result of this success, clergy stipends increased, although salaries continued to be low.[8] Income generated also supported clergy pensions, pensions for their widows, the furnishing and maintenance of parsonages, stipends for cathedral clergy, and the improvement of cathedral buildings.[9] 'This reorganization,' writes David Edwards, 'together with a clear appeal to the laity for new giving, came just in time to rescue the parish clergy from real financial hardship. Fisher, the son of a rector, had never grown out of touch with such facts of life.'[10]

---

    [5]   Trevor Beeson, *The Church of England in Crisis* (London, 1973), p. 153; Chandler, *The Church of England in the Twentieth Century*, chaps. 2, 4.

    [6]   Beeson, *Church of England in Crisis*, p. 153.

    [7]   Ibid.

    [8]   Welsby, *History of the Church of England*, p. 30.

    [9]   Beeson, *Church of England in Crisis*, p. 155; Chandler, *The Church of England in the Twentieth Century*, p. 2.

    [10]   David L. Edwards, *Leaders of the Church of England, 1828–1978* (London, 1978), p. 361.

Reconstruction I: The Clergy Stipend

Before this practical reform in church finance, wide disparities in clergy pay existed. These differences were not based on the clergyman's needs or his worth; they simply grew out of the differing incomes of the various parish endowments. To reduce extreme inequalities, the Church Commissioners pooled all these endowments and moved to bring about a stipend scale based on fairness. By 1958 the result was a minimum stipend of £550 per year for almost every benefice. The reforms also enabled funds to be directed to maintain clergy and to construct church buildings in the new postwar housing areas.[11]

Although this venture in ecclesiastical reorganization produced unquestionable benefits, it did have a downside. Fisher and the Church Commissioners had gone a long way in wrenching the church's administration out of the world of Jane Austen and into the modern world of industrial capitalism. But this transformation brought with it a new set of relationships (which the political economist Max Weber would have recognized): increased bureaucratization, a more centralized administration, more boards and committees. Inevitably, this new machinery could seem impersonal and high-handed, albeit efficient. It 'often seem[ed] to the parishes,' notes the historian Roger Lloyd, 'as though the Church ha[d] become rather like an ecclesiastical civil service, governed not by its bishops but by a string of committees against whose decisions no appeal lies.' Possibly this was so. On the other hand, the steady increase of stipends for the clergy would not have been possible if the Church Commissioners had not had the freedom to take the action that they did. 'The price to be paid for skipping a century and a half and bringing the Church's administration suddenly into line with modern requirements was heavy,' Lloyd concludes, 'but the cost of failure to do it would have been heavier still.'[12]

Reconstruction II: Education

Schools were thought to be Fisher's strength. After all, he had been the headmaster of one for some years. Although his teaching career has been narrowly located in two public schools, he had cultivated an understanding of the school system at large. He saw the future of society to be in the schools. The place of the church

---

[11] Trevor Beeson, *The Bishops* (London, 2002), p. 128; Chandler, *The Church of England in the Twentieth Century*, pp. 64–76.

[12] Roger Lloyd, *The Church of England in the Twentieth Century, 1900–1965* (London, 1966), p. 472.

in that future demanded a presence there. It was in this important context, too, that Fisher was well placed to succeed Temple.

In the year in which Fisher became archbishop of Canterbury a new Education Act was passed by Parliament. Substantially the work of a progressively-minded conservative politician, R.A. Butler, it sought to recast the relationship between schooling and religion and to achieve a powerful improvement in the educational standards achieved by the poor. This act would be a landmark in the history of postwar reconstruction. Secondary education must be offered to all free of charge; local education authorities would reorganize the schools under their jurisdiction into grammar, secondary modern, and technical, and children would be examined at the age of 11 to see to which of the three they should go. In financial terms schools in the public sector now came in the forms of voluntary, aided, controlled, and wholly supported. A number of private schools would be able to receive their grants not from the local authorities but from central government itself if they made a proportion of their places free to selected children. The school-leaving age was raised to 15 years with a declared intention to raise it further to 16 years. The bill was seen to foster the advancement of girls and poorer children altogether. Daily prayer would be compulsory. All children could receive a daily bottle of milk. The Butler Act represented a bold simplification of what had existed before: now every child fell into the framework of a national plan. Its distinctions and divisions, above all between the brighter grammar-school children and the rest, would recreate the old themes of privilege and alienation in a new form. A working-class child who attended a poor rural school was hardly likely to be conscientiously prepared for a public examination at the mere age of 11 – but there would be no way into a grammar school thereafter. Children who attended a secondary modern school had at least as many reasons to doubt themselves as grammar-school children had to believe in themselves.

As he was setting to work on all of this, Butler had found an important ally in Archbishop Temple.[13] Temple could see the bill only as a step forward, an opportunity. Another ally was the bishop of London. One significant aspect of what now occurred was that the churches found themselves having to work ecumenically to maintain the place and character of religious instruction. Only 50 years before, the schools had been the greatest battleground for interdenominational conflict that British society knew. Much of the discussion which took place between the politicians and the church leaders became preoccupied by the subject of religious instruction. The churches affirmed that

---

[13]   See F.A. Iremonger, *William Temple, Archbishop of Canterbury: His Life and Letters* (Oxford, 1948), pp. X.

this must be compulsory, unless families chose to withdraw from it. The position was accepted by almost everybody, evidently regardless of the state of their own opinions. Indeed, the act gave religion an explicit place which it had never before possessed, and a unique one too insofar as it was the only compulsory feature of the new curriculum.[14] But how was the subject was to be taught and who was to teach it? The bill was clear that it should not be the clergy. Fisher, the National Society, and Bishop Bell of Chichester protested, but Butler also had the National Union of Teachers to face and he held firm. Meanwhile, the schools which were owned by churches were now to be 'voluntary aided' institutions. The Roman Catholics wanted their schools to be both entirely denominational and entirely funded by the government. Fisher thought this unreasonable and argued that all church schools would do well to receive 50 percent of their costs. He wanted those schools owned by the Church of England to remain as they were but also knew that most of them simply could not afford to be 'voluntary aided' institutions, not least because many were old and in dire need of modernization. But Fisher saw a further option. If such schools acquired a new status as 'controlled institutions' they would receive state support while the authority of the parish, largely represented by its priest, and the religious wishes of parents would be maintained and the financial burdens made bearable. Out of 144 diocesan schools, 105 chose this status and survived.[15]

Much of the stake which the Church of England had in the realm of education was represented by the National Society. This organization represented a powerful interest in its own right. Though thoroughly respectful, Fisher felt this body was obsolete. He wanted its responsibilities to be assumed not by a society established in the reign of Victoria but by the Church Assembly created in the twentieth century. Education was one area which required a national strategy fashioned within the chamber of a national synod. Yet, at the same time, the mood of the National Society was both despondent and defiant. It would not go lightly, and Fisher wanted no fighting. In the event, it took all of Fisher's patience and ingenuity to wrest a workable compromise from this complication. The National Society survived, but it was now run by the same people who ran the education board of the Church Assembly.

The financial pressure on church schools did not evaporate. It intensified. The theme of education gained ground in the Church Assembly with remarkable force. In 1955 a motion looked to the Schools Council, the Central Board of Finance, and the Church Commissioners to invest in the church schools with

---

[14] For a focused overview, see Keith Robbins, *England, Ireland, Scotland, Wales: The Christian Church, 1900–2000* (Oxford, 2008), pp. 303–6.

[15] See Edward Carpenter, *Archbishop Fisher: His Life and Times* (Norwich, 1991), pp. 428–39.

a new seriousness. One thousand, three hundred and fifty controlled schools now bleakly faced extinction. If the church wanted its schools to survive it would have to pay for them itself. Simply to maintain them would require a new £590,000 a year.

The Central Board of Finance was uninterested in this. But by this time the Church Commissioners had acquired a conspicuous reputation for making money through judicious investments. It was hardly surprising that because of their success they were attracting growing attention from those who wanted money to spend. When approached, the Commissioners were at first evasive: they did not have the power to support schools. If they were given that power it would be a different matter. In November 1956 a new motion was presented to the Church Assembly empowering the Commissioners to make a grant of £1 million over 25 years to fortify the church schools and to attract a further £2 million raised in the parishes and dioceses. This motion won through, but it was now also clear that a debate was raging across the church between those who believed that without this grant the schools would perish, and the future of the church along with it, and those who feared that the funds of the Church Commissioners were being turned into a general fund to support the enthusiasms of the Church Assembly.

The Parochial Clergy Association, led by that old foe of Fisher, the hectoring Edward Courtman, threatened to campaign against the measure when it came to Parliament. This £1 million should be for the needy clergy. 'The Laity,' Courtman argued, 'must not let the Clergy pay the Church's bills.'[16] This attitude was soon winning an audience; Fisher was warned that the Ecclesiastical Committee in Parliament was looking troubled. Moreover, the basic principles of the business looked increasingly murky. By their General Fund, the Church Commissioners were entitled to make grants to support the 'Cure of Souls'. Did the financing of a school truly fall within the terms of this phrase? While Fisher and his allies worried, Courtman – who was himself one of the 95 Church Commissioners – lobbied more furiously than ever. When Fisher summoned Courtman to Lambeth he found that he was quite unable to shift him. He assured him that the terms of the General Fund to which the Church Commissioners answered did not even mention the clergy. Whether the money could be spent in such a fashion was simply a matter of politics, not law. Courtman simply reaffirmed that the Cure of Souls was receiving a quite new interpretation and he was merely defending the old, accepted one. Fisher accused Courtman of errors; Courtman replied that the archbishop had made quite a few himself. Fisher deplored Courtman's discourtesy; Courtman was unbowed. No matter, the

---

[16]   For a more detailed examination of this controversy, see Chandler, *The Church of England in the Twentieth Century*, p. 123.

measure was accepted by Parliament and the immovable Courtman was left to fulminate – not for the first or the last time – while Fisher could smile at that rare thing, a palpable victory.

Reconstruction III: The New Housing Areas

The symbol of social deprivation in early twentieth-century Britain was the slum. By degrees governments and councils had attacked these with a will between the two world wars, but in 1945 it was the view of the country at large that the slum must finally be consigned to the past. Moreover, the need for houses had grown acute: half a million homes had been destroyed during the war. Between 1945 and 1967 two-thirds of a million houses were knocked down in implacable campaigns of improvement across the country. Two million people were displaced. Families in flats or in two-up, two-down terraces watched themselves move up council waiting lists each week and looked to a quite different future in semi-detached homes on large estates. It became an index of political progress to show how many houses were being built each year. The 1945–51 Labour governments held private developers at bay and were widely accused of slowing the business down by reason of ideology. Subsequent Conservative governments had no such compunction. There was something else to consider: by 1951 it had become clear that the population was rising dramatically.

These new estates were often to be found on the fringes of towns and cities. But there were also new towns – between 1946 and 1949 eight of them in the southeast of the country alone.[17] Civic planners understood clearly that their task did not merely involve throwing up new houses but seeing how entirely new communities could be born. There must be schools, shops, libraries, facilities. Who was to provide new churches there? How were new parishes to be created and new parsonages built? Fisher could see that much was at stake in the power with which the old Church of England met the challenge of what was substantially a new society. Other churches recognized the same issue and were soon busily at work.

The task again largely fell to the Church Commissioners, who oversaw the redrafting of borders, the approving of conventual districts, new parishes, and buildings and the financing of new parochial enterprises, and to the dioceses themselves. In 1948 it cost around £40,000 to build a new church large enough to seat 350 or more people. It was soon seen that building neo-Gothic churches

---

[17]   Roger Lloyd called these new estates 'great concentrations of immaturity, with every box-like house entered by the family on the day the last window was filled with glass.' See Lloyd, *The Church of England in the Twentieth Century*, p. 522.

would not only fail to capture the spirit of this new world but would fall short of what was actually needed in the places themselves. There were experiments in dual-purpose buildings, buildings which presented a contemporary character in these contemporary environments.

The Commissioners now offered 20-year interest-free loans. At first this offer attracted little interest. But the atmosphere was soon changing. Furthermore, as Fisher himself had hoped, the dioceses themselves were beginning to modernize their affairs. At the annual general meeting of the Church Commissioners in July 1951, three bishops asked about funds for new housing areas; in that year £100,000 more was allocated. Thereafter, the question of the 'new housing areas' became a popular cause across the church, one that often yielded anomalies and embarrassments. In June 1952 the Church Assembly heard the bishop of Warrington declare that within a single generation a third of the entire population had been rehoused. It could be seen that in such places there was a priest for every 10,000 people. In one diocese, meanwhile, there were 100 parishes with fewer than 500 people, all of them with an incumbent. Yet within only a few years there was evidence that all was not well on the new estates. Was the church too late already? And did this great, migrating population even want the church at all? A priest who worked on an estate of 6,000 found that only six families there proved to be reliable members of his new congregation.

This work created new links between the Commissioners and the dioceses. In 1954 a New Housing Areas Measure was passed by the Church Assembly. Thirty-eight dioceses now queued up to receive their grants, to support the costs of new clergy stipends and interest-free loans for church buildings. By now the Church Commissioners were worried that the burdens of their growing responsibilities had begun to exceed the bounds of their proper obligations. The debate of 1954 once again turned into a contest between those who believed that the Commissioners should give all of their money to the clergy and those who thought that they were free to maintain the Cure of Souls in all other necessary aspects. To this the answer of the Commissioners remained consistent: it was the latter. Fisher agreed entirely with them and made sure that the Commissioners and their allies were not abandoned to fight for themselves alone. In just five years, between 1954 and 1959, the Commissioners offered £3,200,404 to the estates and found this amount matched by £4 million raised by the dioceses themselves and other local sources.[18]

---

[18]   For a fuller discussion of these developments, see Chandler, *The Church of England*, pp. 96–104.

The Limits of Reform

What all churches had achieved across the face of British society in the postwar period was both striking and considerable. Fisher's place in this was fundamental. In a variety of forms he had invested firmly in the cause of reform and modernization, in so doing giving committed individuals as diverse as the loyal tycoon Malcolm Trustram Eve and an energetic young curate in a new parish what they needed in order to collaborate effectively for the same cause. But the very ground on which the cause itself rested was shifting and perspectives soon altered. Some recognized that the work of the post-war Church was not so much replanting an ancient faith in a modern society as marshalling every effort, and every resource, to give the Church a credible chance of survival in a society which was increasingly gazing in other directions. Wherever one looked, be it in the schools, the new estates, or even the old countryside, it became clearer by the year that all the churches were living and working on borrowed time. Nothing solid or enduring could be built if men, women and children were simply turning away from Christian worship. Fisher was realistic about such things – but even he could not see how immense and precipitous the decline of the churches would be, and in only a few years.

Chapter 5
The Anglican Communion, 1945–1961

A Communion of Anglican Churches

Although Geoffrey Fisher indicated that he regarded canon-law reform as his signal contribution to the church, ordinary British men and women probably identified him most closely with the coronation of Queen Elizabeth II. Other observers have viewed his historic meeting with Pope John XXIII as possessing unparalleled significance. But church historians may be justified in seeing Fisher's work on behalf of the constituent elements of the Anglican Communion as this archbishop's greatest achievement. Promoting the unity-in-diversity of this communion of autonomous churches was not only something that Fisher did well; it was an activity that yielded nothing but positive results, both in the present and for decades to come.

Since 1867 the once-a-decade Lambeth Conferences had presented a strong image of Anglicanism as a tradition which understood itself not merely as the established church of one country but as an international communion in which churches of the same tradition could disregard the realities of geography and instead come to think, work, and worship together. Perhaps this attracted Fisher because it so obviously yielded the prospect of order where otherwise untidiness proved the rule. Moreover, in these postwar years it was not yet clear that anything very grave could divide Anglican churches which were, by and large, led by sensible people.

At all events, Fisher was the first archbishop of Canterbury to be able to afford such a vision. Air travel enabled him to visit the churches of the Anglican Communion to an extent previously impossible. Between 1945 and 1961 he traveled all over the world: to Australia and New Zealand in 1950 (Fisher was the first archbishop of Canterbury to visit the Antipodes), to West Africa in 1951, to Central Africa in 1955, to India, Pakistan, Japan, Hong Kong, and Korea in 1959, to Nigeria and East Africa in 1960. His trip with Rosamond Fisher to Asia in 1959 – a strenuous 20,000 miles in five weeks – was the first tour of Asian countries by an archbishop of Canterbury. Several of these trips were to inaugurate new provinces of the Anglican Communion. The new provinces that came into existence after the Second World War – as well as the jurisdiction of the archbishopric in Jerusalem and the East Asian Episcopal Conference –

got under way during his archiepiscopate and at his urging.[1] These visits were not simply evidence of archiepiscopal tourism or an idealized dream of a global communion. In most of these countries Fisher made substantial statements of his own on a wide variety of questions. When Edward Carpenter dutifully published his collection of the archbishop's sermons and lectures in 1958, a stout number of the strongest in the collection turned out to have been made abroad.[2] Fisher would also collect a lengthy list of honorary doctorates from universities as far afield as Rikkyo, Montreal, and British Columbia.

While Archbishop Fisher has often been described as autocratic, this characterization may apply more to his manner than to his meaning. He might dominate a discussion, but the aim of the process might well be to turn over authority for the church in portions of Africa or Asia.[3] When evaluating Fisher, we will have to look not only at his methods but also at his purposes and at the results of his work. In the important instance of his efforts on behalf of the Anglican Communion, he was not an autocrat.

It was fundamentally important that Fisher was the archbishop of Canterbury in the waning days of the British Empire. India secured independence in 1948, a development which Fisher was known to welcome. In Africa, before independent states replaced colonies, Fisher had organized four new provinces of the Anglican Communion. This order of events was appropriate, for in many of these countries Anglican missionary activity preceded British rule. Missionary societies had long maintained structures which were parallel to colonial authorities rather than subordinate to them; the long-held vision of the development of indigenous churches had made great headway.[4] Trevor Beeson has even remarked that in all such things the archbishop of Canterbury proved to be 'ahead of the politicians'; he aided the statesmen, for this work of establishing autonomous churches 'contributed much to the peaceful transition of [these] countries to independence within the Commonwealth'.[5] Because Anglican churches achieved autonomy before the countries themselves became politically independent, the newly structured Anglican churches, by virtue of their cohesiveness, provided a practical benefit to the new nations. Moreover, these new provinces signaled an important change in the nature of the Anglican Communion. African and Asian churches increasingly balanced a

---

[1]   *DNB 1971–1980*, s.v. 'Fisher, Geoffrey Francis, Baron Fisher of Lambeth'.

[2]   Edward Carpenter (ed.), *The Archbishop Speaks: Addresses and Speeches by the Archbishop of Canterbury, The Most Reverend Geoffrey Francis Fisher, PC, GCVO, DD* (London, 1958).

[3]   Edward Carpenter, *Cantuar: The Archbishops in Their Office* (London, 1971), p. 497.

[4]   W.M. Jacob, *The Making of the Anglican Church Worldwide* (London, 1997), pp. 6, 7, 298.

[5]   Trevor Beeson, *The Bishops* (London, 2002), p. 129.

communion that had been dominated by the Western churches.[6] Furthermore, Fisher acknowledged that 'Anglican' had become a misleading name for the communion, for most of its churches were not English. In 1946 he declared:

> [T]he Anglican Communion embraces many national churches .... They are spread all over the world. The name Anglican is already a misnomer; it indicates their remote origin, but it does not at all describe their present condition. They are indigenous churches, not only here and in England and in the British Dominions, but in India, China, Japan, Ceylon, and Africa, East and West.[7]

These words were spoken at a joint session of the American Episcopal church's General Convention, meeting in Philadelphia on 12 September 1946. Fisher had set his sights purposefully on the North American church. He visited the United States not only to greet his American cousins but also to woo them back to Lambeth: the next international conference was but two years away.

What Fisher inherited in transatlantic terms from his predecessors was far from auspicious. The last Lambeth Conference, 18 years before in 1930, had not been an unqualified success in the eyes of at least some of its members who had arrived from overseas.[8] Bishop Henry Knox Sherrill recalled that in 1930 the American bishops felt more like 'onlookers' than 'participants'. Consequently, some of them even grumbled that they would not turn up for another.[9] Aware that this treatment had frayed the ties of friendship, Geoffrey and Rosamond Fisher visited both Canada and the United States in 1946.[10] This would matter. At the Americans' General Convention, held that year in Philadelphia, Sherrill was elected presiding bishop (taking office on 1 January 1947).

In fact, it was Fisher's achievement to convert the doubting Sherill into an ally and friend. The two had first met in St. Paul's Cathedral in April 1945. 'From then onwards', Fisher later recollected, 'we were completely devoted to each other ...'.

---

[6]   Paul A. Welsby, *A History of the Church of England, 1945–1980* (Oxford, 1986), p. 91.

[7]   GF, 'Anglicanism Today', in Carpenter, *The Archbishop Speaks*, p. 87.

[8]   Carpenter, *Cantuar*, p. 497.

[9]   Quoted in William Purcell, *Fisher of Lambeth: A Portrait from Life* (London, 1969), p. 176. In his autobiography, Sherrill writes: 'It was no secret that the American bishops who attended the 1930 Conference came home with the feeling that they had been given scant opportunity to be heard'. *Among Friends* (Boston, 1962), p. 235.

[10]   At the end of this visit, Fisher joked with reporters who had covered his trip: 'In my 32 days in Canada and the United States', he said, 'I have traveled 7,500 miles, I have slept in 22 beds, and I have given 44 sermons. Therefore, for every two sermons I acquired one bed'. Harold A. Ball, 'Archbishop Departs from Halifax as Newsmen Enjoy Last Visit', *The Living Church*, 20 October 1946, p. 6.

Sherill was then in charge of the chaplains looking after the U.S. Forces stationed in Britain. Now both leaders worked hard to ensure enthusiastic American participation in the Lambeth Conference of 1948, the first held in 18 years. Fisher knew that the occasion presented an opportunity for a thoroughgoing international assembly. For many decades, in his eyes, the Conference had not been more than 'a little domestic affair', with 'comparatively few bishops from overseas'. Now he wanted 'to revive the whole idea of the Lambeth Conference as the great family gathering of the Anglican Communion'.[11]

Fisher's genial manner and earnest expression of goodwill won over the American Episcopalians. Time and circumstance had combined to assist the cause of Anglo-American affection: between the 1930 and the 1948 Lambeth conferences lay their shared experience of the Second World War. Anyone who peruses the correspondence back and forth between American and British church figures in this period – the letters of deans and theologians, not just of senior prelates – notices a growing bond, strengthened by the writers' awareness not only of a common heritage but also of jointly held principles now under siege. After Lambeth 1948, American Episcopalians had a clearer perception of themselves as an important part of the Anglican Communion, which they could see was – although rather vaguely defined – at least more than a federation of independent churches. This legacy would endure.

This 1946 visit was the first of several trips that the Fishers would make to North America.[12] Fisher also traveled to the United States for the General Convention of the Episcopal Church in 1952.[13] During this visit, on 7 September he gave an address in Christ Church (Old North Church), Boston, which was broadcast over radio and television.[14] Here he said that at the heart of the spiritual heritage of both the United States and Europe

> are such things as these: belief that each man has a personal worth ...; belief that man is responsible for his brother's good ...; belief that society must be directed first by order and then by freedom, first by duties and then by rights, first by just laws and then by the liberties they secure; belief that society and each member of it is responsible ... to God.[15]

---

[11] Quoted in Purcell, *Fisher of Lambeth*, p. 174. See Sherrill, *Among Friends*, pp. 201, 236, 240.

[12] Charles Smyth, 'In Duty's Path: Fisher of Lambeth', *Theology* 73 (1970), p. 69.

[13] This visit included a three-week vacation in the Hudson River Valley and Massachusetts with Henry Knox Sherrill and his family. Sherrill, *Among Friends*, pp. 244–5. See 'Friends and Bishops', *The Living Church*, 14 September 1952, p. 7.

[14] Carpenter, *Cantuar*, p. 498.

[15] GF, 'Christianity and the Modern World', in Carpenter, *The Archbishop Speaks*, p. 36.

These phrases contain quintessential Fisherian themes: no real freedom outside an ordered structure, no rights apart from duties, and in all things responsibility to God.

In 1954, the year of the General Assembly of the World Council of Churches in Evanston, Illinois, Fisher attended the Anglican Congress, held in Minneapolis and chaired by Bishop Sherrill. He was also present for the meeting of the central committee of the World Council of Churches in 1957. In all, he made four visits to the United States.[16]

The Church of South India

Schemes of union or reunion invariably ended up as schemes alone. There were, perhaps, enough bold words to appeal to idealists and too few solid achievements to antagonize vested interests. A skeptic might very well have felt that this fact revealed a good deal about the Anglican character as it had emerged in its most authoritative quarters: the rhetoric was eloquent and generous, but the reality was firmly conservative. Perhaps the two dimensions simply made one another possible?

But there was one part of the church where action actually caught up with language and inspired a fundamental recasting of arrangements. This was in South India. The Indian context placed all of these questions of church identity and order in a distinctive light. Here missionaries had always known that Christianity was a small minority religion, but one with its own sociology – many adherents belonged to the Dalit caste – and its own regional character. Since the early days of Carey, Heber, and Martyn, Anglican missionaries had collaborated with missionaries from other traditions. They had come to know and trust one another. For generations of Indian Christians what mattered fundamentally was preaching and living the Gospel in a difficult world. Weakness stripped away many of the illusions which Anglicans cherished where they had numbers and strengths to indulge them. Many missionaries who had once imported the divisions of the Western churches could hardly see how to justify or maintain them in this very different landscape. To any pragmatist, to insist on these things seemed to condemn the Christian faith to an accumulation of dismal cul-de-sacs. Indeed, it looked strangely faithless.

Some South Indian churches were Baptist, Methodist, and Presbyterian. Between the two world wars plans were hatched to combine them all. There would be no tortuous debates about the validity of orders, no new ordinations or

---

16   Purcell, *Fisher of Lambeth*, p. 178. See Sherrill, *Among Friends*, pp. 260–61.

re-ordinations. A new church would accept the different patterns of ministry in parallel and, from the time at which the scheme came into effect, all new clergy would be ordained by a bishop. By 1944 this plan had gained a good head of steam. The Anglican province of India, Burma, and Ceylon announced that four dioceses would be free to participate. But then almost at once the archbishops faced a question which required an answer. Would this new church be a part of the Anglican Communion if it had clergy who had not been ordained by a bishop?

Accordingly, it was not India but in other places which must have seemed very obscure to most South Indians, like the Convocation of Canterbury, or the personal studies of Nashdom Abbey and Mirfield, that controversy broke out. For High Churchmen it was quite impossible to accept into full communion a church constituted in this pragmatic manner. Moreover, to do so must discredit the Church of England itself. Fisher's relationship with the Anglican Papalist Dom Gregory Dix was, by and large, brittle. Now it was all the more defensive.[17] These voices of criticism grew louder, more insistent. Was the Church of England going to maintain the cause of episcopacy or abandon it? Even the primus of the Episcopal church in Scotland shoved his oar in. To those who favoured the new church it must have seemed that such protesters were quite ready to see the whole South Indian ship sink beneath the waves as long as a proper bishop could be seen shinnying up the mast as it went down. The proponents of the scheme persevered: the Church of South India would be inaugurated in September 1945.

Fisher had firm views about episcopacy but not fine feelings. He wanted this new church to come to life. If it was forced out of the communion it would be a disaster. At Convocation, on 15 May 1945, he set out his store with meticulous clarity – and was found to be meticulous enough to satisfy even the most ardent and opinionated. The Church of South India would one day, he hoped, be a full member of the Anglican Communion. That may come 30 years hence. Until then they must all accept a state of 'inter-communion' or 'partial communion'. This approach left Anglican priests in South India to their own decisions; to work out where they could properly celebrate communion and where they should avoid it.

Though very much a success, this speech did not end the crisis. The South Indian church was the regular recipient of grants made by the High Church Society for the Propagation of the Gospel. Should those grants continue if the Gospel was being propagated by a church that was not entirely, or properly, Episcopal? Yet without this assistance the new church would probably soon be

---

17   See Simon Bailey, *A Tactful God* (Leominster, 1995), pp. 127–8.

bankrupt. The withdrawal of financial support would be like murdering a young church almost at its birth. The Board of the SPG was divided and attempted a clumsy compromise which made matters still worse. Fisher was embarrassed by it and said so. Supporting the Church of South India was becoming a matter of conscience for him, too.[18] In the event, it was Fisher who proposed that whether grants should be made must be left to the judgment of the society's benefactors. As the problem had arisen because of a belief in bishops, perhaps a gathering of bishops could sort it out? This meeting did not happen. Instead, Fisher had borne the burdens of compromise and alienated both sides of the argument. But he had not worked alone. Bishop Bell had fought a similar battle for the new church at the World Council of Churches, and in 1949 his visit to India brought a timely reassurance to those who lived and laboured there.[19]

The controversy of the Church of South India was packed away for a short while before turning up at the 1948 Lambeth Conference. There Fisher relied on an august introductory letter to defuse the crisis before it could erupt again. No bishop of the Church of South India was invited – and it was made clear that none would be invited in 10 years' time either. The young church was received with open arms by Methodists, Presbyterians, and Congregationalists who were contrastingly content to take a few bishops in their stride without making a song and dance about it. Fisher no doubt looked to time itself to heal and restore. In this approach he proved to be right. In January 1959 he personally chaired a meeting at Lambeth Palace to advance the cause of a new Church of North India. Again he faced eminent and influential critics – but he observed them to be merely 'sniping' at him from all kinds of domestic bunkers.[20] One was the new archbishop of York, Michael Ramsey, who set down a thorough Note. Fisher did not much care for this. At all events, the bishops of the Church of North India were episcopally ordained at the very outset and protests subsided.

---

[18] As Fisher remarked privately to Bishop Rawlinson of Derby. See Carpenter, *Archbishop Fisher*, p. 336.

[19] See R.C.D. Jasper, *George Bell: Bishop of Chichester* (Oxford, 1967), pp. 347–53. See, too, Joseph Mutharaj, 'An Indian Perspective on Bishop George Bell', in *Humanitas: The Journal of the George Bell Institute* 10/2 (October 2008), pp. 73–95.

[20] The word was used of Eric Mascall, the Oxford scholar. Ibid., p. 342.

The 1948 Lambeth Conference

The 1948 Lambeth Conference was arguably one of Fisher's greatest achievements. Attended by 349 bishops and lasting ten days, he ably chaired the lot. The practical consequences accumulated impressively: among its results were the establishment of the Anglican Congress and the creation of the Anglican Cycle of Prayer, which united Anglicans around the world in prayer each day.[21] Although the agenda of the Conference included such weighty topics as the Christian doctrine of man, Christian marriage, church unity, the church in the modern world, and the Anglican Communion, its most important achievement was in the realm of identity and self-awareness.[22] Stanley Eley, Fisher's senior chaplain, said of the Conference: 'It was at this time that the Anglican Communion realized that it was a communion .... When you have over a hundred United States bishops meeting half a dozen Japanese bishops only three years after the war ... ended, the emotional currents are bound to be there'. But the spirit of fellowship present in this conference channeled these currents in a positive direction: '[S]inking all that in their common Anglican heritage, the fellowship ... and the love that grew out of that Conference between the various parts of the Anglican Communion welled up again in the Minneapolis Congress of 1954'. The tenor of the conference was established by its presiding officer, Geoffrey Fisher: 'Within a very few days', Eley observed, 'there was a spirit of informality and yet discipline which is typical, I think, of Fisher'.[23]

Arriving in England for this conference, the presiding bishop of the Japanese church, the Right Reverend M.H. Yasiro, brought with him a beautifully embroidered cope as a gift for the archbishop of Canterbury from the women of the Church of Japan. Indeed, it was offered as a peace gesture. When the cope was held up at the docks, its journey blocked by a £200 import charge, Fisher persuaded the Chancellor of the Exchequer to cancel the fee and let it pass. He wore the cope at the opening service of the Lambeth Conference and wore it again for the coronation of Queen Elizabeth.[24] For this opening service, held on American Independence Day, 4 July 1948, Fisher called on Bishop Sherrill to preach.[25]

Six years later, the spirit of fellowship within the Anglican Communion was further enhanced by the Anglican Congress in Minneapolis, the first meeting of its kind since the Pan-Anglican Congress held in London in 1908.

---

[21]   Welsby, *History of the Church of England*, p. 89.

[22]   Purcell, *Fisher of Lambeth*, p. 180.

[23]   Quoted in Purcell, *Fisher of Lambeth*, p. 181.

[24]   Purcell, *Fisher of Lambeth*, p. 181.

[25]   Ibid.

Bringing together both clergy and lay leaders to discuss the communion, the congress sought to stimulate among all participants the recognition that they were responsible for one another. The more senior members should have special regard for the churches in developing countries which were working toward self-sufficiency.[26] To this gathering each diocese could send one priest and one lay delegate, in addition to its bishops; 657 delegates were present in Minneapolis.[27] Fisher recalled the significance of the celebration of the Eucharist each morning of the congress: 'Every morning we met at the Communion service according to a different Anglican liturgy, and that taught all of us a good deal, too. And always there was this atmosphere of loving trust holding us all together in the united spirit of the Anglican Communion'.[28]

The 1958 Lambeth Conference

The background to the next Lambeth Conference was a difficult one defined by one international crisis and one domestic explosion. But it was also sustained by the fact that many of the bishops of 1948 were still there and they knew and trusted one another.[29] In the end it was widely praised as a success.

The first difficulty emerged in the business of invitations. Fisher, following precedent, invited Makarios III (1913–77), among other Orthodox leaders, to attend the opening ceremonies of the conference. Makarios – Archbishop of Cyprus from 1950 and Cypriot Greek political leader (he would be elected first president of Cyprus in 1960) – was seen by some in the United Kingdom as a supporter of terrorists. He had, in fact, organized a patriotic youth party, some of whose members participated in terrorist attacks. When rioting broke out in Cyprus, Turkey, and Greece in 1955, the British, who controlled Cyprus, sent in troops; and in 1956 they exiled Makarios to the Seychelles Islands. Many in the United Kingdom blamed Makarios for the deaths of British soldiers during the conflict. The feeling was that, while Makarios might not have condoned attacks on British troops, he had not condemned them either. To Fisher's relief, a month before the start of the Lambeth Conference, Makarios announced that

---

[26]   Fisher looked forward, he said, to 'a new understanding by the older Churches of the loneliness, the lack of resources, the need of leadership and learning felt by many of the younger Churches. Their courage and devotion must stir up the whole Communion to come eagerly to their aid'. 'Concluding Words', in Powel Mills Dawley (ed.), *Report of the Anglican Congress, 1954* (London, 1955), p. 217.

[27]   Jacob, *The Making of the Anglican Church*, p. 278.

[28]   Quoted in Purcell, *Fisher of Lambeth*, p. 193.

[29]   Purcell, *Fisher of Lambeth*, p. 194. See Sherrill, *Among Friends*, pp. 266–70.

he would be unable to attend. Earlier, Fisher had gone on television and, during an interview, referred to his fellow archbishop as 'a bad man'. This blunt remark seemed to his critics clumsy, if not maladroit – and it got Fisher into further trouble, this time with the Greek Orthodox Christians. Makarios was not only a high-ranking Orthodox official but also the 'ethnarch' of the Greeks rebelling against British colonial rule.[30] This whole affair would appear to his critics an instance of Fisher's awkward handling of the Fourth Estate.

At home, meanwhile, and within Fisher's own ecclesiastical household, a problematic area was the relationship between the two archbishops, York and Canterbury. Just before the start of the Lambeth Conference, Michael Ramsey did something that Fisher thought demonstrated poor judgment: he gave the inaugural address at a eucharistic congress of the Anglo-Catholic organization, the Church Union. Fisher thought that Ramsey's prominent participation in this congress was the wrong signal to send at decidedly the wrong time. 'At breakfast together', Ramsey's biographer, Owen Chadwick, writes, 'Fisher exploded and attacked the Church Union and all that it stood for and said that they had done great harm and ought to apologize'. For his part, 'Ramsey confessed that they had done a lot of harm and ought to apologize but said that the best of them were trying to, and that the Church of England ought to apologize to the high churchmen for the way in which it had sometimes treated them.'[31]

This incident reveals important contrasts between one archbishop of Canterbury and his successor, but Fisher could not allow these differences of churchmanship and personality to get in the way of his conference. In the Lambeth proceedings, Ramsey was to be a key player. The conference would take up the following subjects: the Bible, church unity, progress in the Anglican Communion, resolving conflicts between and within nations, and the family. But the most central of these themes was probably the first, on the authority of the Bible; and Ramsey was chairman of the committee on the Bible and the person who drafted its final report.

Ramsey's group ended up embracing both modern biblical criticism and the authority of the Bible for contemporary life.[32] Fisher was pleased with the archbishop of York's contributions to the conference; and he was especially grateful for the assistance that Ramsey provided in coaxing the Anglo-Catholic participants at Lambeth to take a friendlier attitude toward the Church of South India, which united a church with the historic episcopate to churches without it in a common structure. 'Yet', as Owen Chadwick remarks, 'nothing

---

[30]   David L. Edwards, *Leaders of the Church of England, 1828–1978* (London, 1978), p. 364; Carpenter, *Cantuar*, p. 507.

[31]   Owen Chadwick, *Michael Ramsey: A Life* (Oxford, 1990), p. 98.

[32]   Ibid., p. 99.

could alter the double personal difficulty – a difference of principles between a low churchman and a high churchman, and an indefinable difference of temperament'.[33]

It was at this Lambeth conference that Michael Ramsey was widely recognized as an outstanding churchman and as Fisher's likely successor. From the opening service of this gathering, the contrast between the tightly organized and supremely aware Fisher and the frequently abstracted Ramsey would have been apparent to anyone looking out for it: 'At the opening service in Canterbury cathedral (3 July 1958)', Chadwick writes, 'Ramsey muddled his instructions and wandered all round the cathedral looking for where he was supposed to sit and stand'.[34]

Among the other accomplishments of the 1958 Lambeth Conference was a recommendation for the establishment of the Anglican Consultative Council. This body was to carry on the work of the Lambeth Conference between sessions and to advise the archbishop of Canterbury and other bishops. The council began functioning after the 1968 conference. Lambeth also called for a revision of the prayer book. And it blessed the religious communities; the Anglican Communion's official acceptance of monks and nuns made it unique among the churches that came out of the Reformation.[35]

A document that received a good bit of media attention was the report of the Committee on the Family in Contemporary Society, which gave its support to the use of birth control for family planning.[36] Stephen Bayne, the bishop of Olympia, Washington, chaired this committee; his successful handling of this task enhanced his reputation. Fisher voiced his approval of the committee's report. It said:

> [T]he procreation of children is not the only purpose of marriage. Husbands and wives owe to each other and to the depth and stability of their families, the duty to express, in sexual intercourse, the love which they bear and mean to bear to each other .... Therefore it is utterly wrong to urge that, unless children are specifically desired, sexual intercourse is of the nature of sin. It is also wrong to say that such intercourse ought not to be engaged in except with the willing intention to procreate children. It must be emphasized once again that Family Planning ought to be the result of thoughtful and prayerful Christian decision. Where it is, Christian husbands and

---

[33] Ibid., p. 100.
[34] Ibid., p. 97.
[35] Ibid., p. 100.
[36] Purcell, *Fisher of Lambeth*, p. 197.

wives need feel no hesitation in offering their decision humbly to God and following it with a clear conscience.[37]

William Jacob notes that this report demonstrated that the bishops 'were speaking from a maturely developed moral theology, and with the benefit of personal experience'.[38] The church historian E.R. Norman points out that this report represents 'quite a volte-face' on the part of the Anglican church, for the 1930 Lambeth Conference had allowed birth control only in cases of exceptional social or medical need. Those qualifications were abandoned. 'Contraception', Norman writes, 'was now to be freely allowed because of the human values implicit in sexual union. This was a revolution in the church's attitude to sexual morality'.[39]

The printed reports of these decennial conferences may or may not be significant or memorable. Stephen Bayne identified what was most important about the Lambeth gatherings when he observed that 'Lambeth is like an iceberg; eight-ninths of it invisible (being the conversation and relationships of 320 bishops from all over); and one-ninth (the reports) doesn't give too accurate an idea of the true depth of our meeting'.[40] It is significant that the 1958 conference was the first one in which many of those who took part in the 'eight-ninths' invisible activity were non-European bishops. The conference was on its way, Adrian Hastings comments, to becoming a truly 'international and inter-racial Christian fellowship, rather than an almost accidental imperial and missionary prolongation of the Established Church of the English nation'.[41] In sum, especially when viewed in the historical rear-view mirror, what the 1958 Lambeth Conference accomplished was more considerable than is often supposed.[42] When it came time to bring the conference to a close, its president, Geoffrey Fisher, good-naturedly directed some humour at his own reputation as a headmaster, saying to the members from overseas: 'Will those who belong to other forms go back to their classrooms'.[43]

Stephen Bayne's appointment as Anglican executive officer was announced by Geoffrey Fisher on 19 April 1959, after Bishop Ambrose Reeves of Johannesburg,

[37]   Quoted in Purcell, *Fisher of Lambeth*, p. 198.

[38]   Jacob, *The Making of the Anglican Church*, p. 280.

[39]   E.R. Norman, *Church and Society in England, 1770–1970: A Historical Study* (Cambridge, 1996), p. 413.

[40]   Quoted in John Booty, *An American Apostle: The Life of Stephen Fielding Bayne Jr.* (Valley Forge, Pa., 1997), p. 64.

[41]   Adrian Hastings, *A History of English Christianity, 1920–2000* (London, 2001), p. 449.

[42]   Jacob, *The Making of the Anglican Church*, p. 295.

[43]   Quoted in Robert T. Holtby, *Robert Wright Stopford, 1901–1976* (London, 1988), p. 53.

South Africa, declined the offer.[44] Fisher and others had become convinced of the need for such an officer, who would travel all over the world, giving further cohesion to the Anglican Communion, helping to hold it together, finding out about and making known the problems and concerns of Anglican churches around the globe.[45] The Lambeth Conference of 1958 created this office. Those who supported the idea recognized that this work needed to be concentrated in the hands of one person, who would have to work well with the archbishop of Canterbury. At the time of Bayne's appointment, the Anglican Communion consisted of 340 dioceses and 40 million church members, including eight million in Africa. There were Anglican prayer books in 170 languages.[46]

New Provinces in Africa

The arrangements by which the Church of England governed itself had by Fisher's lifetime acquired the character of scrambling to catch up with a changing world with as much dignity as possible. Something of this was to be seen in the church's relationships abroad, too. It was not only that the British Empire was retreating. It was that the colonies themselves no longer regarded themselves as dependents. The new generation of African leaders wanted independence. Britain was barely in a position to repudiate this, even if its governments had wished to do so.

To the modern Anglican mind a regional church acquired maturity only when it had become a diocese. Anything less was merely a subordinate part of the whole. After 1945 the arrangements by which the Anglican church in Africa had been maintained were wearing thin. When Geoffrey Fisher became archbishop of Canterbury, there were still many 'Overseas Bishops of the Canterbury Jurisdiction', who remained dependent upon Canterbury for oversight. Fisher felt that the time had come for these Anglican churches to reflect in their organization a new autonomy.[47] He actively assisted them with their formation, personally drawing up the provincial constitutions for the provinces of West Africa, Central Africa, and East Africa. In this process he made use of the model provided by the constitution of the Church of the Province of South Africa. According to its polity, the local archbishop was the focus of unity. He presided

---

[44]   See John S. Peart-Binns, *Ambrose Reeves* (London, 1973), pp. 149, 150, 260.

[45]   Edward Carpenter, *Archbishop Fisher: His Life and Times* (Norwich, 1991), p. 473.

[46]   Booty, *An American Apostle*, pp. 92–7; Jacob, *The Making of the Anglican Church*, pp. 279–80.

[47]   Carpenter, *Archbishop Fisher*, p. 501.

over a general synod to which each diocese sent representatives: clergy and laity as well as bishops.[48]

During Fisher's tenure of office, four new provinces were established in Africa: West Africa in 1951, Central Africa in 1955, East Africa in 1960, and Uganda in 1960. Of this achievement, Bishop William Wand commented: 'Such a record would alone have been sufficient to make Geoffrey Fisher's tenure of the chair of St. Augustine ... of outstanding importance in the long history of the Anglican Communion'.[49] When Fisher journeyed to West Africa in 1951 it marked the first time that a primate had travelled to inaugurate in person a new province of the Anglican Communion. The Church of the Province of West Africa included the dioceses of Lagos, Sierra Leone, Accra, Niger, the Gambia, and the Rio Pongas. Its formation as a province had been initiated by Archbishop William Temple in 1944. The new province, which brought together – not easily – both Low Church and Anglo-Catholic dioceses, was formally inaugurated by Fisher on 17 April 1951, in Freetown, Sierra Leone, when the bishops of the six dioceses signed the preamble and the articles of the constitution. The archbishop of Canterbury then released them from their oaths of canonical obedience to him, and they elected their own metropolitan.[50] 'The granting of independence to the Anglican dioceses in the British West African colonies', notes W.M. Jacob, 'took place significantly before they achieved political independence from Britain – Ghana in 1957, Nigeria in 1960 and Sierra Leone in 1961'.[51]

In May 1955 Fisher again journeyed to Africa, this time for the inauguration of the new province for Central Africa. Fisher was the celebrant at a Eucharist at the cathedral of St. Mary and All Saints in Salisbury (the old name of Harare), Southern Rhodesia (now Zimbabwe). This service marked the culmination of a complex process that Fisher had initiated in 1951: the formation of the Church of the Province of Central Africa, consisting of Anglicans in what are now Zimbabwe, Zambia, and Malawi.[52] It was on this trip, during a visit to St. Michael's College in Blantyre, Nyasaland (now Malawi), that in a discussion with students Fisher made his infamous remark that 'all men are equal in the love of God but not in the sight of God'.[53] His biographer Edward Carpenter has commented, 'It would be impossible to imagine a form of words more calculated

---

[48]   Jacob, *The Making of the Anglican Church*, p. 268; Carpenter, *Archbishop Fisher*, p. 500.

[49]   J.W.C. Wand, *Anglicanism in History and Today* (New York, 1962), p. 44.

[50]   Jacob, *The Making of the Anglican Church*, p. 269.

[51]   Ibid.

[52]   William L. Sachs, *The Transformation of Anglicanism: From State Church to Global Communion* (Cambridge: Cambridge University Press, 1993), p. 315; Jacob, *The Making of the Anglican Church*, p. 269.

[53]   Quoted in Carpenter, *Archbishop Fisher*, p. 518.

to be misunderstood in so highly charged a political atmosphere. Nor is it easy to understand precisely what this comment means – or was intended to mean'.[54] It is just as well that Fisher did not elaborate.

In 1960 Fisher, now aged 73 and still going strong, inaugurated the Province of East Africa in a service at Dar es Salaam (a seaport on the Indian Ocean in what is now Tanzania). Consisting of 12 dioceses, this province took longer to form. Also in 1960, Uganda was established as an autonomous province. This transformation, notes W.M. Jacob, had met with 'considerable white opposition'. Fisher achieved his goal by, in Jacob's words, 'forc[ing] the division of the existing diocese into 11 new dioceses, with the suffragans becoming diocesans, and the former diocese becoming a province'. Once again, the ecclesiastical realm was ahead of the political, Uganda being formed as an independent province two years before the country gained political independence.[55]

Jacob points out that with the formation of the Uganda province, the Anglican episcopate began to undergo an important change. When 1960 began, there were only three black African diocesans; by the end of that year there were seven. Fisher had consecrated four black African suffragan bishops in 1955; they were made diocesans when Uganda became an autonomous province.[56] David Edwards notes that Fisher's efforts in Africa amounted to a 'double success'. His trips 'loosened the constitutional' but 'strengthened the personal links'.[57] Canon Max Warren, general secretary of the Church Missionary Society and an advisor to Fisher on Uganda, later wrote: 'In Geoffrey Fisher Africans saw a great church leader, and a European at that, actually abdicating authority, in Africa an event as yet without precedent in the State'.[58]

These remarkable developments anticipated the era when the Anglican church in Africa would become one of the largest and strongest forces, and surely one of the most vital elements, in the Anglican Communion. By the end of the twentieth century the Anglican Communion was no longer largely Anglo-Saxon; by then, most Anglicans did not have English as their first language. Since 1950 the number of provinces had more than doubled, and the fastest-growing

---

[54]   Carpenter, *Archbishop Fisher*, p. 518. Adrian Hastings comments: 'The Archbishop's statement, in so far as it was true, was rather banal, but it was poor theology (Fisher indeed was no theologian) and it could easily be taken as a defence of racial discrimination on the old grounds of God having set each man in his estate—castle or cottage, affluent white suburb or rickety black shanty-town'. *History*, p. 434.

[55]   Jacob, *The Making of the Anglican Church*, p. 270.

[56]   Ibid.

[57]   Edwards, *Leaders*, p. 362.

[58]   Quoted in Edwards, *Leaders*, p. 362.

dioceses were in Africa and New Guinea.[59] Indeed, by the beginning of the twenty-first century the 'average' Anglican would not be a middle-aged English gentleman but a woman of 22 in sub-Saharan Africa walking several kilometres every day to fetch water for her three or four children.[60] The creation of this global communion had certainly been substantially the achievement of Fisher. It gave the Church of England a place in a new paradigm while simultaneously generating the expectation that the paradigm at large was not only coherent but would look to Canterbury for its identity and various self-understandings. This achievement would be inherited by Fisher's successors and each of them would face his own struggles to maintain the argument.

Australia

In a sermon at Westminster Abbey in August 1947 Fisher affirmed that the church in Australia must no longer be led by the Church of England but must instead stand on its own feet and govern itself. But this was not legally the case. The Australian church was bound by historic trusts. It was obliged to maintain the liturgy of the Church of England. When he did not do this the bishop of Bathurst got into trouble in the courts. In Australia Bishop Batty of Newcastle had longed for the opportunity to set to work on a new independent constitution for his church. Fisher thought he was right. When Australian bishops came to the 1948 Lambeth Conference this was squarely – if secretly – on the agenda.

Prime ministers who experience domestic gloom are widely observed to find rejuvenation on foreign tours. Fisher was the first archbishop of Canterbury who came to enjoy similar compensations. When the bishops of the Anglican church met at Lambeth in 1948 Fisher found himself warmly invited, even pressed, to visit the church in Australasia. It was not difficult to see why this should be accepted. For decades the Anglican church there had been regarded as a very distant realm, something which rested on the periphery of a colonial age. The historical titles by which the church was known looked clumsy or even embarrassing. Australian Anglicans belonged to the 'Church of England in Australia'. A visiting archbishop of Canterbury would now assure it that it did hold a genuine place in the Anglican imagination.

In 1948 it took a passenger ship four weeks to reach the other side of the world. If Fisher were to go to Australasia who would run the domestic office

---

[59]   Jacob, *The Making of the Anglican Church*, p. 298.

[60]   Duncan Reid, review of *Beyond Colonial Anglicanism: The Anglican Communion in the Twenty-first Century*, edited by Ian T. Douglas and Kwok Pui-lan, *Journal of Anglican Studies* 3 (2005), p. 126.

in what must be a protracted absence? Duties were accordingly apportioned to bishops of one sort or another, and the British Council obligingly produced the money for the arcbishop's fare. A convenient pause at Cape Town would give Fisher an opportunity to meet with local bishops there too. The *Dominion Monarch* left on 22 September 1950. On the high seas the churches stoutly maintained their divisions: on board ship Rosamund Fisher was pained to find Anglicans at communion in the lounge and Roman Catholics at communion in the drawing room.

From Perth to Sydney, in civic services and town hall receptions, traveling by motor car through cities and by railways through deserts, the tour was regarded as a remarkable success. Ever the eager tourist, Fisher himself was a brilliant guest – avuncular, inquisitive, and brimful of cheerful experiences and fresh and constructive ideas. A penchant for cricket helped no end. Perhaps, it was mused, visiting English scholars could be sent over to support theological thought in universities and colleges? In Sydney Roman Catholics avoided him while in Brisbane they courted him. Anglican–Nonconformist relations were noticeably warmed. The prime minister, Robert Menzies (a Presbyterian), wrote to *The Times*, 'It deserves to be widely known that the Archbishop's visit stirred men's hearts and minds all over Australia'.[61] A coda in New Zealand was no less successful.

On his return voyage Fisher settled to the congenial task of reading a draft constitution devised by a Constitution Committee appointed by the General Synod of the Australian Church and then devising his own version. This brought out the best in him. The upshot was seen to be clear, bold, and liberal. Perhaps because he was not, at heart, a party man Fisher had the confidence to frame compromises and trust to them, too. The new constitution was approved in convention and the General Synod there in 1955. When its advocates quaked at the prospect of taking it back to the dioceses for final endorsement Fisher fortified them. His stature in Australia proved one of the new constitution's most vital buttresses. The Australian commentator Muriel Porter observes that it is now 'generally acknowledged' that Fisher's 'decisive intervention' saved the day and created a viable, and enduring, constitutional basis for the church in Australia.[62]

---

[61]   See Carpenter, *Archbishop Fisher*, p. 484.
[62]   Muriel Porter, *The New Puritans: The Rise of Fundamentalism in the Anglican Church* (Melbourne, 2006), p. 58.

Chapter 6
Ecumenism, 1945–1961

When Fisher became archbishop of Canterbury he assumed responsibility for a vision of the universal church which had been painstakingly won by his three immediate predecessors. At the onset of the twentieth century Davidson's broad churchmanship had allowed a fair degree of latitude when it came to relations with other traditions: he had taken a pragmatic but generous view of other denominations at home, viewing exchanges of pulpits with no distaste and attracting and readily accepting a spontaneous invitation to pray at the grave of the great Baptist preacher, Charles Spurgeon. Not yet was this a purposeful international dimension of the archbishop's role – but that was already gathering a formidable momentum across the churches at large. In 1895 the World Student Christian Federation had sprung to life. The 1910 Edinburgh Conference on World Mission proved an emphatic landmark, showing how deeply mission and ecumenism were intertwined. The Great War proved only a temporary interruption; within only a few years international ecumenism had come to be largely defined by the Faith and Order and the Life and Work movements and also by the World's Evangelical Alliance, a Protestant association which could look back as far as 1846.

The Church of England had been among the earliest supporters of international ecumenism, starting with the World Missionary Conference held in Edinburgh in 1910.[1] After 1928 Archbishop Lang viewed these initiatives with firm interest. Many of the leading lights in the Church of England could be seen sailing off to one international conference or another. William Temple, meanwhile, had been one of the great ecumenists of his generation, leading the Faith and Order movement abroad, while Bishop Bell achieved no less a stature in the Life and Work movement. The archbishop's relations with other churches had by now become so great a burden that 1933 had seen the creation, in the Church Assembly, of the archbishop of Canterbury's Council on Foreign Relations, a purposeful body which had grown to maturity by the time Fisher arrived at Lambeth Palace. Lang, too, was the first archbishop of Canterbury to seek alliances with other churches across the world in response to the crises of his age. In his two, brief years at Lambeth, Temple had overseen that brief

---

[1] Welsby, *History of the Church of England*, p. 92.

flourishing of Protestant-Roman Catholic accord, the Sword of the Spirit, during the Second World War.

And Fisher? He was hardly to be seen in this landscape. Quite simply, he inherited ecumenism as a responsibility claimed by his predecessors. Yet in time he became deeply committed to it and he would play important roles at key times in its history, showing a fine instinct for what should be done and when. He also had the historical and theological knowledge, the wide personal acquaintance, and the confidence needed to develop fresh proposals and to bring them forward in a useful way. And he managed to carry out this activity while guarding his own flanks.[2] Now his task was to be a constructive one: how was all this idealism and energy to find organization and expression in the postwar world? If Fisher had become archbishop for a single reason it was not because he was viewed as a prophet of high ideals but because he was considered to have a gift for the practical art of building constructively and effectively. What then would he build in the realm of ecumenism?

The ecumenical movements dealt above all in words. They held conferences, passed resolutions, piled up correspondence. Temple was in his element in such a context. But Fisher was never a brilliant public speaker, and for the most part his writings are not memorable. Nor would he prove to be one of the ecumenical giants of the twentieth century – devoted to the movement and thoroughly involved in its processes, as Temple had been or as George Bell was. Perhaps what ecumenism needed now above all was a good dose of unglamorous, practical statesmanship? Some of those who walked onto the stage during Fisher's years – including the new pope, John XXIII – felt that too much theology and too many theologians had so far only got in the way of progress. Fisher was not tempted to add more. Meanwhile, relations between all traditions had invariably stumbled over the recognition of holy orders – arguably because it was the clergy, and not the laity, who dominated these proceedings. While not known as a wordsmith, Fisher had a politician's sense of the right phrase at the propitious moment. Perhaps the two phrases for which he should be most remembered relative to ecumenism are 'full communion' and 'not return'. The first phrase is from the beginning of his archiepiscopate and relates to Protestants. The latter phrase is from the end of his tenure of office and relates to the Roman Catholic Church.

---

2   See William Purcell, *Fisher of Lambeth: A Portrait from Life* (London, 1969), p. 274.

The Cambridge Sermon of 1946

At least one great danger in pursuing the splendid theme of church unity lay in its power to inspire bitter controversy at home. The very terms on which any scheme or dialogue might come to rest inevitably attracted a suspicion of compromised principles. In the company of Roman Catholics an archbishop of Canterbury could look as though he had turned his back on the Evangelicals, while conferences with Free Churches set Anglo-Catholics on edge. By the end of 1945 Fisher was encouraging both parties to nail their colours firmly to the mast, and there was a hope that the Free Churches would do the same. At all events, under the energetic leadership of Dom Gregory Dix it was the Anglo-Catholics who got off to a flying start with a collection called *Catholicity: A Study in the Conflict of Christian Traditions in the West* (1947). To this, Fisher provided a rather detached foreword.[3] The Evangelicals followed with their own collection, *The Fulness of Christ*, in 1950.[4] But to some, at least, it looked more like a riposte to *Catholicity* than an argument standing on its own two feet. Fisher was no doubt glad to see them all kept busy on something broadly constructive while he got on with other things.

Fisher had been active in the British Council of Churches (BCC) since its inception during the war. The British Council brought together members of 16 denominations: the Church of England, the Church of Wales, the Church of Ireland, the Free Churches, the Salvation Army, the Society of Friends, and five interdenominational organizations. As bishop of London, Fisher had served as chairman of the BCC's executive committee; from 1945 to 1961, as archbishop, he served as its president. But probably the most famous address of Fisher's entire archiepiscopate was his Cambridge sermon of 1946. Preached in the University Church in Cambridge, the sermon stemmed from two factors – two historical events – one positive and the other negative. The first was the good experience of establishing full communion with the Old Catholics (via the Bonn Agreement of 1931–32). The second was the bad experience of the American Episcopalians in trying to bring about an organizational union with the northern Presbyterians (via a proposal that Fisher deemed too restrictive).[5]

---

[3] See E.L. Mascall, *Saraband: The Memoirs of E.L. Mascall* (Leominster, 1992), pp. 162–3. Mascall shows how much of the initiative actually lay with Dom Gregory Dix and is critical of Fisher for giving the book 'a patronising beta-minus'.

[4] See Randle Manwaring, *From Controversy to Co-existence: Evangelicals in the Church of England, 1914–1980* (Cambridge, 1985), chap. 10.

[5] Edward Carpenter, *Archbishop Fisher: His Life and Times* (Norwich, 1991), p. 310; GF, 'Archbishop Fisher's Cambridge Sermon, 1946', in R.P. Flindall (ed.), *The Church of England, 1815–1948: A Documentary History* (London, 1972), p. 444; Peter Staples, 'Archbishop Geoffrey

From these experiences Fisher gained a sense of what in the realm of church unity was now workable and desirable. In an era when ecumenists were often still thinking of mergers, Fisher was arguably ahead of his time in wanting to have unity without submerging ecclesiastical identities.

It was from the pulpit of Great St. Mary's, on 23 November, and in a sermon entitled 'A Step Forward in Church Relations' that Fisher proposed that the churches work toward establishing full communion. This arrangement would allow churches to exchange clergy, for the orders of all ordained ministers would be accepted by all participating churches. 'There is', he said, 'a suggestion which I should like ... to make to my brethren of other denominations'; and then he proposed an institutional relationship somewhere between federation and organic union: 'We do not desire a federation: that does not restore the circulation. [And] we are not yet ready for organic ... union. But there can be a process of ... growing alike'. Full communion was the best way forward: 'What we need is that while the folds remain distinct, there should be a movement towards a free and unfettered exchange of life in worship and sacrament ... as there is already of prayer and thought and Christian fellowship – in short that they should grow towards that full communion with one another, which already in their separation they have with Christ'.[6] Full communion would be possible only if each church was willing to accept episcopacy. Thus Fisher proposed that the Free Churches consider 'taking episcopacy into their own systems'.[7] This suggestion was not as bold or presumptuous as it might at first appear, for, as Fisher pointed out, the Free Churches had already said that any future united church would be episcopal, in some form. Cantuar noted that the Church of England was already in full communion with the Old Catholics on the Continent, 'and', he added, 'its relations with the Orthodox Churches ... and with the Churches of Sweden and Finland ... approach ... full communion'.[8]

In Britain, the Cambridge sermon became the most striking contribution to ecumenical hopes since the Lambeth Conference of 1920 had issued its Appeal to All Christian People, an initiative which by now seemed to have

---

Francis Fisher: An Appraisal', *Nederlands Theologisch Tijdschrift* 28 (1974), p. 258. See David Hein, 'The Episcopal Church and the Ecumenical Movement, 1937–1997: Presbyterians, Lutherans, and the Future', *Anglican and Episcopal History* 66 (1997), pp. 4–13.

6   GF, 'Archbishop Fisher's Cambridge Sermon', in Flindall, *The Church of England, 1815–1948*, p. 438.

7   See the comments on this proposal by Vincent Taylor, principal of Wesley College, Headingley, Leeds, in 'Living Issues in Biblical Scholarship: The Church and the Ministry', *Expository Times* 62 (1951), pp. 271–4.

8   GF, 'Archbishop Fisher's Cambridge Sermon', in Flindall, *The Church of England, 1815–1948*, p. 438.

well and truly fizzled out, despite the fact that the British churches had come together for social action, and even though in 1942 the British Council of Churches had been founded. Unwilling to wait for the theologians to finish haggling over the theological details of ecumenical agreements, Fisher was ready to start a process aimed at bringing the Protestant churches of Britain closer together in demonstrable ways.[9] His proposal now did not come completely out of the blue. He had been in conversation with the Free Churches and had reason to suppose that they were interested in reopening discussions. Fisher's manner helped to make his message more palatable. A Free Churchman who was present recalled, 'He was so simple and unaffected in his style, so brotherly and cordial in his attitude that he won all hearts'.[10] Indeed, the Free Churches responded favourably to Fisher's sermon, agreeing to hold conversations with representatives of the Church of England. These discussions took place over the next five years.[11] That fact in itself marks an achievement in church diplomacy. Any practical consequences which might excite men and women in church pews are altogether harder to discern. Roger Lloyd sums up the significance of Fisher's Cambridge Sermon: 'How much is owed to [this sermon] is hardly possible even to guess, but it did take the movement out of the deep freeze and got inter-church discussions started again. There is surely a connection between the sermon and the new proposals for communion and finally organic unity between the Methodist Church and the Church of England'.[12] In the final chapter of this biography we will see what Fisher's reaction was to these proposals for eventual union when they came forward during the archiepiscopate of his successor and former pupil, Michael Ramsey.

The World Council of Churches

Fisher must have known perfectly well that the leading international ecumenists of the Protestant world had longed that Bishop Bell should succeed Archbishop Temple at Lambeth. His own ecumenical credentials were weak. When the Dutch Visser't Hooft, the French Marc Boegner, and the Swiss Alphons Koechlin visited him in London shortly before the end of the war in 1945, Fisher confessed 'simply that he knew little about the World Council, but that he walked in the steps of the two Williams [Temple and Paton] and that he was

[9]   Paul A. Welsby, *A History of the Church of England, 1945–1980* (Oxford, 1986), p. 78.

[10]   Quoted in Carpenter, *Archbishop Fisher*, p. 311.

[11]   Welsby, *History of the Church of England*, p. 79; Edward Carpenter, *Cantuar: The Archbishops in Their Office* (London, 1971), p. 503.

[12]   Roger Lloyd, *The Church of England, 1900–1965* (London, 1966), p. 470.

therefore ready to accept'.[13] But Visser't Hooft would soon come to acknowledge that Fisher gave the great enterprise committed and vital support.

Indeed, Fisher would now play a significant role in the World Council of Churches (WCC) – the first international, interdenominational Christian consultative body – from its earliest days.[14] It was Fisher who was in the chair of the Assembly when the WCC was formally inaugurated on 23 August 1948, in Amsterdam. On this historic occasion, 351 delegates from 147 churches were in attendance. Among the major religious bodies, only the Roman Catholic Church and the Orthodox churches within the Soviet orbit did not send representatives.[15] At this meeting, Fisher was immediately elected one of the World Council's presiding officers.[16] The WCC had decided to have a five-man collegial presidency, in so doing managing to avoid giving offence to any of its constituents and making the office of president more symbolic than substantive. The president functioned more or less as a parliamentary chairman, while the real administrative authority was held by Visser't Hooft, now its first general secretary, and by the committee chairmen.[17] Did all of this really suit Fisher himself? There is at least a touch of Fisherian ambiguity in his remark on the last day of the Assembly that 'the total number of words spoken ... must be something like the numbers which indicate the distance between the earth and the farthest stars'.[18]

On 1 September 1952, *Time* magazine published an article that usefully incorporated Archbishop Fisher's views on the role of the World Council of Churches. The author of this article noted that Fisher 'favors church unity – as an ideal. But, practically speaking, he has his reservations'. Fisher is quoted as saying that the WCC 'is not a church. It is none of its business to negotiate a reunion between the churches'. And if the World Council of Churches tried to force any changes in the creed of the Anglican church, then 'we should clear out'. The author of this piece concluded, 'In this ultimate stubbornness, the archbishop is supported by most Anglican churchmen. In his quiet way, ... Fisher has intensified the predilection of his flock for their middle way in

13   W.A. Visser't Hooft, *Memoirs* (London, 1973), p. 186.

14   Purcell, *Fisher of Lambeth*, p. 189.

15   Welsby, *History of the Church of England*, p. 92.

16   See Peter Staples, 'Archbishop Geoffrey Francis Fisher: An Appraisal', in *Nederlands Theologisch Tijdschrift* 28 (1974), p. 257.

17   Heather A. Warren, *Theologians of a New World Order: Reinhold Niebuhr and the Christian Realists, 1920–1948* (New York, 1997), p. 119.

18   W.A. Visser't Hooft (ed.), *The First Assembly of the World Council of Churches held at Amsterdam August 22nd to September 4th, 1948* (London, 1949), p. 7.

Christendom, and has added to their confidence that it is a true way, a good compromise between Geneva and Rome'.[19]

In 1954 Fisher attended the great Evanston congress of the World Council of Churches and, in the eyes of his confreres, did well. At least one young delegate, a Lutheran from Germany, saw another dimension of him during an interval when both strayed into the local art gallery for respite. Quite alone and evidently lost in reflection in front of a great canvas by Hieronymus Bosch, Fisher suddenly threw his arms around his accidental companion and exclaimed, 'Isn't it *wonderful?*' Another delegate stepped into the room, looked embarrassed, and promptly disappeared.[20]

Evanston was a luminous achievement. It could with justice claim to be 'the most widely representative church gathering ever held' – and it certainly looked it, for 125,000 people attended.[21] It now provided a forum for 163 churches from 48 countries. The theme, *Christ the Hope of the World*, generated six strong reports and a good deal of intense theological business ('They sure is givin' hope a good goin' over', remarked a janitor busy at work in the background[22]). Every participant must have felt at least a strain of exultation that such a formidable rally could come to life. But by now there were doubts in the Church of England. Bishop Wand, Fisher's successor at London, grumbled about the extent to which the enterprise had been preponderantly the achievement of American finance, German theology and Dutch organization. Wand had also fussed over whether or not one of the Council's presidents must always be the archbishop of Canterbury, a demand which Fisher himself evidently viewed with indifference. But Bishop Bell, too, had found the preparatory material somehow lacking in inspiration and had begun to lament 'the almost complete lack of any organization for getting the World Council into the mind of the Church of England'.[23] It was a question which would not go away.

---

[19] *Time*, 1 September 1952, p. 53.

[20] As recounted to AC in conversation by Hans Florin, the young man concerned.

[21] *Evanston Speaks: Reports from the Second Assembly of the World Council of Churches August 15–31, 1954* (London, 1954), p. 7.

[22] Quoted by Jasper in *George Bell*, p. 226.

[23] Ibid., p. 331.

The Methodists

Edward Carpenter has argued that Fisher made a high priority of ecumenism as a deliberate act of policy'.[24] Once the war had ended his sights were firmly set on the Free Churches. While ranks of Anglicans either praised or frowned and puzzled about thes various phrases and meanings of the Cambridge sermon of 1946. the sermon won particular favor in Free Church circles. This support would soon gather its own momentum. A leading Methodist, Leslie Weatherhead, was heard to say that he would become a member of the Church of England tomorrow were it not for its Establishment and its Thirty-nine Articles.

Weatherhead did not mention bishops. Many Methodists did not care for them. For his part, Fisher viewed episcopacy in a thoroughly practical light. It was an important source of authority so that people knew what they were doing. Bishops ordained and defended the true faith. The rest was theory. This judgment attracted many Methodists because, of all the Free Churches, their connection with the Church of England was historically the most ambiguous.

When two Anglican committees, one Anglo-Catholic (under Michael Ramsey) and the other Evangelical (under Donald Coggan) published two further reports on ecumenism Fisher appeared to have more trouble with the views of the Anglo-Catholics. Relations with Ramsey became abrasive. Fisher looked to unity, not the indulgence of party. Ramsey wondered if he could distinguish between the two fairly. For five years conversations with Free Church leaders continued. The meetings were not simply allowed to trundle along in their own manner. Fisher was present at important junctures to give them a prod or to clarify issues. They discussed bishops, establishments and doctrines, and they pondered communion. But Fisher could also see that in the parishes ecumenical activities were sometimes developing quite independently. He was at least vulnerable to the criticism that, while he disavowed centralization, he also possessed an Anglican wariness of local wisdom. Fisher looked to 'an unrestricted inter-communion' between traditions which could look each other squarely and confidently in the eye in the knowledge that they belonged together after all.[25] Each could be distinctive, independent, free. 'Indeed', he remarked to a Birmingham vicar, 'it would be very much like what you find in the early Church at Corinth, and the Church at Athens, and the Church in Jerusalem and in Rome'.[26] While others bickered about principles Fisher went off on holiday to muse about structures.

---

[24]   See Carpenter, *Geoffrey Fisher*, p. 309.

[25]   See Carpenter, *Archbishop Fisher*, p. 317.

[26]   Ibid. The correspondent was W.T.P. Wheeler, vicar of New Basford.

The upshot of all this was predictably indeterminate. But it also produced a curious coda. After 1968 the Anglo-Catholic Archbishop Ramsey became a convinced advocate of union with the Methodists. Fisher, in retirement, would play no mean part in undermining the whole enterprise from his private study in Trent.

The Orthodox

Ecumenically-minded Protestants were divided from the world of Orthodoxy by at least three vast oceans. The first was theological, the second geographical, and the third political. In the twentieth century there had been vital, even inspirational friendships across these divides. Bishop Bell and Bishop Velimirovic maintained an occasional correspondence across decades.[27] Much had occurred in consequence of the flight from Bolshevism after 1917, a great diaspora which saw men like Berdyaev writing a succession of enormous works in Paris and attracting a committed constituency of interest across the West. In Britain the Fellowship of St. Alban and St. Sergius was born in 1928, and for years the Orthodox scholar Nicolas Zernov pleaded the cause of a displaced, and mellow, Orthodoxy from his bastion in Oxford. By the time that Fisher was archbishop the fellowship had a house in west London. This had become a modest, but rich strand in British Christian experience. The Orthodox church in Greece, Cyprus, Yugoslavia, and Bulgaria had long been open to the Church of England. Archbishop Germanos of Thyateira had been a friend of Archbishop Söderblom since 1920, a reliable ally of Archbishop Lang in all statements on world peace, and had long been a committed participant in the ecumenical movements at large. In 1948 he became a President of the World Council of Churches. The ecumenical patriarch of Constantinople, Athenagoras, was a known and trusted friend and ally. But, like the Orthodox in Britain, the Orthodox in Istanbul lived and worshipped as a tiny minority.

The Anglicans who found themselves most fascinated by Orthodoxy were almost invariably found to be High ones. Fisher was not High. He viewed Orthodoxy only partly as an ecumenical adventure. For him the world of Orthodoxy was caught up in the dimension of foreign policy. Throughout his archiepiscopate dealing with Russian Orthodoxy meant dealing not so much with polite, progressive émigrés, for whom ecumenical exchange was a happy enrichment, but an embattled, entrenched, corporate Soviet church which

[27]   See Muriel Heppell, *George Bell and Nikolai Velimirovi: The Story of a Friendship* (Birmingham, 2001).

possessed a quite different mind and inhabited an utterly different landscape. If Fisher wanted the Russian church to join the international ecumenical enterprise, somebody must venture behind the Iron Curtain in the hope that a plausible representative of that tradition could be retrieved. At the time of the Amsterdam General Assembly there was nothing coming out of Russia at all. Because the Iron Curtain fell where it did it was equally difficult now for Orthodox Christians in Romania, Bulgaria, Yugoslavia, and Poland to participate. Stephan Zankov, an eager ecumenist before the war, was now stuck in Bulgaria and quite unable to move. Insofar as these churches sought an international presence, it was in the Communist World Council of Peace.

However severe the discouragements, Fisher thought the ecumenists should persevere. The World Council of Churches needed the Russian church. How could it be authentically international and ecumenical without it? How could the Orthodox world feel anything other than a minority without it? In Geneva, Visser't Hooft was entirely of the same mind. Later he would recall, 'we found it practically impossible under the given circumstances to ensure that the voice of orthodoxy should not be drowned by Western and mainly Protestant voices'.[28] Together the luminaries of the WCC sought to inveigle the patriarchs into the General Assembly of the Council in Amsterdam. In 1946 a flicker of interest simply went out. Little followed. The Soviet ambassador was invited to Lambeth in March 1948, and there launched a battery of questions at the archbishop. None of this appeared to produce anything.

In 1952 this dismal situation began to change. The German pastor, and cause célèbre of the Hitler era, Martin Niemöller, disappeared into Russia on a purely personal initiative. His subsequent reports revived hope. Then, in 1954, Bishop Bell and Visser't Hooft went to Hungary and were told that the head of the Foreign Relations Department of the Moscow Patriarchate, Metropolitan Nikolai, actually wished to learn something of the World Council of Churches.

These activities were all very well, but by the time of Evanston the Cold War was at its bleakest. A number of ecumenists sailing to the United States found themselves anxiously inspecting their own passports to see if the stamps which recorded their various foreign visits to Communist countries might see them refused entry altogether. After the assembly members of the Central Committee argued about whether or not some delegation should seek to visit the Soviet Union. Eventually, they decided to make an approach through the Russian Orthodox bishop in Berlin. The stratagem worked; by February 1955 a line had been established. An American delegation led by Franklin Clark Fry left for Moscow in March 1956. The Hungarian Uprising derailed these endeavours for

---

28   W.A. Visser't Hooft, *Memoirs*, p. 255.

two years, but 1958 brought a meeting in Utrecht, an army of interpreters and several suitcases of gifts. All parties now agreed that the Moscow patriarchate would send an observer to meetings of the Central Committee. In 1959 Visser't Hooft led a delegation to Russia, coming back with a firmly positive view of their prospects for ecumenical dialogue. When the next General Assembly of the WCC met in New Delhi in 1961 the Orthodox churches of Russia, Romania, Bulgaria, and Poland were admitted as members.

The World Council of Churches was to be suspected east of the Iron Curtain for two reasons: it was effectively a Western organization and also a Protestant one. Many Orthodox viewed Roman Catholicism with disapprobation: the churches of the Protestant reformation were hardly worth a contemptful glance. The very notion of entering into respectful conversations about the niceties of Christian doctrine with such people would altogether have failed to occur to them. But here they were together, doubtless with their own reasons and agendas. The extent to which the ecumenically-minded Christians of the West really knew knew what they were dealing with would hang over the WCC for many years to come.[29]

The Journey to Jerusalem

The idea for his last major trip as archbishop came to Fisher 'in one flash ... in my study'.[30] He determined to go first to Jerusalem, then to Istanbul, and finally to Rome. Meeting with the heads of the Orthodox churches on their home turf was the natural next step in a developing relationship that included Fisher's friendship with Archbishop Germanos, the official representative of the ecumenical patriarch in London. In July 1956 nine Anglican and 12 Russian theologians and church leaders had met in Moscow for a theological conference.[31] Thus much important groundwork had already been laid, at least for the Orthodox stages of this journey.

In Jerusalem, in November 1960, Fisher met with the patriarch of Jerusalem, Benedictus, with both the Latin and the Armenian patriarchs, with the governor of Jerusalem, and with the Franciscan Custodian of the Holy Places. He preached in the Anglican cathedral of St. George and visited the traditional pilgrimage

---

[29] For an extended discussion of these themes see Joachim Garstecki (ed.): *Die Ökumene und der Widerstand gegen Diktaturen: Nationalsozialismus und Kommunismus als Herausforderung an die Kirchen Ökumene und Widerstand* (Berlin, 2007) and Dianne Kirby (ed.), *Religion and the Cold War* (London, 2002).

[30] Purcell, *Fisher of Lambeth*, p. 270.

[31] Staples, 'Archbishop Geoffrey Francis Fisher', p. 259.

places.[32] The scholar of ecumenism will note the advances that this trip brought about in Anglican–Orthodox relations. But the student of Fisher's life may find one incident of greatest interest. It occurred at one of these traditional pilgrimage sites. Fisher was reluctant to wear his religion on his sleeve. He would expect an observer to infer his faith from his obvious commitment to Christianity in its traditional, orthodox, institutional expressions – that is, from his participation in its rituals, from his involvement with its sacred texts, from his preaching and sacramental actions, even from his strenuous efforts in church administration. The rest would be private. To the biographer, signs of something else going on may be welcome, therefore, when they do occur.

On a visit to the church of the Holy Sepulchre Fisher had what may be best characterized as a deeply felt experience of participation in the Body of Christ – in the Eucharistic sense in which Body of Christ means both Jesus Christ, crucified and risen, and the body of Christian believers. This experience was so intense that Fisher's normally accurate and detailed memory could not capture the entirety of this occurrence: 'I cannot describe the church', he said later.

> I hardly saw it. I remember the first place I knelt – a stone on which Our Lord's body was supposed to have rested after being taken down from the cross. Why can I not recall all of this with exactitude? Because throughout, in a strange way, I became mentally passive, feeling a kind of victim with Our Lord.

From the moment that Geoffrey Fisher entered the church, he was surrounded by Orthodox monks, Franciscan friars, and others, who virtually carried him from place to place, holding up his arms. There were many steps down to the chapels and then up to the sepulcher. Fisher said that he scarcely walked. Carried along by Orthodox, Franciscans, and Armenians, he hardly had a chance to stumble.

> At a place I would kneel and feel Our Lord looking at us in this strange mixture of past and present; then be borne on again, this way and that, and feeling lovingly at their mercy. And I felt that somehow like this Our Lord was pulled and hustled and felt at the mercy of his unloving guides.

Beyond this powerful sense of being both with Christ and with Christ's followers, Fisher could not recall much at all. 'At intervals the bells would clang again. The whole thing was an astonishing outpouring of every kind of excited motion, all

---

[32]   See H.G.G. Herklots, *Frontiers of the Church: The Making of the Anglican Communion* (London, 1961), p. 80.

flowing round and over me, not me as a person, but as a kind of centre point of that triumphal showing forth of Christian fellowship'.[33]

From Jerusalem, Fisher journeyed to Istanbul, where he met with Athenagoras I, the ecumenical patriarch, head of the Orthodox churches throughout the world.[34] These face-to-face encounters between Fisher and Orthodox leaders helped to move forward Anglican–Orthodox relations. Fisher's visits were an important prelude to the decision taken at the Pan-Orthodox Conference at Rhodes in 1964 to pursue doctrinal discussions with Anglicans. Moreover, Fisher's efforts dovetailed with the interests and commitments of the archbishop of York, Michael Ramsey, who loved the Orthodox tradition and relished participating in theological dialogues with Orthodox churchmen.

Meeting the Pope

In 1956 the confirmed Anglophile Cardinal Montini played host to a modest colloquium of Anglicans and Catholics. This quiet occasion suggested a change in the climate which hung over the relationship between the two traditions. That December, Fisher wrote Montini a cordial letter of thanks: 'I am sure that such personal contacts ... are the best way of creating that spirit of love and understanding ... which is a prerequisite for closer unity in the future'.[35]

Archbishop Fisher's historic visit with Pope John XXIII occurred on 2 December 1960. It took place in a changed ecumenical context. Pope John had called for a Council of the Universal Church, which would become known as Vatican II (1962–65); and the pope had established, as a part of the preparation for this council, a new Secretariat for the Promoting of Unity among Christians. In August 1959 the secretary of this new body, Monsignor Jan Willebrands, as an unofficial Roman Catholic observer, attended a meeting of the Central Committee of the World Council of Churches, held at St. Andrews, Scotland.[36] Fisher talked with Willebrands on this occasion, and shortly thereafter the pope communicated his willingness to meet the archbishop at the Vatican.[37] Fisher's visit was to be one of the first initiatives undertaken in response to this new ecumenical openness on the part of the Church of Rome.[38]

---

[33] Quoted in Purcell, *Fisher of Lambeth*, p. 277.
[34] Fisher was only the second archbishop of Canterbury to visit an ecumenical patriarch, after Lang in 1939.
[35] Frederick Bliss, *Anglicans in Rome: A History* (Norwich, 2006), p. 37.
[36] Carpenter, *Cantuar: The Archbishops of Canterbury in Their Office* (London, 1971), p. 501.
[37] Staples, 'Archbishop Geoffrey Francis Fisher', p. 260; Carpenter, *Archbishop Fisher*, p. 707.
[38] Welsby, *History of the Church of England*, p. 177.

But Vatican officials still viewed the visit of an archbishop of Canterbury with suspicion, handling it, in the words of one Vatican scholar, 'like a guilty secret'.[39] The two poles of opinion there were defined by the pope's Secretary of State, Cardinal Tardini, and the President of the Secretariat for Promoting Christian Unity, Cardinal Bea. In announcing this historic event, the first such visit since that of Archbishop Arundel in 1397, the official Vatican newspaper, *Osservatore Romano*, simply referred to the archbishop of Canterbury as 'Dr. Fisher'.[40] After failing to prevent this visit, Vatican officials suppressed the press coverage as much as possible.[41] The visit would be known, as *Osservatore Romano* phrased it, as 'una semplice visita di cortesia' (a simple visit of courtesy). All of this looked more than faintly discouraging. For his part, once in Rome, Fisher went off to the Anglican church there and preached on the virtues of Anglican collegiality as opposed to Roman papal monarchy.[42] When he arrived for his audience with the pope, his escort rushed him past the Swiss guards and permitted no photographs of the archbishop and the pope together to be taken. Still, Fisher's audience with the pope was unusually long: 67 minutes.[43]

What had brought Fisher to this moment? He later recalled, 'I grew up with an inbred opposition to anything that came from Rome. I objected to their doctrine; I objected to their methods of reasoning; I objected to their methods of operation in this country'.[44] This attitude was noticeable. The archbishop of Westminster, Cardinal Heenan, later admitted that he found Fisher 'a combination of affection and censure'.[45] What changed his attitude? 'Without any doubt, the personality of Pope John. It was quite obvious to the world that

---

[39]   Peter Nichols, *The Politics of the Vatican* (New York, 1968), p. 314.

[40]   Carpenter, *Archbishop Fisher*, p. 708.

[41]   Welsby, *History of the Church of England*, p. 177.

[42]   As noted by Peter Hebblethwaite in *John XXIII: Pope of the Council* (London, 1984), p. 383.

[43]   Owen Chadwick, *Michael Ramsey: A Life* (Oxford: Clarendon Press, 1990), p. 319.

[44]   Quoted in Purcell, *Fisher of Lambeth*, p. 271. An example of one such doctrinal difference was the Roman Catholic dogma of the Bodily Assumption of the Blessed Virgin Mary. In his address to the full synod of the Convocation of Canterbury in 1950, Fisher made his views clear: 'We [the archbishops of Canterbury and York] cannot understand their [Roman Catholics'] insistence on requiring acceptance within their own ranks of doctrines altogether outside the Bible and the ancient universal creeds'. Promulgating such dogma, Fisher believed, 'leads only to the confusion of Christian truth when Roman Catholic theologians draw inference from inference, far removed from any evidence, historical or otherwise'. President's Address, 12 September 1950, *The Chronicle of Convocation: Being a Record of the Proceedings of the Convocation of Canterbury ... in the Sessions of September 12, 13 and 14, 1950* (London, n.d.), p. 355.

[45]   John Carmel Heenan, *A Crown of Thorns: An Autobiography, 1951–1963* (London, 1974), p. 262.

Pope John was a different kind of pope, whom I should like to meet, and could meet, on grounds of Christian brotherhood without any kind of ecclesiastical compromise on either side. Of this I felt certain already'.[46]

When Fisher and Pope John met, the archbishop recalled, the pope, in the course of their discussion, 'quoted to me a passage from a recent address of his in which as it happened occurred a reference to the time when his "separated brethren" would return to the Church of Rome'. When he heard this language being used, Fisher interrupted the pope with a momentous, if brief, word of correction: 'I said, "Your Holiness, not *return*"'. Taken aback, the pope asked his interlocutor to explain what he meant. Fisher replied, '"None of us can go backwards, only forwards. Our two Churches are advancing on parallel courses and we may look forward to their meeting one day'. After a pause, the pope said, "You are quite right" and I never heard him speak again of our "returning"'.[47]

'Not *return*': With that brief interjection Fisher made it clear that he, on behalf of the Anglican Communion, must reject a musty approach to ecumenism which spoke only of separated and errant brethren 'returning' to the One True Church. This meeting was played down by the Vatican officials, but unquestionably it marked the beginning of a new relationship between the two ancient churches – and on new terms. A man who undertook this journey 'late in my life, late in my experience of Christian faith and living', Fisher deserves much credit for keeping his wits about him and for making of this meeting much more than a bland exchange of courtesies.[48]

What did this much-publicized encounter actually amount to? Ecumenists in the Protestant world hailed a great step forward and no doubt took heart. In the Church of England Anglo-Catholics must have viewed the occasion with glowing satisfaction, while Evangelicals looked askance and even trembled a little when they wondered where such things might lead. The new ecumenists in the Roman Catholic church, too, might have found the momentum of their cause at least a little quickened. What might follow? Could real union be sought? Might the principles of centuries be bargained away? The pope himself soon remarked that the visit had provoked 'many fanciful stories'. Turning to St. Luke, Cardinal Bea found that 'one outcome of the meeting has been for "the thoughts of many hearts to be made manifest"'. But, as Bea remarked, Christians already met one another frequently.[49] Was the only difference between this meeting and

---

[46]   Quoted in Purcell, *Fisher of Lambeth*, p. 273.

[47]   GF, *Touching on Christian Truth: The Kingdom of God, the Christian Church and the World* (London, 1971), pp. 187–8.

[48]   GF, quoted in Lloyd, *The Church of England*, p. 587.

[49]   Cardinal Augustin Bea, *The Unity of Christians* (London, 1953), pp. 64–5.

others to be found in the unique positions of the participants and the bustle of an excitable press?

Bea knew that whatever the explicit outcome might be, a 'new atmosphere' was now inhabited by Catholics and Anglicans. He acknowledged that the visit had been Fisher's initiative. He went on: 'It was Dr Fisher who sensed the change of atmosphere; pointed it out; realized the obligations entailed and took the necessary steps to bring the public to a greater awareness of the new atmosphere and to foster their interest'.[50] But in 1960 Bea was prepared to conclude enigmatically: 'We are sincerely convinced that his visit of last December will bear fruit, though we have no wish to specify its nature'.[51]

Following this trip and in anticipation of the Second Vatican Council, Fisher in 1961 dispatched to Rome a representative, Canon Bernard Pawley of Ely Cathedral, to note the preparations for the council and to be available to the Secretariat for Unity to provide information about the Church of England. The two churches, Fisher believed, needed to understand each other as well as possible. These years, when Cardinal John Heenan was archbishop of Westminster and Eugene Cardinale was the apostolic delegate, saw an improvement in Anglican–Roman Catholic relations in Britain.[52]

The Second Vatican Council appears to have recognized this new relationship. In its decree on ecumenism it gives special recognition to the Anglican Communion: 'Among [the churches separated from the holy see] in which some catholic traditions and institutions continue to exist, the Anglican communion occupies a special place'.[53] Roger Lloyd offers this comment on the meeting of Fisher and the pope in relation to Vatican II: 'No one can say, and it would be impertinent to guess, just what was the effect of this famous meeting between these two kind, genial, but very different men. The Second Vatican Council might very well have taken just the same course as in fact it did if they had never met at all'. But, he notes, 'From the English side [this meeting and its aftermath] kindled a respect, even an affection, for Rome which had not existed for centuries before'.[54]

Fisher himself, in retirement, continued to look forward to progress with Rome. He kept up his contacts with leading Roman Catholics, corresponding and conversing with them, always seeking greater Christian unity. He did

---

[50]   Ibid., p. 71.

[51]   Ibid.

[52]   Welsby, *History of the Church of England*, p. 178.

[53]   Decree on Ecumenism, para. 13, in Walter M. Abbott (ed.), *The Documents of Vatican II* (Piscataway, N.J., 1966), p. 356.

[54]   Lloyd, *The Church of England*, p. 587.

not seek union with Rome. But with his English Roman Catholic friends he hopefully discussed possible approaches to full communion.[55]

What had Fisher learned from this last trip of his archiepiscopate? Or at least, what was his most vivid memory? Interviewed upon landing in London on 3 December 1960, he said that his strongest memory was of 'a camel which looked at me with most ineffable scorn. A donkey smiles. Roughly speaking, all humanity is a donkey or a camel'.[56] A simple parable but one that may indicate why the pope and the archbishop got on as well as they did.

Coda: Reaching Out to Non-Christians

Ecumenism, the subject of this chapter, typically refers to efforts to achieve unity among the various Christian bodies. The term does not denote interreligious dialogue, which appears to have engaged Geoffrey Fisher's attention to no appreciable degree. But there was a large and perhaps growing population of non-Christians in Britain of whom an archbishop of Canterbury could not fail to take note: men and women all around him, alienated or indifferent, to whom Christian beliefs were literally incredible. Did the archbishop of Canterbury have anything to say to them? Were all these doubters simply beyond the pale of God's kingdom and even damned forever? Not a bit of it. Fisher's attitude toward these non-Christians was decidedly irenic and understanding.

In 1959 an interviewer asked Fisher about those who try to follow the ethical teachings of Jesus but cannot believe in the divinity of Christ or even in the existence of God. What about them? Fisher replied that, if they could accept only Christ's moral teaching, then they should try to live by these principles: 'Christ will be with them in their honest endeavour'. A Christian, he said, respects those who live good lives, even though these individuals do not accept the divinity of Christ. Although they are not believers, they 'are walking in the Light of Christ'. For both Christians and non-Christians, Fisher observed, 'there is only one true Light of the world .... Christ is the Light of the World and He rejoices ... when non-Christians walk in it'. And so, he suggested, 'in the Kingdom of God, there is ... a place for the agnostic, as there certainly is for the sinner'. It was the atheist whom Fisher could not understand. 'The atheist says there is not, there cannot be, God or a Kingdom of God: his reason tells him so.

---

[55]   Ted Arblaster, "'All the world's a stage...'", *St. Mark's Review*, no. 152 (Summer 1993), p. 46.

[56]   Quoted in Purcell, *Fisher of Lambeth*, p. 268.

But reason doesn't. Reason cannot prove that there is not a God, any more than it can prove finally that there is'.[57]

At this point Fisher drew both a distinction and a connection between faith as Christian belief and faith as the walk or life of a Christian: 'The believer has weighed the probabilities and made an "inner choice"'. But that is not the end of the affair. In living the life of faith the Christian grows into a deeper understanding of God's purposes and indeed into a deeper awareness of God's own life. God may in a sense still be a hypothesis, 'since we walk by faith and not by sight', but Christian conviction increasingly becomes a 'certainty beyond a peradventure'. The test of Christian truth-claims cannot be made at the very beginning, apart from life, in an antiseptic laboratory, but only in the muck of one's actual existence, with all its challenges, griefs, joys, travails, loves, and repentances.[58]

This connection between faith and life has ramifications for those who have trouble with Christian belief. At least, Fisher said, such persons can 'believe in the purpose of Christ and the kind of creative life He exhibited, and the Kingdom which He preached'. They can make Christ's loving and healing purpose their own commitment. What happens next? Then 'they will be so busy *doing* these creative things, or rather finding out by trial and error what to do and how to do it, that they will not spend too much time asking and answering questions (which becomes sometimes an excuse for not committing oneself)'. Fisher pointed out that 'Our Lord said, "Come, follow Me" into this creative pattern of responsible life. If they do that they will almost certainly find that they come to believe' in the overcoming of brokenness and the raising of new life through Christ, and hence come to know the meaning in and for their own lives of the Crucifixion and Resurrection of Christ.[59] 'Doctrine and life', Fisher noted, 'come to be inextricably part of the same loyalty, each connecting the other and informing it'.[60]

Fisher inherited from Temple the patronage of the Council of Christians and Jews, which had been established in the conditions of wartime, in 1942. This, too, represented a contribution to Christian ecumenism insofar as the archbishop now shared the presidency of the council with the Moderator of the General Assembly of the Church of Scotland, the cardinal archbishop of Westminster and the Moderator of the Free Church Federal Council. As the council proceeded to issue statements on the situation in Palestine, this drew criticism from those with loyalties there. Did Fisher understand this as a

[57] GF, quoted in Kenneth Harris, *Conversations* (London, 1967), pp. 81–2.
[58] Ibid., p. 82.
[59] Ibid., pp. 82–3.
[60] Ibid., p. 84.

theological responsibility or one commended by the responsibility of leading a national church? In its early days the council had been a far from steady body. The chief rabbi, J.H. Hertz, was viewed by the Christian participants as decidedly defensive and even difficult. But Hertz died in office in 1946 and was succeeded by the more amenable Israel Brodie, a figure far more recognizable to the civic-minded Fisher. He, too, was a leading Freemason (and grand chaplain to the United Grand Lodge of England) and he would be the first chief rabbi to be knighted (although Hertz had become that rather superior thing, a Companion of Honour).

Ecumenism and the Visible Church

By 1961 Fisher's stature as an ecumenist was considerable and widely acknowledged. Yet he remained a surprising ecumenist, lacking that sense of theological adventure which had so often defined the other pioneers of movements for church unity. In this realm his essentially practical virtues cleared a good deal of space for pragmatic and constructive achievement. Undetained by theological trench-fighting, he was capable of viewing the ecumenical vision as something greater than a contest over the legitimacy of Orders. His perceptions were not narrowly clerical. He related superbly well to people who could be regarded as reasonable, amenable, and moderate, almost – if not quite – regardless of the tradition which produced them. Furthermore, he saw clearly the public responsibility which the churches at large bore in a world of politics, controversy, and confrontation. At large, Fisherian ecumenism was an expression of religious maturity and civic obligation and an extension of international duty. It spoke of a confidence that the church mattered to more than itself and of a conviction that its leaders had no right to disappear into their own dimension of existence. From this temptation, ecumenists as a breed would be found to be no more immune than Christians of any other variety.

Chapter 7
Church and State, 1945–1961

The Established Church

In the Fisher era, the church historian E.R. Norman observes, 'The principle of Established religion was very much taken for granted .... During the 1940s and 1950s very few within the Church of England questioned it; and the few Nonconformists or secularists who spoke of disestablishment were responding to historical instincts which were not live politics ...'. Both William Temple and Geoffrey Fisher 'assumed the existence of the National Church .... Nearly every leading churchman in these years felt the same'.[1]

This principle of Church Establishment which was so widely accepted has traditionally been interpreted in such a way that it has more to say about responsibility than about authority; it has more to do with reciprocal obligations than with special privileges. It signifies, on the one hand, the responsibility of the state to God; and, on the other hand, the responsibility of the Church of England to all the people of the land, whether they are Anglicans or not. The archbishop of York, Cyril Forster Garbett, devoted much energy to working out what Establishment properly stands for. 'The Church of England', he said in 1947, 'still in many ways represents the religious aspect of the nation. This is most notably seen at the Coronation .... The Church, hallowing the King, calls upon the State to remember that it is the servant of the spiritual order, and that all its power and glory are a trust from God to be used for His purposes'.[2]

At the same time, as Garbett said in a book on the relationship of church and state, published in 1950, the Church of England is specially obliged to look after the spiritual welfare of the nation. 'It is one of the glories of the Church that its clergy minister not only to a congregation, but to all who live within the parish'.[3]

---

[1]   E.R. Norman, *Church and Society in England, 1770–1970: A Historical Study* (Cambridge, 1996), p. 397. As GF put it, 'the Free Churches have discovered that the Establishment has positive advantage both for them and for the country as serving well the whole place of the Christian religion in the life of the nation'. GF, 'Church and State', in *Touching on Christian Truth: The Kingdom of God, the Christian Church, and the World* (London, 1971), p. 140.

[2]   Cyril Forster Garbett, *The Claims of the Church of England* (London, 1947), pp. 189, 190.

[3]   Cyril Garbett, *Church and State in England* (London, 1950), p. 129. '[E]very citizen lives in some parish', Fisher wrote, '... and can claim the spiritual counsel and ministrations of the parish

The church had a 'duty of making spiritual provision for the whole nation ...'.[4] Beyond providing pastoral care, representatives of the Church of England have a duty to give moral guidance to the state on a wide range of questions. 'An Established Church', Garbett wrote, 'has the responsibility of arousing and educating the conscience of the State and the nation on matters of public policy and administration. It must show that Christianity has a message not only to the individual but also to society. It must proclaim God's laws of justice, mercy, and love, and at the same time show their relevance to current politics'.[5]

For his part, Fisher was sure that when people spoke of 'church and state' they had put the two parts in the right order.[6] The state was unthinkable without the mission and guardianship of the church. But he also took a high view of the state: 'secular authority is sacramental just as the Church is sacramental'.[7] Fisher frequently spoke out, in Parliament and elsewhere, on the issues of his time. Although he was politically to the right of his predecessor, William Temple, he accepted the Welfare State. But he warned against the danger of too much state control and the consequent loss of concern for the whole person: the moral and spiritual as well as the physical and material needs of human beings.[8] He was equally sure that an industrial society needed to draw on Christian principles of faith, hope, and charity if it was to avoid strife, even war, and achieve justice and prosperity.[9]

Fisher was not an uncritical admirer of Conservative governments. Here his personal relationships were suggestive: he got along best with the Labour premier Clement Atlee and least well with a Tory one, Harold Macmillan

---

priest; and this pastoral duty of the clergy ... still remains as the first care and privilege of the Church'. GF, 'The Beliefs of the Church of England', in Edward Carpenter (ed.), *The Archbishop Speaks: Addresses and Speeches by the Archbishop of Canterbury the Most Reverend Geoffrey Francis Fisher* (London, 1958), p. 55.

[4]   Garbett, *Church and State in England*, p. 130.

[5]   Ibid., p. 131. When he was enthroned as archbishop of Canterbury on 19 April 1945, Fisher said, 'All through our history ... the Church has been organically related to the nation, charged with the duty of bringing into the secular life of our people the sanctities of the faith and fear of God, by teaching them to fashion their characters and their policies by the obedience which Christians owe to their Lord. For long indeed Church and nation were different names for the same body of people, the one describing them on the side of their heavenly, and the other of their earthly citizenship'. GF, 'Church and Nation', in Charles Smyth, *The Church and the Nation: Six Studies in the Anglican Tradition* (London, 1962), p. 13.

[6]   See Carpenter, *The Archbishop Speaks*, pp. 95–6.

[7]   Ibid., p. 97.

[8]   William Purcell, *Fisher of Lambeth: A Portrait from Life* (London, 1969), p. 210; Norman, *Church and Society*, p. 377.

[9]   See Carpenter, *The Archbishop Speaks*, pp. 109–13, 114–21.

(who would do better with Fisher's successor, Michael Ramsey). Attlee was an undemonstrative, practical man who thrived on getting big things done. This was no doubt how Fisher saw himself, though he happily allowed himself a little more ostentation. Meanwhile, he proved a persistent critic of Macmillan on matters related to both domestic and foreign policy, finding particularly distasteful the Conservative premier's 1959 campaign slogan, 'You Never Had It So Good'. This he thought simply 'dreadful', saying it was used to justify 'a smug contentment which ignores the peril of our own situation and the appalling conditions of people in other countries'.[10] Yet Fisher's instincts were fundamentally conservative. Thus, Christie Davies, a commentator on 'the death of moral Britain', considers him an emblematic 'reminder of a social and moral world we have lost and of the strange death of Conservative England, despite the decisive victory of capitalism over socialism'.[11] Fisher was indeed a respecter of authority and of established institutions, as well as firmly anticommunist. Referring to Fisher's famous remark to Pope John, David L. Edwards says of him, 'Although with his head he knew that "none of us can go backwards", he was at heart content with the Establishment he had entered on becoming a headmaster

---

[10]   GF to R.A. Butler, 16 February 1960, R.A. Butler Papers (Trinity College, Cambridge), G35, fols. 39–43, quoted in Kevin Jefferys, *Retreat from New Jerusalem: British Politics, 1951–64* (New York, 1997), pp. 198–9. For his part, Macmillan characterized GF as 'silly, weak, vain and muddle-headed'. See Peter Catterall (ed.), *The Macmillan Diaries: The Cabinet Years, 1950–1957* (London, 2003), p. 577 (entry for 21 July 1956). He also found Fisher to be an unengaging conversation partner: 'I try to talk to [Fisher] about religion', the premier commented in his diary. 'But he seems to be quite uninterested and reverts all the time to politics'. See Peter Catterall (ed.), *The Macmillan Diaries: Prime Minister and After, 1957–1966* (London: Macmillan, 2011), entry for 8 February 1957, quoted in Peter Hennessy, *Having It So Good: Britain in the Fifties* (London, 2006), p. 502. Hennessy points out, however, that Fisher and Macmillan had much in common. Both had misgivings about the moral changes taking place in British society. 'Fifties Britain', notes Hennessy, 'tends to be viewed through early-twenty-first-century eyes as stuffy and staid, but for Macmillan's and Fisher's generation, their standard of a tranquil, self-ordering society was that of pre-1914 England' (p. 517). A devout Anglican, Macmillan worried about the spiritual costs of 'having it so good' (p. 516). To an interviewer in 1959, Fisher spoke with concern about the multiplication in an affluent society of 'temptations to self-indulgence (which accounts for a great deal of the world's sin and misery)' and about the weakening of 'many of the time-honoured defences against bad thinking and bad doing'. GF, quoted in Kenneth Harris, *Conversations* (London, 1967), p. 85.

[11]   Christie Davies, 'The British State and the Power of Life and Death', in S.J.D. Green and R.C. Whiting (eds.), *The Boundaries of the State in Modern Britain* (Cambridge, 1996), p. 374. See Christie Davies, *The Strange Death of Moral Britain* (New Brunswick, N.J., 2004), pp. 67–78, 113–14, 117; and Harry Potter, *Hanging in Judgment: Religion and the Death Penalty in England from the Bloody Code to Abolition* (London, 1993), pp. 124, 151, 166, 168–9, 178–9, 193. Capital punishment would be abolished in Britain in 1969.

less than ninety years after Thomas Arnold, and he was confident that this old England could be brought alive by hard work – such as he himself gave without stint all his life'.[12]

The Coronation of Queen Elizabeth II

Geoffrey Fisher had an exalted view of the monarchy and hence of the ceremony in which the king or queen is crowned. He saw the coronation service as far more than a major public event; or, if it was inescapably that, then a media event whereby the message of Christianity – in particular, the message that England was still a Christian state, responsible to God – could be delivered to millions. Writing of the coronation service in 1953, E.C. Ratcliff, the Ely Professor of Divinity at Cambridge University, made exactly this point about the larger meaning of the ceremony: 'The Coronation Service ... reflects the persistent English intertwining of sacred and secular, of civil and ecclesiastical. It reflects particularly the historic English conception of the mutual relations of Sovereign, Church and People, and of all three to God .... [It] symbolises national continuity ... *sub specie Christianitatis*'.[13]

Most of all, then, Geoffrey Fisher viewed the coronation service as a quintessentially religious ceremony. He 'possessed a fine and eminently audible voice', notes Edward Carpenter, 'though he lacked Lang's rare quality of lifting a ceremony into a world of drama and mystery. What he could do was to introduce a straightforward spiritual intention. Supremely was this the case with the Coronation'.[14] The Queen, Fisher said, is 'called by God' and 'consecrated by God'.[15]

The British sovereign no longer possessed much temporal power, but this fact only increased, in Fisher's view, her spiritual authority. That was part of what he wanted to convey before and during the service. 'The executive power, the

---

[12]   David L. Edwards, *Leaders of the Church of England, 1828–1978* (London, 1978), pp. 365–6.

[13]   E.C. Ratcliff, *The Coronation Service of Her Majesty Queen Elizabeth II* (London, 1953), p. 23. 'Our Coronation Order expresses in the most vivid way the ideal relationship between Church and State; the archbishop representing the Church, and the king the State ...'. Garbett, *Church and State in England*, p. 121.

[14]   Edward Carpenter, *Cantuar: The Archbishops in Their Office* (London: Cassell, 1971), pp. 508–9. See Roy Strong, *Coronation: A History of Kingship and the British Monarchy* (London, 2005), p. 472.

[15]   GF, 'Majesty', in *I Here Present Unto You: Addresses Interpreting the Coronation of Her Majesty Queen Elizabeth II* (London, 1953), p. 21.

power to rule and govern, to order and compel, has been steadily taken from our monarchs', he declared. 'But this diminution of temporal power has given to the Sovereign the possibility of a spiritual power far more exalted and far more searching in its demands: the power to lead, to inspire, to unite, by the Sovereign's personal character, personal conviction, personal example; by the simplicity of a sincere heart, by the sympathy of a generous soul; by the graces of God'.[16]

The young queen largely shared her archbishop's view of the sacred character of this event. To help prepare her spiritually, Fisher put together for her use *A Little Book of Private Devotions*. A historian of the monarchy has said of Elizabeth: 'Both the oath and the anointing were viewed by her as pivotal events in her life, seen as acts of personal dedication to the service of the nation'.[17] The anointing was the most solemn and sacred part of the coronation ritual. It took place out of view of both the cameras and the congregation. Divested of royal robes and adornments and wearing a simple white dress, the Queen moved to St. Edward's Chair. With the oil of chrism the archbishop anointed her by making a sign of the cross on her palms, on her chest, and on her head, saying:

> By thy Head anointed with holy Oil: as kings, priests, and prophets were anointed.
> And as Solomon was anointed King by Zadok the priest and Nathan the prophet, so
> be thou anointed, blessed and consecrated Queen over the Peoples, whom the Lord
> thy God hath given thee to rule and govern ....[18]

Shortly thereafter, the archbishop of Canterbury lifted the royal crown above the head of the seated queen, held the crown aloft for a few moments, and then dramatically brought it down upon the sovereign's head. After homages to the queen by prelates and nobles, there was the acclamation, 'God Save Queen Elizabeth. Long live Queen Elizabeth, May the Queen live for Ever!'

The coronation of Queen Elizabeth II took place on 2 June 1953. It was the first major royal celebration to be televised. In these early days of the medium, only 3 million Britons owned television sets, but the ceremony reached an audience estimated at 20 to 27 million people, which was half the adult population. Another 12 million people followed the coronation on the radio.[19]

---

[16] GF, 'Majesty', p. 22.

[17] Strong, *Coronation*, p. 431.

[18] Ibid., p. 488; Ben Pimlott, *The Queen: A Biography of Elizabeth II* (New York, 1997), p. 213.

[19] Sandbrook, *Never Had It So Good*, p. 41.

A recent writer in the *Times Literary Supplement* refers to this event as 'the most magnificent public spectacle of twentieth-century Britain'.[20]

The coronation of Elizabeth II arrived at a propitious moment in the history of the British monarchy. 'When George died in 1952', notes Dominic Sandbrook, 'the Windsors were far more popular than they had been at his accession, and his daughter Elizabeth succeeded to the throne with probably as much public goodwill as any that had gone before her'.[21] Rose Macaulay, however, could not resist issuing a demurral: 'No doubt all pleased by the coronation service and its ceremonies', she wrote to an English priest in the United States, 'though its expense must seem to them wildly excessive, as indeed it does to me, when money is so badly needed for our old and only barely subsisting poor people, and so many other things'.[22]

Macaulay's comment adumbrates a time only a few years hence when the fortunes of the monarchy would start to decline, and people would indeed begin to ask if it was worth all the money expended. Being tied together with the church as central parts of 'the Establishment' turned out to be a mixed blessing for both venerable institutions. The coronation service, writes A.N. Wilson in *After the Victorians*, 'was in part a splendid piece of religio-patriotic pageantry to celebrate great things which deserved celebration: peace, freedom, prosperity'. But, he says, this service 'can now be seen as a consoling piece of theatre, designed to disguise from themselves the fact that the British had indeed, as Dean Acheson so accurately remarked nearly a decade later, lost an empire and failed to find a role'.[23]

---

[20]   Nigel Saul, 'The Pomp of Power', *Times Literary Supplement*, 25 November 2005, p. 26. See also Hennessy, *Having It So Good*, pp. 233–49. Hennessy is particularly good on the reaction of the people of Scotland, where nationalist sentiment was strong. When the dean of Westminster, Alan Don, a Scotsman, suggested that the Moderator of the (Presbyterian) Church of Scotland have a role in the Coronation, GF saw the wisdom of this accommodation and readily agreed (p. 247).

[21]   Sandbrook, *Never Had It So Good*, p. 41.

[22]   Rose Macaulay to Reverend Hamilton Johnson, 5 December 1952, in *Last Letters to a Friend, 1952–1958*, ed. Constance Babington-Smith (New York, 1963), p. 56.

[23]   A.N. Wilson, *After the Victorians: The Decline of Britain in the World* (New York, 2005), p. 528.

Pronouncing: Marriage and Divorce

Until 1853 a divorce required nothing less than an act of Parliament. In 1857 a Matrimonial Causes Act carried divorce out of the church courts and into the secular courts. In 1912 there was a Royal Commission and a new liberalization. Then divorce found its prophet in the lawyer A.P. Herbert. In 1935 Herbert was elected Member of Parliament for Oxford University, and two years later the new act which he so perseveringly promoted had done much to alter the legislative landscape in which the issue rested. Both its friends and its enemies remarked that the rules governing divorce had now become easier and fairer. There was certainly far more of it about. Subsequently, the experience of war provoked many weddings but proved no ally of matrimony at large: hasty marriages could turn out to be brittle, and long absences did not always make the heart grow fonder. Attitudes altered still more. In short, when Fisher became archbishop it was widely perceived that the number of divorces was spiraling upwards. In 1945 there were 25,000 and in 1947, 40,000. The judges felt submerged by this onslaught; timetables sagged under the weight of the growing numbers of applications.

Fisher upheld – indeed insisted upon – the church's traditional teaching on marriage and divorce. Marriage, as he found it in canon law, was a holy, indissoluble state. His views on marriage did allow room for pragmatic accommodations. But the overall effect was rigid and dogmatic. In this he stood stoutly beside the leadership of the Mothers' Union, of which his wife was a president. Divorce, to his mind, was both a private failing and a public menace. When a Labour Member of Parliament sought approval for allowing a seven-year period of marital separation to count as an additional ground for divorce, Fisher condemned the proposal as a sop to a morally sick society bent on rejecting marriage for life.[24]

By the end of the Second World War a bill was prepared to make the granting of divorces quicker by giving registrars powers to deliberate over cases where no defence was offered. Fisher would have none of it. He spoke of 'marriage discipline'. The phrase was revealing: divorce must be proof of something like indiscipline. He ventured his own proposals to preserve the role of the judges and to slow down the speed of an individual application until six years of marriage had passed. By 1946 he was marshaling evidence meticulously and appearing

---

[24] Ibid., p. 150. Fisher's position was absolute and unbending. He was distressed, for example, by Anthony Eden's remarriage after divorce, even though Cantuar acknowledged the absence of any moral error on Eden's part. GF to Peter Winckworth, 8 October 1952, GF Papers 99, fol. 299; D.R. Thorpe, *Eden: The Life and Times of Anthony Eden, First Earl of Avon, 1897–1977* (London, 2003), p. 378.

before a new committee chaired by Lord Denning. He set up a committee of his own, with no fewer than five bishops, to look into civil marriages. The work that came of this did much to confirm Fisher's sense that they merely produced 'a dingy, casual occasion'.[25] In 1949 a further bill attempted to extend the provisions of the 1907 act by allowing a man to marry his divorced wife's sister (which appeared logical if the wife had become, in effect, dead). Fisher was beginning to feel that the institution of marriage was under attack.

Indeed, Fisher's task was not an easy one. He was poised precariously between parties and opinions of different kinds and had to hold together a church of Anglo-Catholics, for whom marriage was virtually a sacrament, and liberals and evangelicals; the Mothers' Union, canon law, Convocation and Church Assembly; the tasks of theology and pastoral practice, civil law and Parliament. It was too personal a matter for everyone to take, as Fisher himself advanced, a detached and rational view: those who were happy in marriage could hardly imagine how anyone could be otherwise, except by some weakness or shortcoming, while those who were unhappy in marriage found the language of the church unhelpful or frankly irrelevant. Meanwhile, those who were not married could be superbly open-minded or utterly blinkered. Little wonder, as Carpenter has observed, that no fewer than six files of voluminous correspondence now take their place in the Fisher archive at Lambeth Palace Library. In one exchange Fisher banned a supplicant, a town mayor, from communion for three years, to the bewilderment of his own chaplain. Fisher could always reply that, however stern his judgments, they were not made without compassion. This claim did not always convince. In 1946 he was proposing the creation of panels of clergy, doctors, and lawyers to support returning servicemen and their wives to adjust to the new life which peace would bring. He became president of the Marriage Guidance Council.

Marriage was a public institution and Fisher proceeded to make politics of it. He now got into trouble with politicians, who found him dogmatic, and with lawyers, who found him obfuscating – and even rude. There was an awkward public scuffle with the President of the Probate, Admiralty and Divorce Divisions, Lord Merriman. Hardly surprisingly, when there was a Royal Commission on Marriage and Divorce, no archbishop, bishop or minister was found to be sitting upon it. Fisher had to console himself by lobbying its chairman, Lord Morton of Heryton. There was, at least, a submission by the Church of England Moral Welfare Council.

Fisher owned the Church's pastoral duties to divorcees. But such watchful principles could in private circumstances relax amiably into an unabashed

---

[25]   See Edward Carpenter, *Archbishop Fisher: His Life and Times* (Norwich, 1991), p. 382.

authoritarianism. He won little love amongst the public when the Queen's sister, Princess Margaret, wanted to marry Group Captain Peter Townsend – who had been the innocent party in the dissolution of his marriage. Fisher made it clear what the church's position was. On 27 October 1955, Margaret had an hour-long private conference with the archbishop in his study. Four days later she issued a press statement which said that she was 'mindful of the Church's teaching that marriage is indissoluble' and that she would not be marrying the Group Captain.[26] People naturally supposed that Fisher had put some pressure on the princess to call off the marriage, an allegation that the archbishop vehemently denied. But 'it is scarcely likely', observes a biographer of Queen Elizabeth II, 'that the purpose of such a meeting *à deux* between a Primate and a Princess at such a time was to make small-talk, and the Archbishop was not reticent about his firmly held opinions on the subject of divorce and re-marriage'.[27] In the event, Margaret married Antony Armstrong-Jones, a marriage that was seen to fail. It was impossible for observers not to wonder: would she have been better off with the Group Captain? Perhaps the Archbishop of Canterbury should have been more attentive to the human beings actually involved and less beholden to his sense of what the rules were in this case? The breakdown of Princess Margaret's marriage, writes Ben Pimlott, 'carried the savage message that the Archbishop, the editor of the *Times*, the Cabinet and other moralizers who had advised the Queen about Peter Townsend's suit had, in human terms, been wrong; and that the Queen might have done better to have stood up to them'.[28]

In 1954 and 1955 Fisher held conferences on marriage and divorce at Lambeth, and the constituents were found to be diverse. These at least showed that however disinclined Fisher was to view favourably, or even sympathetically, the breaking asunder of marriages, he was not content to be merely a law unto himself. In the church there were priests who wanted to know if they could marry divorcees as well as priests who had themselves divorced and married again. This state of affairs looked disorderly. Fisher did not care for disorder in any form, least of all in a matter about which he greatly cared. In 1957 he supported the position of the Convocations in forbidding the clergy from holding a second marriage in the church.[29] But he conceded that priests who were by now marrying divorcees should be viewed with a 'charitable understanding'. Bishops should decide whether a Christian divorcee could be admitted to communion.

---

26   Norman, *Church and Society*, p. 411.

27   Ben Pimlott, *The Queen: A Biography of Elizabeth II* (New York, 1997), p. 236.

28   Ibid., p. 437.

29   See his statement on the remarriage of the divorced in the *Chronicle of Convocation: Being a Record of the Proceedings of the Convocation of Canterbury ... in the Sessions of May 21, 22, 23 and 24, and October 1, 2 and 3, 1957* (London, n.d.), p. 208.

Fisher himself proved a firm sponsor of a quiet service of blessing which adopted parts of the 1928 Prayer Book for marriages, and this proposed service was accepted. It was duly integrated into Canon Law, and in 1957 and 1958 the convocations of Canterbury and York accepted the new understandings framed by the conferences. For all this, there was now a powerful sense in the air that the views of the Church were obsolete. When the Divorced Wife's Sister Bill appeared again before Parliament in 1959, Lord Kilmuir stood up to Fisher; and when Fisher criticized the bill in Parliament the *Daily Herald* newspaper ridiculed his arguments as 'antiquated'. [30]

Fisher was opposed to artificial insemination. Here there was another powerful public debate and yet another commission (in 1948). In the late 1940s, Fisher saw AID (Artificial Insemination by Donor) as immoral, even suggesting that it be made a criminal offense. He reasoned that AID was a breach of the marriage contract, a violation of the exclusive relationship between husband and wife. [31] His speech in the House of Lords on 16 March 1949 was not without influence. It found him again to be the advocate of marriage. Artificial insemination by the husband (AIH) could surely be allowable, but artificial insemination by a donor (AID) was simple adultery. In this debate lay a quiet, but crucial innovation. Contraception was permissible within marriage as part of the orderly planning of family life, but not outside marriage. In such a way did Fisher become the sponsor of the 1948 Lambeth Conference statement which set the Anglican church apart from the Roman Catholic church. A decade later, Fisher held the same views. In his presidential address to the full synod of the Convocation of Canterbury in January 1958, Fisher remarked that, if AID were not made a crime, then at least some legal restrictions ought to be imposed upon it, including the registration of the names of donors. [32]

In the discussion of all such questions Fisher gave the impression of an almost obdurate clinging to principles, however inoperable, and also a practical advocate of realistic reform. Striking is his response to the Wolfenden Report of 1957, which posited a distinction between a sin and a crime. Fisher warmed to this approach and also sought to integrate a due acknowledgement of rights

---

[30]   Carpenter, *Archbishop Fisher*, p. 386.

[31]   G.I.T. Machin, *Churches and Social Issues in Twentieth-century Britain* (Oxford, 1998), p. 155; Purcell, *Fisher of Lambeth*, pp. 213–14; Edward Carpenter, *Archbishop Fisher*, pp. 391–2; *Church Times*, 30 July 1948, p. 423.

[32]   GF, 'President's Address', 14 January 1958, *Chronicle of Convocation: Being a Record of the Proceedings of the Convocation of Canterbury ... in the Sessions of January 14, 15 and 16, 1958* (London, n.d.), p. 4. See GF Papers 235, fol. 140, and two newspaper cuttings that follow: one from the *Daily Mail*, the other from the *Daily Mirror*, both articles from 21 January 1960; Purcell, *Fisher of Lambeth*, p. 214; Edward Carpenter, *Cantuar*, p. 506.

and liberties into the argument. Far from disdaining his subject as a simple reactionary, Fisher's principal biographer, Edward Carpenter, turns to the October 1957 number of Fisher's *Canterbury Notes* and finds in there 'a breadth of view, a liberal approach, and respect for the individual within society' striking for its day.[33]

Contesting: Premium Bonds

In at least one other debate Fisher would appear to fight a noisy battle against a public innovation which seemed to the broad public largely innocuous. In the mid 1950s an issue of personal morality and state policy arose which sharply divided the archbishop of Canterbury and the Conservative government. 'It was when [Fisher] touched on the question of Premium Bonds', writes William Purcell, 'that he became formidable, launching out into a tremendous polemic, which was neither forgotten nor forgiven by some in the Government of the day'.[34]

Announced on 17 April 1956 as part of Chancellor of the Exchequer Harold Macmillan's budget proposals, premium bonds were designed as a way to reduce inflation and to encourage savings by those who might be attracted by the prospect of winning cash prizes. Interest earned by investors' money would go not to the individual bondholders but toward a pool of cash awards. Bondholders, in other words, were gambling with their interest payments, which were collected into a central fund and then awarded as prizes. The first premium bond was purchased on 1 November 1956. By the end of that day, men and women, in pursuit of the top prize of £1,000, had spent £5 million on premium bonds. The first drawing was held on 1 June 1957; by then £82 million had been invested. People participated in Macmillan's new state savings scheme not only because there was no risk – their initial capital investment was inviolate; it could be recovered at any time – but also because it was one of the few games in town.

Because the cash prizes were distributed by chance, the scheme met with opposition from those, including the British Council of Churches, who viewed it as gambling. The government, Fisher pronounced in the House of Lords, 'have chosen ... a rather second-rate expedient, which may attract savings but which adds nothing to the spiritual capital of the nation', relying as it does on 'motives of private gain'. Fisher was against '[p]rivate gain divorced from responsibility', and so he was against premium bonds. The government should be certain

---

[33] See Carpenter, *Archbishop Fisher*, p. 393.

[34] Purcell, *Fisher of Lambeth*, p. 215. See Harold Macmillan's comments in Peter Catterall (ed.), *The Macmillan Diaries: The Cabinet Years, 1950–1957*, p. 554 (entry for 26 April 1956).

that 'money gained shall be truly earned and that money earned shall be used reasonably, thoughtfully and for the general good'. [35] Fisher's challenge to the government drew few others in Parliament to his side, however, and of course the government's proposal was adopted.[36]

Debating: Capital Punishment

Fisher believed that the state had the right to take life.[37] He supported the death penalty in certain cases of murder, for example, and attributed this stance to his belief in the dignity of human life and in the right of society to defend itself.[38] He in no way questioned the system or the conventions of law which he inherited. They were empirical, rational, necessary. The prison system appeared to balance acceptably the principles of removal from society and reform of the offender. They were creditably humane and appropriately austere. There was no very urgent sense that any of this was crying out for reform. Yet for years now a busy lobby had been deploring the execution of murderers as an offence against civilized values. In the House of Commons Richard Stokes had persevered in presenting one private member's bill after another. The campaigning publisher Victor Gollancz had taken up the cudgels against it. The great editor of the *Observer* newspaper, David Astor, had begun to work with Arthur Koestler against the death penalty. Public opinion still seemed to favour hanging, but controversial cases now and then shook that consensus. In time it could be seen that the abolitionists were gaining allies, public attention, momentum. Fisher had not been part of this. Increasingly, he found himself in the position of defending an established practice as the very ground on which it rested steadily diminished.

This pattern could be observed clearly in the House of Lords. When the Criminal Justice Bill of 2 June 1948 appeared there, only one bishop, Bell of Chichester, supported abolition. But by 10 July 1956 a further abolition bill had attracted far more impressive support, not least from the bishops' bench. Fisher looked, and sounded, clearly uncomfortable. He wanted to see reform, but not abolition. Those who thought capital punishment wrong were simply mistaken.

---

[35] GF, Speech on the Small Lotteries and Gaming Bill, 26 April 1956, *The Parliamentary Debates (Hansard): House of Lords Official Report* (London: Her Majesty's Stationery Office, 1957), 196:1303–4.

[36] Machin, *Churches and Social Issues*, pp. 148–9.

[37] For an overview of the subject of the Church of England and capital punishment, see Harry Potter, *Hanging in Judgment: Religion and the Death Penalty in England* (London, 1993).

[38] GF Papers 167, fols. 201 and 204 (8 March 1956).

In cases of proven murder it performed 'a terrible, irrevocable and cleansing witness'. But he saw how clumsy and equivocal the whole business had become. At least half of those solemnly condemned by a judge to hang were reprieved.[39] By the end it could be seen that the Christian consensus had shifted from Fisher to Bell. In his final speech in the House of Lords Fisher looked beleaguered and isolated.

The debate on capital punishment showed the limits of Fisher's pragmatic morality and the strengths of those who found in the matter a fundamental principle which could not be compromised and which would endure all weathers. But here, as in other matters of public dispute, Fisher proved consistent in viewing his responsibilities to Parliament with seriousness. Indeed, he had shown a zest for politics and entire confidence that his position as archbishop of Canterbury brought him to matters of state from a high, firm position. He was significant enough to be an ally to his friends and an obstacle to his foes and sufficiently a figure of weight to be widely known in both guises by the national public. He had readily inherited the broad ground claimed by Davidson, Lang, and Temple before him, occupying it with conviction and exploiting it with vigour. In preserving and developing that inheritance he left much to his successors.

---

[39] H.L. Deb., 5s, cols. 746–52 (10 July 1956).

Chapter 8
The World's Tumult: Foreign Affairs, 1945–1961

The era in which Fisher's archiepiscopate occurred was vivid with international dramas. The war against the Axis powers was concluded with eventual occupation or nuclear bombs. Europe began the steadfast work of reconstruction but in the context of a cold war between a communist East and a liberal, and usually democratic, West. India became independent in 1947; the British administration in Jerusalem concluded its affairs in February 1948, and the United Nations brought to life the state of Israel that May. China became a communist land in 1949 and Christian missionaries were ejected. By the mid-1950s South Africa was moving inexorably towards apartheid while the legacies of colonialism across Africa mounted dolorously. On all these matters Fisher was pressed for a view, by men and women in the places themselves, by politicians, church people, and journalists. As he inherited so many obligations from his predecessors, he inherited their bulging postbags, too. Fisher might have had every confidence in his powers at home, but when it came to volatile, even dangerous, matters abroad he must have sensed how little experience he brought to such things. Archbishop Lang had come wearily to the verdict that an archbishop of Canterbury could do little effective good in such a world as this. But he could easily do significant harm.

Deliberating: Nuclear Weapons

In his attitude to the use of nuclear bombs Archbishop Fisher displayed his essential realism. He deplored the awful nature of these weapons but acknowledged that the West was facing an enemy both remorseless and relentless, who would stop at nothing, except equal or greater counterforce. Responding to a Sheffield union leader who urged the church to 'raise her voice [against] these horrible weapons', Fisher affirmed his belief that '[t]he greatest difficulty is that the Soviet government openly proclaims that it does not believe in God or in spiritual laws, or in prayer or in the obligation of men and nations to seek peace and ensure it. Thus, there is a fundamental distrust created in the nature of things'. Nuclear weapons were needed, therefore, as a deterrent and a bargaining lever: 'It may be that the existence of the H-Bomb will be a more powerful agent in leading to some kind of agreement than anything else'.[1] Because he held Soviet communism to be a real threat to freedom and world peace, he would not go along with those who called for a ban on nuclear weapons. He saw the Bomb as a tragic but necessary resource in the world as it actually existed.[2]

Just as Fisher clearly measured himself against Temple, he must also have been deeply conscious that Bishop Bell continued to present the possibilities of Christian idealism in questions of foreign affairs. When Bell wrote to *The Times* on 5 April 1954, arguing against nuclear weapons, Fisher told the bishop of Winchester:

> I have a horrible feeling that there ought to be a motion down on the Convocation Agenda about the Hydrogen Bomb. It is not that anything we say will do anybody any conceivable good, but if we say nothing there will be protests that the Church gives no lead and that when the world is in jeopardy talks about nothing but its own Canons.[3]

The Convocation did express its apprehension about the hydrogen bomb, calling the existence of this new weapon 'a grievous enlargement of the evil inherent in all war and ... a threat to ... humanity and civilisation'. But the Convocation also recognized that 'statesmen[,] in the discharge of their responsibilities and in the existing conflict of international interests and beliefs, cannot separate consideration of the Hydrogen Bomb from that of other weapons of war or from the total state of international relations' – thus appearing to accept the maintenance of these weapons for as long as the conflict lasted. The motion called upon 'all statesmen urgently to seek agreement' on the reduction and control of arms.[4]

The church's official pronouncements continued to come in for heavy criticism from those who considered the use of nuclear arms to be fundamentally at odds with Christian principles.[5] In a letter to *The Times* on 17 January 1956,

---

[1]   J. Hunt to GF, 3 April 1954, GF Papers 142, fol. 371; GF to Hunt, 5 April 1954, GF Papers 142, fol. 372.

[2]   Dianne Kirby, 'The Church of England and the Cold War Nuclear Debate', in *Twentieth Century British History* 4 (1993), pp. 250–83. For other letters and papers related to the topic of nuclear weapons and the church's response, see GF Papers 142, fols. 368, 373–408.

[3]   Fisher to Mervyn Haigh, 26 April 1954, GF Papers 142, fols. 384–85.

[4]   *Chronicle of Convocation: Being a Record of the Proceedings of the Convocation of Canterbury ... in the Sessions of 11, 12 and 13 May 1954* (London, n.d.), pp. 22–3.

[5]   Kirby, 'The Church of England', p. 282.

Bishop Bell opposed these weapons on solid just-war grounds: the same ethical platform from which he had launched his protest against the Allied saturation-bombing campaign in the Second World War. Hydrogen bombs, he said, 'are morally indefensible'. They not only 'inflict destruction on a colossal scale altogether out of proportion to the end desired'; they also fail to discriminate between military targets and civilian populations. Indeed, the 'poison' of their radioactive fallout could end the human race. The bishop of Chichester called upon the American president and the British prime minister 'at least to pledge themselves to renounce all further tests, and never to be the first to use hydrogen bombs'.[6] The month before Bell's letter appeared, Fisher, in an address to the Royal United Service Institute, had stated his view that the enemy needed to be kept in check by any means necessary: 'I believe that every deterrent to Communism – even the Hydrogen Bomb – is good so long as it deters'.[7]

But Fisher's developed position on nuclear weapons was more nuanced than this utterance (and similar statements) suggests. His basic ethical stance always was that the value of factual truth – for example, the facts disclosed by scientific discovery – must be examined and weighed in the light of moral truth. In their ethical judgments, Christians must seek out and employ a higher law than that to which a purely functional reason points: just because we can do something – such as build a bigger bomb – does not mean that we ought to. Factual truth should not be considered an end in itself: rather, something is good, Fisher believed, if it can be used for the larger human good. Love, he said, 'must condition what uses we make of truth', including the powerful truths of nuclear energy.[8]

As the years went by, then, Fisher grew more concerned about the ethical justifiability of nuclear weapons, more skeptical of the power of these weapons to prevent conflict, and hence more eager to seek peaceful ways of ending the arms race. To Prime Minster Anthony Eden, Fisher wrote of 'an anxious and growing opinion among the Churches that the British and American Governments must take a fresh initiative *now* in the field of disarmament and atomic warfare if the situation is to be kept under any kind of moral control'. In this lengthy letter of 23 January 1956, Fisher told the premier that possessing the hydrogen bomb was justifiable as a deterrent. But all knew that its employment would be suicidal – it 'would ... devastate both sides beyond endurance' – and so use of this tool of war was, in both moral and strategic terms, unthinkable. The 'Christian conscience', he said, revolts 'against the very existence of such an inhuman and

---

6   George Bell, 'The Hydrogen Bomb' (letter), *The Times*, 17 January 1956.

7   GF, 9 December 1955, quoted in Kirby, 'The Church of England', p. 279.

8   GF, quoted in Kenneth Harris, 'Dr. Geoffrey Fisher, 1959 [interview]', in *Conversations* (London, 1967), p. 71.

nihilistic weapon'. Great Britain, therefore, should work for arms control and reduction, as well as for the prohibition of certain classes of nuclear weapons. By such means both Britain and the United States might 'recapture the moral initiative in this field', for the sake of the safety and security of the world.[9]

Protesting: The Suez Crisis

The foreign-policy debate with which Archbishop Fisher is most closely identified occurred in the House of Lords during a spirited exchange which occurred with the Lord Chancellor, who was attempting to defend the policy of the British government during the Suez Crisis. Fisher's remarks on this occasion were critical of Britain's armed intervention – carried out in collusion with the French and the Israelis – aimed at regaining control of the Suez Canal.

Built by the international Suez Canal Company and opened in 1869, this 106-mile waterway connected the Mediterranean Sea with the Gulf of Suez (and thence with the Red Sea). In 1875 Great Britain became the largest shareholder when Prime Minister Benjamin Disraeli bought 40 percent of the shares for the government. The Convention of Constantinople, signed in 1888 by all the major European powers, declared the canal neutral and promised free navigation in peace and war. In June 1956, in response to pressure from Egypt, the British completed their evacuation of armed forces from Egypt and the Canal Zone. But in July 1956, after Britain and the United States withdrew their pledges of financial support to help Egypt build the Aswan High Dam, President Gamal Abdal Nasser nationalized the Suez Canal, replacing the privately owned company that had managed the canal with the Egyptian Canal Authority. On 29 October 1956, Israel, which had been denied passage through the canal since 1950, invaded Egyptian territory. Then Britain and France dispatched armed forces to retake the canal.

Fisher's remarks in the House of Lords on Thursday, 1 November 1956, came the day after British attacks had begun. Following Egypt's refusal to comply with an ultimatum to withdraw from the canal, British and French troops moved in, with Canberra bombers swooping down from bases in Cyprus. The British government alleged that the invasion was to keep the peace; in fact its aim was to topple President Nasser, who had closed the canal. The day after Fisher's intervention in the Lords, the United Nations General Assembly met in

---

GF to Anthony Eden [copy], 23 January 1956, National Archives FO 371/123119/ZE 112/39 1956. Used by permission.

emergency session and approved an American resolution calling for a ceasefire. This Fisher favoured.[10]

Fisher regarded the British action as a violation of his nation's responsibilities under the United Nations Charter.[11] In the House of Lords, he persistently questioned the Lord Chancellor, Lord Kilmuir, trying to induce the government to admit that Britain was an aggressor, not the defensive power. 'The point I remember', Fisher later said, 'is that Kilmuir made a great speech in defence of Government policy. At some point he asserted that we were only going into Egypt as a fire-engine to extinguish a blaze'. Like many other observers, Fisher had doubts about this characterization of the circumstances. He launched into the Lord Chancellor:

> I intervened and asked a question, referring to the fact that the forces of Israel were twenty miles or more inside Egyptian soil. But the Lord Chancellor would not see it, and so I went on trying to make him admit that Great Britain and Israel were both invading Egypt as an act of war. A fierce exchange followed, embalmed now in the pages of *Hansard* [the official record of Parliament].[12]

Lord Kilmuir asserted that Egypt was the attacking power and refused to acknowledge that Great Britain, France, and Israel together had undertaken this attack. 'Embalmed' in *Hansard* are Fisher's pointed comments and questions: 'We cannot ignore the fact that the President of the United States thinks that we have made a grave error. We cannot ignore the fact ... that world opinion on the whole ... is convinced that we have made a grave error ...'. Fisher believed that a 'strong case' could be made 'for saying that our action is a contravention of the United Nations Charter'. He acknowledged the existence of 'a good argument for taking the action that Britain took, but he had serious concerns. The British people, he remarked, were 'perplexed and alarmed'.[13]

Then the archbishop directly challenged the Lord Chancellor, the Right Honourable Viscount Kilmuir. 'My Lords, the noble and learned Viscount referred to the attacking Power against which we have to exercise self-defence. Who is the attacking Power?' The Lord Chancellor answered that self-defence

---

[10]   Dominic Sandbrook, *Never Had It So Good: A History of Britain from Suez to the Beatles* (London, 2005), p. 17; Edward Carpenter, *Archbishop Fisher: His Life and Times* (Norwich, 1991), p. 405.

[11]   Carpenter, *Archbishop Fisher*, p. 402.

[12]   Quoted in William Purcell, *Fisher of Lambeth: A Portrait from Life* (London, 1969), pp. 261–2.

[13]   GF, 1 November 1956, *The Parliamentary Debates (Hansard): House of Lords Official Report* (London: Her Majesty's Stationery Office, 1957), 199: cols. 1294, 1295.

can mean 'the protection of nationals on someone else's territory'. He argued that if, after 'a peaceful landing', the nation we are invading 'says that they will resist with all their force', then we have a right to defend ourselves. 'Which is the attacking Power in this case?' Fisher asked. '[T]he person who threatens to use force in answer to a proffered peaceful intervention', Lord Kilmuir replied. 'Who is this attacking Power?' Fisher persisted. 'Egypt', the Lord Chancellor said. Fisher led Lord Kilmuir to acknowledge that there were actually two stages of attack and defense, the first initiated when Israel invaded Egypt. 'You omitted to mention the first', he told the Lord Chancellor. 'I have now inserted it'.[14]

Lord Jowett, who had been a schoolmate of Geoffrey Fisher's at Marlborough, said to the archbishop on their way out, 'Well, Fisher, that's one of the best pieces of cross-examination I've ever heard'.[15] But Fisher himself later appeared to regret that his cross-questioning of the Lord Chancellor had been as stinging as it was.[16] It could soon be seen that Fisher's position was not widely popular; many criticized him for speaking out as he did. But he continued to insist that the British people were divided on Suez and that their misgivings should be openly acknowledged. Throughout November and December of 1956 Fisher was remarkably well informed, through his own well-placed sources in Downing Street, about what had been happening behind the scenes. Fisher's involvement was an instance of a key Establishment figure not only expressing an opinion in public but also possessing key intelligence to back it up: information, for example, about Britain's confidential negotiations – collusion – prior to the Suez military operation.[17]

The British government, led by Sir Anthony Eden, thought that the American government, led by Dwight D. Eisenhower, would give them support.[18] But Eden badly misjudged the amount of American and other international backing he would receive. Most of the world viewed the Suez invasion as a serious blunder, an aggressive action wrong in itself and undertaken at precisely the wrong moment in world history. In early November 1956 Soviet tanks rolled into Budapest, Hungary, to put down the popular anticommunist revolution that had broken out there.

Certainly the U.S. president had no intention of being pulled into a conflict in the Middle East. He and his secretary of state, John Foster Dulles, were

---

[14] Ibid., cols. 1352–54.

[15] Quoted in Carpenter, *Archbishop Fisher*, p. 404.

[16] Carpenter, *Archbishop Fisher*, p. 405.

[17] Thorpe, *Eden*, pp. 524–5, 540–41.

[18] See Tony Judt, *Postwar: A History of Europe since 1945* (New York, 2005), p. 295.

totally against using force to settle the dispute.[19] In fact, what pushed the British out of Egypt was economic pressure from the American government.[20] On 22 December the British and the French completed their withdrawal from Suez, and on 9 January 1957, an ailing and exhausted Sir Anthony announced his resignation as prime minister.[21]

Diplomacy: The Buganda

The British churches all had a stake in what happened in the end of empire because their missionary societies had by the mid twentieth century set down deep roots across Africa and Asia. They had built churches, hospitals, schools, colleges, and universities; they had studied indigenous patterns of life, created dictionaries, translated between languages. All of this activity made the Christian mind in Britain an international one. It was also often found to be extraordinarily well-informed. Fisher once remarked that the colony of Uganda had fascinated him since boyhood.

As archbishop, Fisher viewed his essential task in Africa as the creation of a new framework for the Anglican church there.[22] But, while the provinces of West, Central and East Africa and finally Uganda were brought to life, it was all too clear that Africa had become a continent caught between the volatility of colonial and postcolonial politics and the new aggression of cold war competitions. More than this, Protestants and Roman Catholics viewed one another with distrust there. Fisher had no illusions about the activities by which the Catholic church promoted its political interests in postcolonial Africa.[23] The Church Missionary Society had been embedded in Uganda for generations. But the bishop, Cyril Stuart, now found himself stranded in a country which looked

[19] Sandbrook, *Never Had It So Good*, pp. 11–12.

[20] Ibid., p. 21.

[21] For an overview of the Suez affair in its various aspects – legal and financial, as well as political and military – see Hennessy, *Having It So Good*, pp. 405–57. The strained relationship between GF and Anthony Eden went back at least to December 1955, when Cantuar and the prime minister differed on important ecclesiastical appointments. The chief point of disagreement concerned the translation of Michael Ramsey, the bishop of Durham: Should he go to York (Eden's view) or to London (Fisher's preference)? See Thorpe, *Eden*, pp. 446–7.

[22] This section owes much to Edward Carpenter's committed discussion in *Archbishop Fisher*, pp. 524–40.

[23] See Kevin Ward, 'African Nationalism, Christian Democracy and "Communism"', in Katharina Kunter and Jens Holger Schjørring (eds.), *Changing Relations between Churches in Europe and Africa: The Internationalization of Christianity and Politics in the 20th Century* (Wiesbaden, 2008), pp. 84–6.

very different from the one he had first come to as bishop in 1934. He confronted petitions accusing him of conspiring with the government to defraud the church of mineral rights. The situation looked increasingly dangerous. In May 1948 there were riots in Kampala.

The great symbolic authority for thousands of Bugandans was the Kabaka, Mutesa II, effectively a king over half a million subjects, but also an impressionable and susceptible young man who had been duly furnished with an education at Cambridge but whose private life looked more likely to maintain the traditions of polygamy than to uphold the church's teaching on marriage and monogamy. Fisher was soon involved in all this, not least in the support of the hard-pressed Stuart. When the Kabaka visited Britain the archbishop met him but the two steered clear of what Fisher called nicely 'his matrimonial affairs'.[24] Stuart held out as best he could. In January 1953 Southwark Cathedral saw the consecration of a new bishop of Uganda, the much-travelled Leslie Brown. While Bishop Brown threatened the unrepentant Kabaka with excommunication, the Kabaka prepared to attend the forthcoming coronation in London. Fisher met him at a garden party in Buckingham Palace.

While these things were going on in London, British colonial administrators were tussling with the task of creating a viable East African state in which the Buganda would have only a place. Inevitably, Mutesa II and his nation feared a loss of identity, dignity, and power. When he refused to submit to British policy, he found himself taken off to London. This could only make matters worse. Fisher was again in touch with him while he was in the country and sought to be practical. A Bugandan deputation came to Lambeth Palace – strikingly, before going on to see the Colonial Secretary, Oliver Lyttelton. Within weeks Fisher was being lobbied by Bugandans to take a stand against the British government. Fisher was predictably evasive but offered an assurance that he would do what he could to see that Uganda was not simply incorporated within a larger federation in which the interest of its people might be compromised. Under the surface he grew crosser about the indiscretions of other parties, not least Lyttelton himself and the now retired Bishop Stuart, who were now at loggerheads in the correspondence columns of newspapers. There was a further, constructive meeting between the archbishop and the deputation, which wanted the Kabaka back. Fisher tried to secure a meeting with Lyttelton, but the Colonial Secretary would have none of it. Fisher stood up for himself. He managed to secure a meeting between the deputation and the Secretary of State for the Colonies. By now he was being advised by a former missionary, John Taylor, that the Christian institution of marriage was more likely to be undermined by Mutesa's absence

---

[24]   Carpenter, *Archbishop Fisher*, pp. 525–6.

from Kampala than by his presence there. Even a local member of the Mothers' Union was saying so.

The labyrinth into which Fisher had purposefully stepped now fused almost every imaginable aspect known to political life – empire, sovereignty, ethnicity, democracy and arbitrary power, constitution-making at large and marriage in particular – and almost every form of activity known to the art of politicians at large – correspondence, both public and private, monarchs, delegations and assemblies, speeches and public letters. It was also clear that the Buganda expected much from the Church of England. In the midst of all this Fisher's own sympathies were becoming more distinct – and they did not tend to favour the view of Whitehall. He found Lyttelton obstructive just as Lyttelton found him meddlesome. He wondered if the Governor of Uganda, Sir Andrew Cohen, was about to suffer a nervous breakdown. Yet the Bugandan deputation found him a sensitive advocate and gracious host. Fisher had come to count its leader, Kaluli Sempe, as a friend. Meanwhile, in Uganda itself the chief of the C.M.S., Max Warren, was instrumental in securing the creation of a new committee chaired by the director of the Institute of Commonwealth Studies, Sir Keith Hancock, to devise a solution to the constitutional impasse. The Warren–Hancock axis would prove a highly constructive one.[25] Fisher made his support known in all the quarters which he now touched. By now British trade was being boycotted in Uganda itself. Riots followed. On 31 May 1954 a state of emergency was declared in Buganda.

It was high time that Whitehall changed course. It did. There was a new Secretary of State for the Colonies – Lennox Boyd. Fisher met him, sent him a letter of 1,700 words, and found that he got on well with him. But a significant change also occurred in Kampala: on 5 November the Chief Justice of Uganda found that the British government had exceeded its powers in deporting the Kabaka in the first place. Fisher found this judgment an answer to prayer and invited Mutesa to Canterbury for Christmas. When the House of Lords met to discuss the crisis 11 days later, Fisher made sure that he was there to praise the 'exemplary patience of the Lukiko [the parliament of Buganda] and of the people of the Buganda'.[26]

All this time Hancock and Warren had been busy with the steady labour of compromise. It worked. The Lukiko accepted the sum of their efforts, while proposing certain amendments of its own. A settlement drawn up by a delegation in London and Lennox Boyd was adopted by the Lukiko that July. *The Times*

---

[25]   See Caroline Howell, 'Church and State in Crisis: The Deposition of the Kabaka of Buganda, 1953–1955', in Brian Stanley and Alaine Low (eds.), *Missions, Nationalism and the End of Empire* (Grand Rapids, Mich., 2003), pp. 203–4.

[26]   H.L. Deb., 5s, vol. 189, col. 1512.

looked to Lambeth Palace and recorded 'a personal triumph'.[27] The historian Caroline Howell has judged, 'That the church played a vital role in the conclusion of a new, highly significant constitutional settlement is incontestable'.[28]

Mutesa went home the next summer and processed into the cathedral in Kampala. He soon returned to London to participate in negotiations to settle the future of the whole protectorate. Fisher was perfectly amenable to the idea that Bugandans should retain as much self-governance as possible within a new state, but he found the implacable demands of their representatives hard to assimilate, even within the breadth of his eirenic wisdom. On 1 January 1961 the Lukiko voted to secede from the protectorate altogether. Fisher lamented, but his time as archbishop was now running out. It was after his retirement that a settlement was reached, in March 1962, whereby Buganda and a cluster of other western districts of Uganda enjoyed a semi-autonomous place within the new independent state and Muesa II became president of the country. In February 1966 he was deposed by his prime minister, Milton Obote, and, after a flurry of gunfire in Kampala, sent scuttling into exile. A tragic remnant, he died, under mysterious circumstances, in London three years later, leaving behind an autobiography (*The Desecration of My Kingdom*) and 18 children by 11 wives.

Intervening: South Africa

The government of South Africa was regarded by wartime Britain as a staunch ally and its prime minister, General Smuts, as one of the great statesmen of the age. Indeed, the man who had fought for the Boers at the turn of the century had become a British field marshal and a member of the War Cabinet. He was often to be seen in influential quarters in London. A committed internationalist, he was first a bold advocate of the League of Nations and then a prophet of the United Nations Organization. At home, Smuts was certainly no prophet of righteousness: he thought the segregation of races meet and right. Yet under his government South Africa presented a political spectacle which was just about presentable in the opinion of an embattled liberal democracy. But by 1948, when Smuts lost a general election in which only white voters participated, many countries were feeling distinctly unhappy at what was going on in the country he had by then served as prime minister for a solid decade.

In 1948 British opinion, insofar as it noticed what was happening in South Africa at all, observed the fall of Smuts but not the coming of his successor,

---

[27]   Carpenter, *Archbishop Fisher*, p. 534.
[28]   Caroline Howell, 'Church and State in Crisis', p. 204.

Dr Malan. In fact, this election marked a watershed in the history of South Africa. From then onwards the construction of a system of racial discrimination (known by the euphemistic term *apartheid* – or separate development) by an Afrikaner National Party proved relentless. 'Mixed' marriages were prohibited in 1949; so too sexual relations between those of different races. In 1950 two fundamental acts of legislation, the Population Registration Act and the Group Areas Act, provided the cornerstone for a new society. Men, women, and children were now classified and divided with the kind of bureaucratic precision and thoroughness which had marked the methods of the most deplorable regimes of the European twentieth century. The separation of the races was not simply defined by the allocation of resources – an allocation which affirmed the supremacy of white South Africans and the oppression and exploitation of the so-called 'Non-Whites' – but by the occupancy of land. Vast campaigns of dispossession were conducted with unyielding determination. Sophiatown, a vivid, brilliant but brutal district in which 50,000 black men, women and children lived, was simply demolished in 1955. This act of forced removal proved to be the first of many. 'Non-White' families were pressed in shambolic 'homelands'. In 1958 black South Africans lost their right of citizenship altogether. When the Appeal Court sought to overturn a number of apartheid acts, the government simply populated it with their allies and sympathisers. To this there was resistance. The African National Congress was both fortified and radicalized, but it was also divided as arguments as to how best to oppose the great tide of segregation grew more bitter and frustrated.

It was not simply the politics of this which found its way into Fisher's postbag. Apartheid created a veritable world of complications, dilemmas, and dangers in the everyday lives of ordinary families. The Anglican church counted 1,400,000 members in South Africa, the great majority of them now categorized as 'black' or 'coloured'.[29] As Keith Robbins has remarked, this presence, and the many official connections which it engendered with Lambeth Palace, meant that 'no other body in British public life could match the "knowledge on the ground" which the Church of England possessed'.[30]

In the year in which the National Party had defeated Smuts the church had appointed a new archbishop of Cape Town, Geoffrey Clayton. Clayton found himself appalled by what was now going on and was sure that the church must confront it. The bishopric which he had vacated, that of Johannesburg, was now taken by a Liverpool priest named Ambrose Reeves. Fisher himself had suggested

---

[29] For a thorough overview, see Michael E. Worsnip, *Between Two Fires: The Anglican Church and Apartheid, 1948–1957* (Natal, 1996).

[30] Keith Robbins, *England, Ireland, Scotland, Wales: The Christian Church, 1900–2000* (Oxford, 2008), p. 330.

to Reeves that he read Alan Paton's prophetic novel *Cry, the Beloved Country*. But Fisher went further than this. Reeves, he wrote, should only accept the see if he was prepared to marshal a 'crusade against the evil side of the colour problem'.[31]

However much provoked in an age of communism, Nazism, and fascism, Archbishop Lang had seldom been encouraged by foreign churchmen to intervene in the domestic political affairs of a sovereign state. Now, when it came to South Africa, Fisher found himself caught between Clayton, who pressed that the church in South Africa must speak and act for itself, not least to prove that it was not simply an imported church from a different country, and priests like Michael Scott and Trevor Huddleston, who urged that the Church of England must speak out its own protests and stand by the oppressed. In 1956 Huddleston published his book *Naught for Your Comfort* and it became one of the most widely read polemics of its day.[32] Fisher seldom hesitated to support the decisions made by those in senior positions. But he was not immune to feeling the awkwardness of these dilemmas. Meanwhile, letters from South Africans of all kinds tumbled into Lambeth Palace, reporting, protesting, deploring. Anglican congregations faced segregations; Anglican schools faced closure; Anglican hospitals found the most rudimentary practicalities unworkable. The fact that the dean of St. Paul's Cathedral in London had become a vigorous and effective participant in the controversy showed that this was not only a dispute locked away within the borders of another church and another country.[33] British opinion against apartheid was gathering force. Under the bold and principled leadership of its editor-proprietor, David Astor, the *Observer* newspaper had not only fortified its commitment in African affairs large but begun to support actively critics of apartheid itself. One was Michael Scott.[34]

The crisis wrought by apartheid showed that an archbishop of Canterbury still possessed weight in public affairs. It also showed that Fisher, in particular, was choosing to work not merely denominationally but ecumenically. When fears arose that the South African government would lay claim to mandated territories currently under British control, Fisher readily associated himself with a firm resolution of warning by the British Council of Churches. When Clayton produced a great memorandum setting down a long list of unequivocal objections to all that was happening in South Africa, he sent it to the South African prime minister, Dr Malan, to the Minister of Justice and also to the archbishop of Canterbury. It was now impossible, pressed Clayton, to keep silent. It was after this intervention that Fisher made a bold speech under the aegis of

---

31 Carpenter, *Archbishop Fisher*, p. 546.
32 Trevor Huddleston, *Naught for Your Comfort* (London, 1956).
33 See at large Valerie Collins, *Partners in Protest* (London, 1992).
34 See Richard Cocket, *David Astor and the Observer* (London, 1991), pp. 178–202.

the British Council of Churches in Birmingham in April 1953, pointing to 'sub-human' living conditions and to 'a sort of slavery'. These remarks provoked a formal protest by the South African government. They might threaten South Africa's membership of the Commonwealth; it might precipitate a withdrawal from the coronation of the queen. Did the archbishop of Canterbury speak for the British government? Fisher replied: 'I cannot always keep silence; and from time to time I am bound to declare what is the prevailing Christian opinion on world or Commonwealth affairs in which Christian opinions are involved'.[35] By now Bishop Reeves was under police surveillance and counting how many of his black clergy were being arrested. His friends thought that he should be spared more and brought home. Fisher wanted him to stay where he was. A withdrawal would look too much like a victory for the South African government. For his part, he made a further stand in the House of Lords and spoke to both Houses of Convocation. These speeches were categoric and assertive. They were adopted by the *Observer*, as a call for action.[36]

Fisher can have had no illusions about the cost of Clayton's witness. The price could only grow heavier still. On 6 March 1957 the archbishop of Cape Town organized and dispatched a collective protest by all bishops of the province against the forced segregation of church congregations. It was Ash Wednesday. The next day he was dead.[37] Fisher could only send a telegram of condolences to South Africa, but to the secretary of the British Council of Churches, the Methodist Kenneth Slack, he wondered how to make a memorial service into 'an organised demonstration against the policy of the South African government'.[38] Clayton's death precipitated a correspondence between Fisher and Malan's successor, J.G. Strijdom, in which the archbishop sought to engage the politician in the precisions of the controversy. Strijdom soon tired of this.

The new archbishop of Cape Town was the bishop of Stepney, Joost de Blank. Like Clayton, de Blank had no doubt whatsoever that apartheid was unacceptable to the Christian conscience. He was also ready to campaign against it.[39] Nobody could doubt that the years between 1957 and 1961, when Fisher retired, saw a dreadful deterioration. In 1960 the Sharpeville massacre left 69 dead, and photographs of the mayhem covered newspaper pages across the world. Archbishop de Blank now insisted that the Dutch Reformed Churches of South Africa must be excluded from the World Council of Churches – and

---

[35]　Carpenter, *Archbishop Fisher*, p. 551.

[36]　Ibid., p. 553.

[37]　The standard study of Clayton is by Alan Paton, *Apartheid and the Archbishop: Geoffrey Clayton* (London, 1974).

[38]　See Carpenter, *Archbishop Fisher*, p. 556.

[39]　See John S. Peart-Binns, *Joost de Blank: Scourge of Apartheid* (London, 1987).

that if they were not the Anglican Church of South Africa would withdraw from the organization rather than remain a part of it in such company. This campaign went too far for Fisher; and also for the General Secretary of the W.C.C., the redoubtable Willem Visser't Hooft. But it also created a new framework for the debate at large, and, while Fisher was a part of it, the dynamic force of the controversy had moved away from him and into a new forum. A consultation took place at Lambeth Palace. It achieved very little. Fisher was beginning to doubt that de Blank was quite what the crisis demanded: he seemed intent on provoking new and unnecessary crises himself. While Fisher laboured to calm the dispute, de Blank persisted in intensifying it. A long correspondence between the two men began to show signs of wear and tear. In April 1960 Ambrose Reeves was informed that he would soon be arrested, and he escaped to London via Swaziland. He returned to Johannesburg soon after only to be deported. Fisher publicly deplored the deportation of a bishop as 'vicious'. But he resisted suggestions that the affair should provoke a new joint pronouncement on behalf of the primates of all the provinces of the Anglican Communion, finding such a gesture 'embarrassing and dangerous'.[40]

When South Africa announced to the world that it had become a republic, in May 1961, nobody could doubt what kind of a state this was. In October 1960 the country withdrew from the Commonwealth. Before the year ended the South African member churches of the W.C.C. met at Cottesloe and issued a statement which affirmed that no provision of apartheid could be upheld by Scripture. Predictably, the Dutch Reformed Church disassociated itself from this statement. When Geoffrey Fisher retired the future looked bleak indeed.

---

[40]   Carpenter, *Archbishop Fisher*, p. 570.

Chapter 9
Retirement, 1961–1972

Deciding to Retire

In early 1961, as he approached his 74th birthday, Geoffrey Fisher decided that it was time to retire. He had held episcopal office for almost 30 years – in an era before bishops took sabbaticals – and his customary ardor for committees and conferences was cooling. He was in good health, but he felt mentally fatigued and his famous energy was starting to flag. Upcoming events that would require his participation – the Third Assembly of the World Council of Churches in New Delhi, 1961; the Anglican Congress in Toronto, 1963 – he did not look forward to with his usual good humour.[1]

Sometimes when a man or woman reaches a certain age, the personality's internal governor becomes less constraining, more complaisant, in relation to the less attractive impulses of the self. So it was with Geoffrey Fisher in the last year or two of his archiepiscopate. He talked more and listened less. He became more impatient, more prone to dominate discussions, less willing to hear opposing views. Particularly was this the case at Bishops' Meetings, where he might speak for a full hour without letup. At such times he must have been all but insufferable to those whom protocol obliged to sit quietly and look attentive. The archbishop's domestic chaplain boldly ventured to tell him he was talking too much. Graciously, Fisher took this message to heart, assessed the situation, and decided to resign. On 17 January 1961, he announced his retirement to the Convocation of Canterbury.[2] When he stepped down on 31 May, he was offered a life barony, which he accepted. He and his wife became Lord and Lady Fisher of Lambeth.

Whom should the prime minister appoint as his successor? Fisher preferred the evangelical Donald Coggan, bishop of Bradford, to the more obvious choice, Michael Ramsey, archbishop of York. The latter, Fisher believed, was too much a party man – too closely allied with the Catholic wing of the Church of England – to be either a strong supporter of church reunion efforts or a consistent opponent of Catholic liturgical extremes. As we have already seen, Ramsey did

---

[1]   Edward Carpenter, *Archbishop Fisher: His Life and Times* (Norwich, 1991), p. 748.

[2]   Ibid., p. 747; Owen Chadwick, *Michael Ramsey: A Life* (Oxford, 1990), p. 106.

not share Fisher's positive view of canon law as a means of bringing about order in worship.[3] Also, Fisher doubted that Ramsey possessed the requisite managerial skills – or the commitment to administration – to deal effectively with the huge workload at Lambeth. In Fisher's opinion, Ramsey spent too much time on theology and too little time on administrative business. For these reasons, Fisher did not feel that he could urge Harold Macmillan to recommend to the queen that Michael Ramsey be translated from York to Canterbury.[4]

But, if Fisher supposed that Macmillan shared his view of what was needed in an archbishop of Canterbury, then he badly mistook his man. The prime minister was looking for a spiritual leader first and foremost; he was not unduly bothered by the fact that Ramsey was an indifferent administrator.[5] The church 'had had enough of Martha and it was time for some Mary', Macmillan is reported to have commented later, explaining his decision.[6] The premier drew his analogy from the story in Luke's Gospel (10:38–42) which offers the contrast between Martha, busy about her many tasks, and Mary, the type of contemplatives.

Thus, Macmillan made up his mind, according to his own lights; the opinion of the outgoing Primate of All England mattered little to him. Michael Ramsey relished telling the story of his conference with the premier concerning the selection of Geoffrey Fisher's successor. Several different accounts of this meeting have been handed down. This one is Owen Chadwick's version: 'Macmillan said to Ramsey, "Fisher doesn't seem to approve of you". Ramsey defended him. "Fisher," he said, "was my headmaster and he has known all my deficiencies for a long time". "Well", said Macmillan, "he is not going to be my headmaster"'.[7]

In 1961 Geoffrey and Rosamond Fisher moved to Dorsetshire, a county in south-west England on the English Channel. At first they lived in the small town of Sherborne, but in 1962 they took up residence in a redundant rectory in Trent, a village of 300 people in rural Dorset; and there they remained. Geoffrey Fisher became curate-in-charge of the parish church, taking services on Sundays and calling on parishioners during the week. He followed a standard routine. After breakfast he would go to his study, write letters, and read *The Times*. In mid-morning the rector of the parish was likely to call, and the two men would

---

[3]   Chadwick, *Michael Ramsey*, p. 103; Margaret Pawley, *Donald Coggan: Servant of Christ* (London, 1987), p. 126. Fisher also may have questioned Ramsey's commitment to Church Establishment. Michael De-la-Noy, *Michael Ramsey: A Portrait* (London, 1990), p. 140.

[4]   Chadwick, *Michael Ramsey*, p. 104.

[5]   Ibid., p. 105.

[6]   Quoted in Chadwick, *Michael Ramsey*, p. 107. Chadwick takes this reported statement to be an authentic utterance by Macmillan.

[7]   Chadwick, *Michael Ramsey*, p. 107. Cf. De-la-Noy, *Michael Ramsey*, p. 139; and Carpenter, *Archbishop Fisher*, p. 750.

talk over matters both civil and ecclesiastical. After lunch and a brief rest, Fisher would go for a walk, visiting the people of the village. Soon he knew all of them, not only their names but also their circumstances. If on his walkabout he encountered someone he did not recognize, he would ask him or her, 'And who are *you*?' Decades after his own youth, he experienced in Trent something like the community he had known and felt secure in as a boy. He was always good with young people, easy and natural with them. One evening each week he played chess with a boy in the village. With everyone he was approachable and friendly. If he was out walking and thought he would like a cup of tea, he could knock on a cottage door and enjoy it with one of his neighbours.[8] The way that he lived his retirement in Trent gave Geoffrey Fisher's career as an Anglican clergyman a rounded-off quality, as he embraced an opportunity in parish ministry that his early turn to schoolmastering had denied him.

Both Fishers loved the life of this English country village. In 1967 they celebrated their golden wedding anniversary and Geoffrey Fisher's 80th birthday. In April of that year Queen Elizabeth and Prince Philip entertained them at Windsor Castle, and in May the residents of Trent held a reception in the Fishers' honor in the hall of the local church school.[9]

A Loose Canon? Anglican–Methodist Reunion

If Geoffrey Fisher had confined himself to the modest life sketched above, then he would have offered to posterity the very model of an archiepiscopal retirement: an active man's graceful withdrawal from high office followed by humble service on behalf of his adopted community. Even for Christian leaders, however, the self is more often a chiaroscuro of light and dark than an unbroken plane of radiant goodness. To the portrait of Geoffrey Fisher, retired, the shadow of pride adds depth, making the subject more interesting, if not more appealing.

Episcopal prerogatives and the habits of authority must be hard to leave behind. In retirement, Fisher still insisted – against standard practice – on being addressed as 'Your Grace' and on being referred to as Archbishop – rather than Bishop – Fisher.[10] Worse, he could not manage to do the right thing and refrain from interfering with the efforts of his successor. No one, including his wife, could prevail upon him to hold back.[11] Now Fisher did everything he could to torpedo the chances of the Anglican–Methodist reunion scheme. He campaigned against

---

8   Carpenter, *Archbishop Fisher*, pp. 754, 767, 770.
9   Ibid., p. 753.
10 De-la-Noy, *Michael Ramsey*, p. 140.
11 Carpenter, *Archbishop Fisher*, p. 756.

the proposal, wrote letters denouncing it, and published articles and pamphlets criticizing its terms. In July 1969 the Methodist Conference approved the plan, but the Church of England turned it down, declining to affirm the proposal by the necessary majority.[12]

Ironically, Geoffrey Fisher, the Protestant-leaning archbishop who had reached out to the Free Churches in his Cambridge sermon of 1946 opposed the union scheme; while Michael Ramsey, the Anglo-Catholic who Fisher feared might drag his feet on ecumenism, endorsed it. Fisher's excessive involvement in the debate and his public disagreement with his successor embarrassed Archbishop Ramsey.[13] Apparently Fisher could not stop thinking of himself as Ramsey's headmaster, providing needed direction to his pupil.[14] 'The Trent postmark', Ramsey would mutter in retirement; 'now, the Trent postmark always filled me with a feeling of doom'.[15] Ramsey sometimes simply dropped the disquieting item into the wastebasket.[16] At all events, he stopped answering these epistles, leading Fisher to register a formal complaint with the Standing Committee of the General Synod that he was not being properly treated by his successor.[17]

In his opposition to Anglican–Methodist amalgamation, Fisher was more consistent than he might at first appear. He had always preferred full communion to union – thereby anticipating the path of successful ecumenism over the next quarter-century. He had never supported a total merger of the Church of England with any Protestant church. What he did favour was a federation of autonomous churches, which – once the Protestant bodies had incorporated episcopacy into their systems – would share ministries and the sacraments but hold on to their distinctive liturgies and historic identities.[18]

---

[12]   Ibid., p. 757. Fisher set forth his objections to the proposal in a pamphlet titled 'Covenant and Reconciliation', published in 1967. Wanting to make certain that the scheme would have sufficient backing in both churches if the measure did pass, the Methodist and the Anglican churches decided that a 75 percent majority would be necessary for the proposal to be approved. On 8 July 1969 the Methodist Conference approved the reunion scheme with 77 percent in favour, but that same day the Convocations of Canterbury and York could muster only a 69 percent majority. The proposal was revived and voted on by the General Synod (established in 1970) in May 1972, when it received less than 66 percent in favour, and therefore was allowed to lapse.

[13]   David L. Edwards, *Leaders of the Church of England, 1828–1978* (London, 1978), p. 366.

[14]   Chadwick, *Michael Ramsey*, p. 115.

[15]   De-la-Noy, *Michael Ramsey*, p. 200.

[16]   Jonathan Mantle, *Archbishop: The Life and Times of Robert Runcie* (London, 1991), p. 125.

[17]   Chadwick, *Michael Ramsey*, p. 115.

[18]   Peter Staples, 'Archbishop Geoffrey Francis Fisher: An Appraisal', *Nederlands Theologisch Tijdschrift* 28 (1974), p. 258. See GF, *Covenant and Reconciliation: A Critical Examination of*

Fisher worried that organic union would mean the end not only of the Church of England as the Established Church but also of the Church of England as the center of the Anglican Communion. Consequently, he risked offending many of his natural allies in the church by lending his name and stature to a group of reunion opponents who, without his assistance, might have failed to defeat the union scheme when it came up for a vote in the Convocations.[19]

Death

In 1972 Geoffrey Fisher's health began to decline, and on Thursday, 14 September at age 85, he suffered a stroke. When his wife, Rosamond, came to his side as he lay prostrate, he said to her, 'Don't bother me, dear, I'm busy dying'. He was taken to the hospital in Sherborne. Fortunate to the end, he had an easy death, dying peacefully in his sleep just one day after being stricken. Five days later, his funeral service was held in the Trent church.[20] In 1982 Lady Fisher moved to Wimbledon to live with a member of her family.[21] She died in 1986 and her body was interred alongside her husband's in a vault beneath the cross in the churchyard at Trent.[22]

the First Report of the English Standing Conference on 'Covenanting for Union' and of the Interim Statement of the Anglican-Methodist Unity Commission Entitled 'Towards Reconciliation' (London, 1967), pp. 5–6.

[19] Edwards, *Leaders*, pp. 366–7. Edwards observes that a difficulty with Fisher's approach to ecumenism was that while Fisher did not support proposals for union with the Free Churches, none of the Free Churches would have been interested in taking episcopacy into its system unless doing so did result in union with the Church of England.

[20] Carpenter, *Archbishop Fisher*, p. 762.

[21] Ibid., p. 763.

[22] Ibid.

Chapter 10

Assessment

The most famous appraisal of Fisher's leadership came from the pen of the prominent theologian Donald MacKinnon (1913–94). His comment appeared in a footnote to an article that he published in *Theology* in 1963: 'The historians of the Church of England', he said, 'may yet recognize that the worst misfortune to befall its leadership in the end of the war was less the premature death of William Temple than his succession by Fisher of London, and not by Bell of Chichester'.[1] Weighty words, but they should be taken with a heavy discount, for D.M. MacKinnon was predisposed to deplore almost everything about Geoffrey Fisher. The Norris-Hulse Professor of Philosophical Theology at Cambridge University, MacKinnon, in the words of Iris Murdoch's biographer, 'certainly had instinctively radical social and political principles – the oft-repeated tale of his climbing under the table to bite the calf of a visiting Anglican bishop has only symbolic truth: he was at odds with what would later be termed the Establishment'.[2] Frequently iconoclastic, MacKinnon naturally preferred the more liberal bishop of Chichester, whose 'steadfast fidelity in protest against the policy of obliteration bombing' he particularly admired.[3]

Even with a substantial discount, MacKinnon's words carry heft and warrant a response. Every biographer of Fisher or historian of the postwar Church of England has had to ask if MacKinnon was right: was Bell preferable to Fisher? The question is unavoidable, but the answer is elusive – not only because it relies on guesswork but also because the two men appear to have been roughly equal in their varying qualities. Indeed, although MacKinnon's phrasing of the issue makes it sound as if the truth of the matter is clear and that even church historians would eventually recognize it, both Fisher's strengths and Bell's weaknesses were greater than MacKinnon acknowledged. It is doubtful that Bell would have been significantly better than Fisher in the role of archbishop of Canterbury. But MacKinnon was essentially correct: Bell probably was the wiser choice. The reason why this is so points up the unfairness of the question itself, however, for

---

[1]   D.M. MacKinnon, 'Justice', *Theology* 66 (1963), p. 102n.

[2]   Peter J. Conradi, *Iris Murdoch: A Life* (New York, 2001), p. 130.

[3]   Donald M. MacKinnon, *Themes in Theology: The Three-Fold Cord* (Edinburgh, 1987), p. 124.

the answer must take into account what no one in 1945 could have foreseen: the period of the tumultuous 1960s and beyond.

People used to quote Ralph Waldo Emerson's dictum from 'Self-Reliance' (1841) that '[a]n institution is the lengthened shadow of one man'. Properly understood, this statement merely reminds us of the large impact, for good or ill, of the person at the top. Misinterpreted, Emerson's saying can gull the unthinking into supposing that the finest leadership is the most unitary and self-reliant; or that the best leader is a dominating figure, seeking to control everything. But as every good administrator knows, these mistaken conclusions overlook the vital yin-yang of leadership. Like the author of Ecclesiastes, the wise leader knows that to everything there is a season: a time to cast a shadow and a time to stand out of the light.

The yang of academic leadership, for example, is accomplishing good by actively working to bring about the best conditions for teaching and learning. The yin of academic leadership is accomplishing good by hiring an excellent staff and then making space for their distinctive contributions. In liberating others, the withholding is as crucial as the giving.

Early in his professional career, as a young headmaster, Geoffrey Fisher must have grasped these basic principles. In fact, one of his biographers notes precisely this point. In his book *A Class of Their Own*, which discusses headmasters who became archbishops of Canterbury, Bernard Palmer points out Fisher's skill in choosing faculty leaders who could effectively manage their own shops. Palmer writes that in Fisher's view, 'the key to the successful running of a school curriculum ... lay in the choice of really good heads of department. He flattered himself that he had been successful in his selection of first-rate men, particularly in the middle period of his headmastership'. The result was 'a steady flow of university scholarships' and an improvement in the intellectual tenor of the institution. Several men who had been staff members under Fisher at Repton went on to preside over their own schools.[4]

Geoffrey Fisher's positive achievements as headmaster – and especially as archbishop – are best understood in terms of both doing and not-doing. Of course, the world being what it is, someone proficient in the Tao of leadership may not receive all the recognition that he or she is entitled to. Charles Smyth recounts the following story about Fisher and his reputation:

'Mark my words', observed a well-known dignitary of the Church of England, who had been closely associated with the Primate at one stage of his career: 'when Geoffrey was

---

[4] Bernard Palmer, *A Class of Their Own: Six Public School Headmasters Who Became Archbishop of Canterbury* (Sussex, 1997), p. 163.

Headmaster of Repton, everybody said 'What a good school Repton is', but nobody ever said 'What a great Headmaster Fisher is!' When he was Bishop of London, everybody said: 'How well the Diocese is running' but nobody said 'How admirably Fisher is running it!' And it will be the same all his life.[5]

Both this statement and the earlier one by Bernard Palmer about choosing capable department heads contain clues to the nature of sound leadership and insights into the biography of Geoffrey Fisher. Indeed, Fisher's 18 years at Repton would seldom be left behind. They would be far more often invoked by his critics than by his admirers. Archbishop Ramsey, who arguably suffered the worst of Fisher, once recalled how, as a boy, he had accompanied his headmaster on a walk through the grounds of the school. They encountered a gate there which would not open. Rather than considering the cause and setting carefully to work, Fisher simply kicked it open and carried on blithely. This Ramsey found suggestive.[6]

But it is important to go far beyond what has become the conventional assessment of Fisher as a headmasterly archbishop who enjoyed indulging a penchant for order and discipline merely as though the Church of England presented some kind of elongated classroom. Fisher was first and last an administrator who sought to live by practical arts. In 1947, when the cottages in the grounds of Lambeth Palace were being rebuilt, the foreman of Concrete Limited, Bill Allen, bumped into a figure dressed in gaiters, knee breeches, and clerical hat. A brief conversation followed:

Archbishop:	Who are you?
Allen:	I am the foreman for Concrete Ltd. I am fixing Bison floors.
Archbishop:	Oh good. And are you going to get results?
Allen:	Yes sir.
Archbishop:	That is more than I can get. Results is what I cannot get.
Allen:	Well, sir, Concrete Ltd gets 'em.

A scholarly bishop may be judged by his wisdom and a prophetic bishop by his courage *contra mundum*, but an administrator-bishop must be judged chiefly by his results. In Fisher's case this quest for results was fundamentally important. He inherited a church whose arrangements were in large part archaic, meaningless,

---

5   Charles Smyth, 'G.F.F.: An Appreciation', in Bernard Thomas (ed.), *Repton, 1557–1957* (London, 1957), p. 112.

6   See John G.B. Andrew, 'Michael Ramsey – Archbishop Extraordinary and Contemporary Prophet: Personal Recollections of His Chaplain', in *The Anglican: A Journal of Anglican Identity* 39:1 (2010), p. 11.

or irrelevant, and one that was in danger of slipping into a state of societal irrelevance in a time of vast upheaval. The task of reform and reconstruction was an administrative one, but one fired by a clear purpose. To say that Fisher was merely an administrator would be like consigning the Labour prime minister Clement Attlee to the same category. Both men had a clear sense of what they sought to achieve, and they understood the practical arts by which they could pursue their goals. They also had an unsentimental view of the cause to which they belonged and the men with whom they worked. Fisher had little time for prima donnas, intransigent dogmatists, and self-advertisers. But there were times when he could overlook the genuine claims of those who looked for change. The story of a fruitless meeting with a number of discontented bishops at Westcott House in Cambridge in 1958 leaves an awkward impression.[7] In the appointment of new bishops his mind was often set against the creative possibility. Bernard Palmer suggests that Attlee, as prime minister, would have given the Church of England a more lively new generation of bishops than Fisher was prepared to allow.[8] Arguably Fisher's view of the church as a corporate reality freed him from at least some of the mystique, the rhetoric, and the illusions which distracted so many others when matters of substance came into view. Alan Webster has observed how attractive a figure Fisher could be to a laity that was not blinkered by the fascinations of church parties.[9] Yet Fisher's apparent immunity from the new, and often rich, perceptions of theological thought across the traditions surely limited the store of ideas from which he drew. Over a long archiepiscopate this fact began to show.

For all this, Fisher's archiepiscopate is most vulnerable to criticism in those areas in which he might have asserted a more imaginative style of leadership or in which he dominated or interfered when he should have let go. He was most successful when, informed by the virtues of prudence and temperance, he handled the yin-yang of leadership like an adept. As archbishop his ecumenical achievements were impressive. The Cambridge sermon of 1946 relaunched ecumenical debates at home while Fisher played a committed and vigorous part in the early history of the World Council of Churches. He also knew when the time was right to initiate a meeting with the pope. His parallel enterprise, the creation of a convincing Anglican Communion, showed his qualities again: he brought American Episcopalians and Australian Anglicans into the framework with brio and was happy to encourage and assist Anglicans in Africa as they

---

[7]   As observed by Alan Webster, in 'Geoffrey Francis Fisher (1887–1972)', in the *Oxford Dictionary of National Biography* (Oxford, 2004), p. 673.

[8]   Bernard Palmer, *High and Mitred: A Study of Prime Ministers as Bishop-Makers, 1837–1977* (London, 1992).

[9]   Webster, 'Geoffrey Francis Fisher', p. 672.

formed autonomous provinces. William Jacob, an authority on the history of the development of the Anglican Communion, makes a significant observation about this aspect of Fisher's leadership: 'his experience as a headmaster probably made him willing to risk delegating responsibility'.[10] By loosening the bonds, he not only preserved but also strengthened the unity of the Anglican Communion.[11] In time it could be observed that these two global investments – the one ecumenical and the other denominational – were, if not quite at odds, at least competing for the devotion of the Anglican imagination. Yet, if the ecumenists would be left to one side, the empire of Anglicanism would within only 40 years be wracked by bitter controversies because it could find no way of adjudicating, or at least accepting, its disagreements.

In sheer statistical terms, the Church of England under Geoffrey Fisher fared reasonably well. Although the number of baptisms continued to drop in the 1950s, the number of confirmations rose steadily until 1960.[12] Taking a long view and putting the data of the various communions into perspective, Adrian Hastings notes that 'there had been no very sharp statistical alteration in the religious practice of England between 1890 and 1960: Free Church figures fell fairly considerably, Roman Catholic figures rose, [and] the Anglican decline was pretty steady but seldom appeared calamitous'. He points out that 'in 1895 there were 641 Anglican baptisms per thousand live births; in 1960, 554. They had first risen and then fallen in the meantime, but not dramatically so'. In addition, 'over 60 per cent of all marriages were in an Anglican church in the 1890s; they were still almost 50 per cent in 1960'. Nor did the number of Easter communicants drop precipitously. 'The Newcastle diocese in 1960 had 39,977 Easter communicants – the highest it had ever had; this represented 6.4 per cent of the population over fifteen, just about the same proportion as that of the 21,216 Easter communicants of 1891'. The Church of England had experienced a drop in participation in the interwar years, but this decline was 'somewhat reassuringly, if really only rather slightly, reversed in the 1950s, so that there was no expectation of the sort of sudden statistical collapse which was ... to take place [in the 1960s and 1970s]'.[13]

---

[10] W.M. Jacob, *The Making of the Anglican Church Worldwide* (London, 1997), pp. 267–8.

[11] Charles Smyth, 'In Duty's Path: Fisher of Lambeth', in *Theology* 73 (1970), p. 70.

[12] Grace Davie, *Religion in Britain since 1945: Believing without Belonging* (Oxford, 1994), p. 52.

[13] Adrian Hastings, *A History of English Christianity, 1920–2000* (London, 2001), p. 551. For more statistical data on religious participation in the 1950s and 1960s, see Callum G. Brown, *The Death of Christian Britain: Understanding Secularisation, 1800–2000* (New York, 2001), chaps. 7–8.

In assessing the church's leadership, perhaps the most telling statistic is the number of men going into the Anglican ministry. This measure might provide the best indication of the perceived vitality of the church, for who would want to sign on with the crew of a sinking ship? And, as we have seen, Fisher himself had worked hard to improve the lot of the parish clergy. In 1958 the number of men ordained was 505, the highest number in several years. Two years later, 599 men were ordained. In 1962 there were more men ordained – 628 – than in any year since before the First World War.[14] In the mid-1960s the numbers started to go down again: 592 in 1965, 436 in 1969, 392 in 1971.[15] By 1976 there were only 273 ordinations.[16] Fisher gave the parochial clergy more reason to be grateful than any other archbishop of Canterbury in the twentieth century. But it is likely that he failed to observe how quickly the place of the parish priest was already weakening in the life and moral understandings of a local community. Within only a decade it would be seen to be receding very quickly indeed.

Any number of cultural factors lie behind these changes, and scholars have made themselves busy with them ever since. But the robust role played by Archbishop Fisher should not be entirely overlooked. He conveyed the impression of having the ecclesiastical situation well in hand; where there were problems, he would search them out and tirelessly work to find solutions.[17] He was the type of useful administrator who is often most preferred by those who do the main work of an institution. By the end of Fisher's tenure of office, the late 1950s, the Church of England appeared to be doing well. Trevor Beeson calls this period 'an Indian summer for the church'. He notes the data that we have also remarked: 'The number of Confirmation candidates and, more significantly, the number of ordinations began to rise'. He comments that the parish clergy felt these changes and welcomed them. A new breed of quite able clergymen 'believed that the Church of England was ripe for a new reformation .... An editorial in the *Church of England Newspaper* in 1960 informed its readers that "A new Church of England is being born, a church efficient, sophisticated and progressive, a church with money enough and to spare"'.[18] This was substantially the work of the Church Commissioners, whom Fisher had steadfastly supported, and of the new diocesan organizations, whose emergence Fisher had actively

---

[14]   *Men for the Ministry, 1963* (London, n.d.), n.p. (*Men for the Ministry* booklets, with ordination statistics, are available in LPL); Anthony Sampson, *Anatomy of Britain Today* (London, 1965), p. 183. See Cyril Garbett, *Church and State in England* (London, 1950), pp. 278–9.

[15]   Trevor Beeson, *The Church of England in Crisis* (London, 1973), pp. 46–7.

[16]   Hastings, *History*, pp. 551–2.

[17]   See William Purcell, *Fisher of Lambeth: A Portrait from Life* (London, 1969), pp. 93, 94.

[18]   Beeson, *Church of England in Crisis*, p. 174.

encouraged.[19] It is no wonder that Fisher declared, when he was about to retire, that he left the Church of England 'in good heart'.[20] Grace Davie believes that 'there was, in the 1950s at least, a distinct feeling of well-being, of revival even, within church circles'.[21]

How well did Fisher prepare the church for what came afterwards? This is the question raised in the introduction. There we heard the central character in Rose Macaulay's *The Towers of Trebizond*, a young woman named Laurie, speak of the Church of England as 'a great empire on its way out'.[22] In fact, Fisher deserves much credit for his work to ensure that the church was not on its way out. 'None of Fisher's predecessors', correctly notes one commentator on his career, 'witnessed the dismantling of an empire and its conversion into a commonwealth, none of his predecessors divested himself of responsibility for and oversight of churches and people in so many parts of the world or on so large a scale'. In addition, '[n]one travelled so far or so often, none worked so long to see his own church become part of a coming, greater church'.[23]

Yet a sense of certain deficiencies and missed opportunities in this impressive career hangs in the air. Fisher's reliance upon rules and traditional structures of authority was excessive. Overly involved in canon-law reform, he left the church inadequately prepared to meet the crises of the 1960s. If, in his episcopal appointments, he typically played safe; his undue caution probably cost the church farther down the road.[24] 'The price of his wholesome disapproval of slackness or eccentricity in the clergy', an admirer, Charles Smyth, writes, 'was a tendency to favour docile subordinates, a tendency from which the Church suffered in proportion as the Archbishop's influence on ecclesiastical appointments grew'.[25]

---

[19] Andrew Chandler, the historian of the Church Commissioners, comments that GF may not have been loved by those who go in for flashy campaigns, but the archbishop's 'worth was better known by those who undertook the workaday task of institutional reform'. Fisher 'perhaps found his element' in his work with the Church Commissioners. The Commissioners themselves 'would not see the like of [GF] again, and they would be fortunate to see much at all of those who succeeded him'. *The Church of England in the Twentieth Century: The Church Commissioners and the Politics of Reform, 1948–1998* (Woodbridge: Boydell, 2006), p. 148.

[20] Quoted in Hastings, *History*, p. 452.

[21] Davie, *Religion in Britain since 1945*, p. 31.

[22] Rose Macaulay, *The Towers of Trebizond* (1956; reprint, New York: New York Review Books, 2003), p. 234.

[23] Ted Arblaster, "'All the world's a stage ....'", *St. Mark's Review*, no. 152 (Summer 1993), p. 45.

[24] Trevor Beeson, *The Bishops* (London: SCM, 2002), p. 131.

[25] Smyth, 'G.F.F.: An Appreciation', in Thomas, *Repton, 1557–1957*, p. 112.

Especially during the final years of his archiepiscopate, neither his standard meeting agenda nor his manner when presiding was open to much dissent. 'During the latter part of his reign', notes Trevor Beeson, 'many of the bishops became frustrated and critical of the amount of time taken at their meetings by small administrative matters. They also resented being treated as if they were public school housemasters subject to an increasingly talkative and dictatorial head'.[26] A rule-oriented headmaster, he had a low tolerance for opposition to his authority and for too much questioning of his judgment.[27] 'Once he had reached a conclusion himself', wrote Eric Kemp, 'he saw it almost as moral obliquity in others not to accept that he was right'.[28] A leader who has been called 'the last true representative of the old order', Fisher was vulnerable to the criticism of Erastianism.[29] He did identify himself too closely with the settled arrangement of society.[30] He was, quite unapologetically, a Freemason (as 16 other bishops of the Church of England were found to be in 1953) who evidently saw no reason to question either the organization or his own part in it.[31] Nowhere was this identification more clearly stated than in the coronation of Queen Elizabeth. This event, the sociologist Grace Davie writes, 'embodied in high-profile form what might be termed the establishment spirit of the 1950s'.[32] When this establishmentarian ethos came under attack in the 1960s, Fisher and the church he represented were rendered that much more vulnerable. Even the traditional garb that Fisher wore associated him with what many looked upon as an irrelevant past. 'Dressed', David Edwards notes, 'in the episcopal costume of apron and gaiters (and rebuking fellow-bishops who preferred trousers), he began to look, while holding office, a figure out of a dead world'.[33]

The Established Church was allied not only with the state but also with the higher strata of English society. Trevor Beeson comments: 'Whatever the effect of the marriage [of church and state] has been upon the life of the English nation as a whole – good men are divided on the matter – it cannot be denied that the effect upon the Church of England has been to link it permanently with

---

[26]   Beeson, *The Bishops*, p. 131.

[27]   Paul A. Welsby, *A History of the Church of England, 1945–1980* (Oxford, 1986), p. 10. See Palmer, *A Class of Their Own*, p. 187.

[28]   Eric Kemp, 'Chairmanly Cantuar', *Times Literary Supplement*, 10 April 1992, p. 24.

[29]   As made, for example, by Robert Jeffery in his reviews of David Hein's earlier text. See the *Expository Times*, June 2008, p. 456.

[30]   Hastings, *History*, p. 664.

[31]   See Dianne Kirby, 'Christianity and Freemasonry: The Compatibility Debate within the Church of England', in *Journal of Religious History*, 29 (February 2005), pp. 43–66.

[32]   Davie, *Religion in Britain since 1945*, p. 31.

[33]   Edwards, *Leaders*, p. 366.

the most privileged sector of English society'.[34] When Fisher stepped down in 1961, three-quarters of the bishops had been to public schools, all but three were graduates of Oxford and Cambridge, and two of the others had gone to Trinity College, Dublin.[35]

Cultural historians describe an accelerating pace of change in British society and culture starting in the second half of the 1950s. The popular films of the first half of the decade, such as *Genevieve* (1953) and *Doctor in the House* (1954), have a bright, cheerful tone. After 1955 this upbeat temper gives way to a darker mood of disillusionment and protest. John Osborne's play *Look Back in Anger* is representative. First produced in London in 1956, the year that Suez shattered British confidence and illusions of empire, Osborne's play was made into a film in 1958.[36] Fisher's final year as archbishop of Canterbury saw the first publication of a magazine of political and social satire, *Private Eye*, as well as the staging of an irreverent revue, *Beyond the Fringe*, in London's West End. The latter was the work of a group of Cambridge graduates: Alan Bennett, Peter Cook, Dudley Moore, and Jonathan Miller. Large numbers tuned in the following year, 1962, to watch a new program on television: *That Was the Week That Was*, which aided and abetted the spirit of iconoclasm taking hold across the land. None of the venerable institutions of society was safe from ridicule.

While Fisher's episcopal costume may have put the archbishop at increased risk of caricature, a deeper problem for the church was that his style of religion was so readily dismissible, particularly in an age grown intolerant of conventional wisdom and suspicious of traditional practices. In his seminal work *On Religion: Speeches to Its Cultured Despisers* (1799), the German theologian Friedrich Schleiermacher voiced his concerns about the dangers inherent in a religion that has lost its animating spirit. The church is then reduced to relying on its forms and creeds, while the experience that gave rise to them is lost sight of. In the event, the empirical church fails to be the true church. It will have, Schleiermacher said, 'a school-mastering, mechanical nature, which indicates that [its members] merely seek to import religion from without'.[37] The actual church may also fail

---

[34] Beeson, *Church of England in Crisis*, p. 25.

[35] Sampson, *Anatomy of Britain Today*, p. 180.

[36] Tony Judt, *Postwar: A History of Europe since 1945* (New York, 2005), p. 300. John Osborne wrote in a widely remarked essay: 'My objection to the Royalty symbol is that it is dead; it is the gold filling in a mouthful of decay'. John Osborne, in Tom Maschler (ed.), *Declaration* (New York, 1958), p. 58.

[37] Friedrich Schleiermacher, *On Religion: Speeches to Its Cultured Despisers*, trans. John Oman (New York, 1958), p. 161.

to be the true church when it accepts 'special privileges' for itself and becomes intimately connected with the interests of the state.[38]

Too often in his administrative manner and almost always in his language Geoffrey Fisher gives the impression of someone who has retained the form but lost touch with the initial impulse – what Schleiermacher called the 'sense and taste for the Infinite' – which inspired the form.[39] This impulse, Schleiermacher said, 'appears as a surrender, a submission to be moved by the Whole that stands over against man'.[40] When we do witness an expression of this heart of true piety, such as when Fisher is literally moved in Jerusalem, it is a striking event, altogether exceptional. Pope John XXIII recognized in him 'a straightforward man, of high ideals and great sincerity' and he added, 'I see many people here from kings to the least of men; but I knew at once that he was a man of God'.[41] Evidence exists in Fisher's life-story that he saw himself as a disciple of Jesus. Trying to determine what to do about the offer of the London bishopric, he agonizes before finally deciding, during Holy Week, to say yes to the question 'Lovest thou me?' Along the Via Dolorosa, he experiences himself as a participant in the life of Jesus and in the lives of those who make up the Body of Christ.[42] But this vibrant awareness does not come through in his desiccated, mechanical prose. Geoffrey Fisher, said one of his chaplains, F.C. Synge, was 'a lover of smoothly running diocesan machinery. Law, rather than Gospel, was the stuff of his sermons'.[43] Undoubtedly Fisher meant for us to take his entire life as a witness to his deepest convictions: reorganizing church finances is as holy a work as anything else. But the 'school-mastering, mechanical nature' of his religion – and of aspects of his leadership – could not have commended itself to many who came after him. And it soon struck a society which was soon questioning so many inherited manners and mores as striking the wrong chord. Here, too, the longer term would not flatter Fisher.

Another way of stating this concern is to ask whether Geoffrey Fisher had sufficient imagination for the challenges he faced. Clearly in a number of areas he did. But perhaps, as Peter Kirk writes, he (or someone else) could have done more 'to capture the public imagination for the Church'. Writing in 1958, Kirk acknowledges that, in an increasingly secular age, getting across to people 'the eternal Christian verities' is not easy. When Fisher speaks, what he says 'is often

---

[38]   Ibid., p. 167.

[39]   Ibid., p. 39.

[40]   Ibid., p. 37.

[41]   Webster, 'Geoffrey Francis Fisher', p. 675.

[42]   Carpenter, *Archbishop Fisher*, p. 772.

[43]   Quoted in Purcell, *Fisher of Lambeth*, p. 88. Synge was his domestic chaplain when Fisher was bishop of London.

very sensible'. But 'when Temple pronounced on these things, he somehow made them seem not only right but inevitable; Dr. Fisher, for some strange reason, lacks this touch'.[44] The view of Bishop E.W. Barnes may be jaundiced but it is nevertheless of interest. To the author of *The Rise of Christianity*, Fisher also seemed to lack the ability to impart the essence of the Christian faith in a compelling manner. His son, John Barnes, sums up his father's perception by recalling that, to the bishop, 'Fisher never seemed quite as real as his three predecessors'. He may 'have appeared to be more like a puppet operated by red tape'.[45] Bishop Bell may have had his particular faults, but he had more imagination than Fisher, and for this reason – as well as for his other virtues, especially the courage he demonstrated in wartime – he might have made a more luminous archbishop of Canterbury.[46] Bell was more drawn to the works of the imagination, to the presence of the holy in art, drama, and literature.[47] Thus, he might have found ways to speak to those unmoved by the rituals and structures of the Established Church.[48]

When Fisher retired, he was succeeded by someone who was indeed a Mary to his Martha: a person renowned, then and since, for his deep spirituality. We can admire Michael Ramsey at the same time that we can appreciate the distinctive achievements of Geoffrey Fisher. We heard F.C. Synge describe Fisher as a 'lover of smoothly functioning diocesan machinery', whose sermons contained more law than gospel. We should note that in this same quotation Synge goes on to speak of Fisher as 'a very English Anglican, full of common sense and wisdom and kindness and prudence and shrewdness'.[49] Those nouns are well chosen and help to round out a review of Fisher's strengths and weaknesses. In an era that included the theologians Austin Farrer and Eric Mascall, the poets T.S. Eliot and W.H. Auden, the writers Dorothy L. Sayers and C.S. Lewis, the philosophers Ian Ramsey and Donald MacKinnon, the novelists Barbara Pym and Rose Macaulay, and many other Anglicans of significant accomplishment, Fisher's contribution was both notable and usefully complementary.

---

[44] Peter Kirk, *One Army Strong?* (London: Faith Press, 1958), pp. 72–3. See Peter Staples, 'Archbishop Geoffrey Francis Fisher: An Appraisal', *Nederlands Theologisch Tijdschrift* 28 (1974), p. 253.

[45] John Barnes, *Ahead of His Age: Bishop Barnes of Birmingham* (London, 1979), p. 420.

[46] Staples, 'Archbishop Geoffrey Francis Fisher', p. 240.

[47] See Ann Loades, 'The Vitality of Tradition: Austin Farrer and Friends', in David Hein and Edward Hugh Henderson (eds.), *Captured by the Crucified: The Practical Theology of Austin Farrer* (New York, 2004), pp. 28–9.

[48] See David Brown, *God and Enchantment of Place: Reclaiming Human Experience* (Oxford, 2004), pp. 2, 407–8.

[49] Quoted in Purcell, *Fisher of Lambeth*, p. 88.

PART II
Documents

The following collection finds Archbishop Fisher at work in a number of diverse contexts: in private correspondence, in sermons, in Convocation, in the House of Lords, and at public occasions. Some here are drawn from Edward Carpenter's admirable 1958 compendium, *The Archbishop Speaks*. Carpenter occasionally allowed himself to re-present statements which, in their original form, were clearly framed in longer paragraphs or divided into distinct sections. Occasionally, too, he refashioned stray sentences where the grammar was dubious or removed sentences which he found superfluous. At large, however, he was a rigorous, adept and sensitive editor of Fisher's words and in all but one speech here ('Partnership in Industry') the present editor has readily adopted his versions. It may be added that Fisher himself – who in 1958 was still very much archbishop of Canterbury – must surely have given Carpenter's work a firm approval.

1

The Atomic Bomb

A public statement, 1945[1]

The discovery how to employ atomic energy would have come sooner or later in any case. We must be thankful that we found the method before Germany. I think we should be thankful that the discovery came when it did. If it had come in peace-time, every nation would have tried to develop it in secret for military purposes, while the ordinary citizens would have had no realisation of its deadly possibilities. Now we know as a dreadful fact that man has a weapon that could be used to destroy civilisation. The use already made of it has shocked us all. Not only the Christian conscience, but every conscience is afraid and ashamed.

Opinions will differ as to whether the bomb ought to have been used at all. It can be argued that its use has in fact saved more human lives than it dreadfully destroyed by bringing the war to a sudden end, that ethically it is no *more* evil than any other weapon of total war, that a fearful demonstration of its power was necessary to convince men that its first use must be its last.

The argument on the other side is on two different levels. On the one, the use of this weapon has given Japan an excuse for saying that she has not really been defeated at all. If the plot against Hitler had succeeded, it would have shortened the war; but the extra cost in lives and suffering, we may believe, was necessary if Germany was to acknowledge defeat and learnt its lessons. So it may be believed that the bomb has been too successful, and has prevented the people of Japan from learning through the slower but already inevitable process of defeat to abjure militarism. On a deeper level, history shows mankind ever accommodating its conscience to more deadly and inhuman forms of war, abandoning one restraint after another. Another long step has been taken to the abyss, and the shame of taking it is upon us.

Whether rightly or wrongly, what has been done has been done. The question now is this: Having looked into the abyss, can mankind recover itself? Not if there is another major war. Not if every nation secretly seeks to exploit atomic energy to more efficient military uses, against the day of another war.

---

[1]   First printed in the *Canterbury Diocesan Gazette and Leaflet* and subsequently published by the Press and Publications Board of the Church Assembly, 1945. Copy in London, Lambeth Palace Library, Fisher Papers 2, fols. 17–18.

The way of deliverance is in the Charter of the United Nations. Every nation which signs it must live by it and between them there must be no military secrets. The trust which now exists between them must grow and be fortified. Nations outside the Charter must be so controlled that they cannot develop this weapon. And the United Nations must suppress not merely war, but the intention to resort to war, in whatever quarter, at its first manifestation. The nations must be lovers of peace and discipline themselves to it, and must control the lawless, if civilisation is to endure.

2

A Step Forward in Church Relations

A sermon preached before the University of Cambridge,

3 November 1946[1]

I am the Door: by me if any man enter in, he shall be saved and shall go in and out, and find pasture. The thief cometh not but for to steal and to kill and to destroy: I am come that they might have life and that they might have it more abundantly.

St. John 10: verses 9 and 10

This parable 'of the Sheep, the Shepherd, and the Brigands' echoes all the main themes of the Christian Gospel. Our Lord is the Door, through whom we men can know God in His true Fatherhood: He is the one Saviour who calls men to follow Him, calls them individually and by name: those who hear His call and obey it, not only enter through Him but possess His life. He is the Shepherd as well as the Door. And in Him they become one flock with one Shepherd who has given His life for the sheep.

That is our Lord's divine answer to human need. That is what all Christians find in Him.

It is of matters relating to the unity of the Church that I wish to speak: and therefore I have put first the unity which already exists before speaking of that which does not. In every main Christian denomination are found in abundance those who have entered by the one Door, have found the one Saviour and draw from Him their life. Of all such Christ is the Shepherd and all such belong to His flock; but they are in different folds, fenced off from one another by barriers, some trivial enough, some reaching up (as it would seem) to heaven itself, which the long course of the Church's history has erected.

So while in each fold the followers of our Lord draw their life from Him, that divine life does not freely circulate between the folds in the life-giving operations of worship to Him who is the Head of the Church and of sacramental fellowship between His members. In the temporal sphere, in the historical Church, the circulation of the Church's life-blood is impaired or blocked: and thereby of

[1]   Reprinted in Edward Carpenter (ed.), *The Archbishop Speaks* (London, 1958), pp. 63–71.

necessity its work and witness are enfeebled. Even though many of the divisions had their historical justification and their conscientious cause, even though God has used them to preserve this part or that of the riches of Christ from being lost, to our Lord and to his people they are a scandal and a rock of offence to be removed, that the life of His Church may be more abundant.

The imperfections of the Church caused these disunities and every denomination has its imperfections still. But at last the minds of Christians are turned earnestly towards recognising in one another the manifest signs of the faith and life of Christ and towards praying that he many may again become visibly one in the Holy Catholic Church of Christ.

It has been the great achievement of the past two generations, of the Oecumenical movement, of Lambeth Conferences and of countless faithful souls, to focus attention upon that which all denominations hold in common and receive from Christ, their one Shepherd. Rome alone remains officially unwilling to acknowledge other folds under the one Shepherd or even to join in prayer with them. Between all the others there is an interchange of fellowship and prayer and thought and a searching to overthrow the barriers between them. On the theology of Redemption and Grace, of the Scriptures, the Creeds, the Sacraments, even of the Church itself, there are no barriers that reach up to heaven.

It is round the theology of the ministry that the tensions most exist: some would regard the ministry of the Church as solely derived from and subject to the will of the Church, the Spirit-bearing Body, while others regard it as the original gift of Christ to His Church to be preserved in unbroken succession: and the synthesis of these not necessarily contradictory views has not yet been found.

But there are all sorts of other barriers, not of theology but of habit which, when it comes to living together, have a great importance and which because they are matters of habit widely diffused and long valued are not readily amenable to change. Each denomination has its own idiom of worship within the framework of the Christian verities, its own idiom of thought and speech, of procedure and government, of family life. Two neighbouring households may be friendly and yet not at ease at the prospect of living in one household. And the inertia in the minds of many people of many denominations as regards steps to unity is due less to theological reasons than to dislike of a merging of domestic habits.

In what I go on to say, I am thinking simply of the situation in Britain. There have been years of conversations between the Church of England, the Church of Scotland, and the Free Churches. There has been great growth in understanding: there have been sketches of a united church, outlines of reunion schemes. Then came the war and put an end to that period.

How shall we begin again? I sense a certain reluctance to begin at all.

A distinguished theologian has recently expressed the opinion that all schemes of reunion should be postponed until further study, theological thinking and prayer in all Christian communions have led them to a recovered apprehension of the integrity and balance of Christian truth, alike in the sphere of faith and in that order, based on a renewed understanding of the Scriptures of the Old and New Testaments and of the witness of Christian antiquity.

That is to suggest that nothing should be done until the theologians have begun all over again and reached agreed conclusions. The past does not suggest that such theological unanimity will come in any foreseeable future. But meanwhile there is the life, the life of Christ, visible in every denomination: and its circulation impaired or blocked. There is the one Shepherd, and the separated folds. In the history of the Church the divine life creates, and the theology is controlled by, the life as much as the life is controlled by the theology.

I believe the difficulty of beginning again lies elsewhere. Schemes of reunion have generally been what I will call constitutional. They posit between two or more denominations an agreed constitution by acceptance of which they become one. Its articles must be such as to satisfy and to bind the negotiating parties. They must contain all that each negotiating party specially values and omit anything which it stubbornly resists: they must be non-committal where there is unresolved difference of opinion: they must set out an organisation and a method of government: with this new constitution in their hands the negotiating denominations are to lose their formerly separate identities and become a "new Province of the Universal Church", unsure at its birth what will be its relations to other Christian communions and whether former affiliations of the uniting bodies will be impaired or not. I think that reluctance is caused partly by fear of that loss of identity which is a precious thing to those concerned, partly by fear of compromises, the full implications of which cannot be foreseen, partly by fear of unfamiliar forms of government, and all the time by fear of a written constitution. It is designed to help denominations to 'grow together' in the unity of the life of Christ. But a constitution is an artificial thing and may imperil the life it seeks to promote.

In this country I think there are three special reasons which make the constitutional method the most difficult of all ways to reunion.

In the first place the Church of England is an established Church; it has a very complicated legal nexus with the State, which enters deeply into its machinery of government.

The Free Churches would certainly not accept the establishment as it is. And while they might agree that a reunited church could valuably retain some measure of State connection, the process of extricating the Church of England from what it was not desired to retain and of accomplishing its transference to a newly devised constitution would be a work of even greater magnitude and difficulty than the scheme of reunion itself.

Secondly its position in the Anglican Communion requires that the Church of England should not confuse its own identity. It is the nodal point of that Communion. It is one thing for four dioceses in India to go out of the Anglican Communion into a province with a constitution of its own and a position within the Catholic Church still to win. But for the Church of England to go out of the Anglican Communion would disrupt that Communion itself, by depriving it of its nodal point. The Church of England by the nature of the case can only move along with its fellow-churches in every part of the world. It cannot submit itself to any constitution convenient for these islands unless it is one which in principle its related churches can adopt for themselves. The time may come when in the service of the unity of the Church, the Anglican Churches can cease to exist as a distinct group. But that time is not yet in sight for us and the Free Churches might well say the same for their own groups.

Thirdly, there are tensions within the Church of England itself which are not resolved: it has its own problem of recovering its own spiritual authority over itself and of re-ordering its own life. As I believe, the Church of England is being called and led to resettle its own inner life in loyalty to the tradition and the task which God has entrusted to it. But when it is thus engaged in a delicate task, it is unwise at the same time to involve it in questions of constitutional affiliation to other denominations. We need to have, as I believe we are getting, a surer hold upon our own tradition before it can be offered to, or accepted by, others as their own.

If then procedure by constitutional reunion is so beset by difficulties, is there any other way of advance? Any other means by which we can get towards that free circulation of the life of Christ between the folds of His flock?

There is a suggestion which I should like in all humility to make to my brethren of other denominations. We do not desire a federation: that does not restore the circulation. As I have suggested the road is not yet open, we are not yet ready for organic or constitutional union. But there can be a process of assimilation, of growing alike. What we need is that while the folds remain distinct, there should be a movement towards a free and unfettered exchange of life in worship and sacrament between them as there is already of prayer and thought and Christian fellowship – in short that they should grow towards that full communion with one another, which already in their separation they have with Christ.

The Church of England is in full communion with the Old Catholics on the Continent: and its relations with the Orthodox Churches on the one hand, and with the Churches of Sweden and Finland on the other, already approach, if they do not yet reach, full communion. My longing is, not yet that we should be *united* with other churches in this country, but that we should grow to *full communion* with them.

As I have said and as negotiations have shown, no insuperable barrier to that remains until we come to questions of the ministry and government of the Church. Full communion between churches means not that they are identical in all ways, but that there is no barrier to exchange of their ministers and ministries. Every Church's ministry is effective as a means by which the life of Christ reaches His people. Every church's ministry is defective because it is prevented from operating in all the folds of His flock. For full communion between churches there is needed a ministry mutually acknowledged by all as possessing not only the inward call of the Spirit but also the authority which each church in consequence requires.

At the Lausanne Conference of Churches in 1927, it was said that in view of the place which the Episcopate, the Council of Presbyters, and the Congregation of the Faithful, respectively had in the constitution of the early Church, in view of the fact that these three elements are each today and have been for centuries accepted by great communions in Christendom, and that they are each believed by many to be essential to the good order of the Church, 'We recognise that these several elements must all ... have an appropriate place in the order of life of a reunited Church'.

Every constitutional scheme has proceeded on those lines. The non-episcopal churches have accepted the principle that episcopacy must exist along with the other elements in a reunited Church. For reasons obvious enough in Church history, they fear what may be made of episcopacy. But they accept the fact of it. If they do so for a reunited Church, why not also and earlier for the process of assimilation, as a step towards full communion?

It may be said that in a reunited Church they could guard themselves in the constitution against abuses of episcopacy. But they could do so far more effectively by taking it into their own system. The Church of England has not yet found the finally satisfying use of episcopacy in practice: nor certainly has the Church of Rome. If non-episcopal churches agree that it must come into the picture, could they not take it and try it out on their own ground first?

It is not of course quite as simple as all that. There are requirements and functions which Catholic tradition attaches to the office of a bishop in the Church of God, which, if our aim is assimilation and full communion, must be safeguarded. Negotiators in the past have been able to agree upon them, and could with hope enquire into them further, if our non-episcopal brethren were able to contemplate the step I suggest.

As it seems to me, it is an easier step for them to contemplate than that involved in a union of churches: and if achieved, it would immensely carry us forward towards full communion, without the fearful complexities and upheavals of a constitutional union. In such a giving and receiving of episcopacy, there would be a mutual removal of a barrier between the folds.

Nor would any fresh barriers be raised, such as may be by a constitutional scheme. For no previously existing affiliations would be impaired. The Church of England can be in communion with the Church of Sweden which in its turn is in communion with the Church of Norway, although as yet the Church of England is not in communion with the Church of Norway. That may be illogical, but it is the way of Christian life and love. William Temple used to quote Fr. Kelly as saying that we must not regard the churches as we regard a row of separate boxes, but as rays of coloured lights shading into one another.

In putting forward this suggestion, I am presupposing that between the churches which concerned themselves with it there would be found to be agreement upon the essential principles of the Church, the Scriptures, the Creeds, the Sacraments and of the Ministry itself as 'a gift of God through Christ to His Church, essential to its being and well-being, perpetually authorised and made effective through Christ and His Spirit' (Lausanne, Report 5): and I believe that presupposition to be reasonable. Differences of interpretation are not such as to forbid communion and indeed are to be found within each body.

If then non-episcopal churches could thus take episcopacy into their systems, I hope that that step would not stand alone. I should hope that in preparation for it, along the lines of recent Canadian proposals, each communion, episcopal and non-episcopal, should contribute the whole of its separate ministry to so many of the ministers of the other as were willing to receive it. By that means there would be assimilation at work from the start at the presbyteral level as well as at the episcopal level.

I love the Church of England, as the Presbyterian and the Methodist love their churches. It is, I think, not possible yet nor desirable that any church should merge its identity in a newly constituted union. What I desire is that I should be able freely to enter their churches and they mine in the sacraments of the Lord and in the full fellowship of worship, that His life may freely circulate between us. Cannot we grow to full communion with each other before we start to write a constitution? Have we the wisdom, the humility, the love and the spirit of Christ sufficient for such a venture as I have suggested? If there were agreement on it, I would thankfully receive at the hands of others their commission in their accustomed form and in the same way confer our own; that is the mutual exchange of love and enrichment to which Lambeth, 1920, called us.

3

Canon Law

From a speech in the Convocation of Canterbury,

20 May 1947[1]

... I wish to refer to the Report on Canon Law which will come before you tomorrow.[2] The importance of that report and our debt to the Archbishop of York and his colleague who have produced it is universally recognised. Without trespassing on to-morrow's business, I would make these brief comments:

1. The reform of Canon Law is, I believe, the first and most essential step in the whole process of Church reform. For reasons which you know well, our canons are antiquated, obscure and largely irrelevant. Canon Law is the law required 'for the ordering of the public spiritual affairs of the Church of God'. Because we have no body of operative Canons to turn to, the Church has lost its sense of obedience to its own spiritual ordinances. With no law of its own, it has lost the sense of being law-abiding; and solemn oaths of canonical obedience have been evacuated of their true meaning. The ill consequences of this condition, practically and morally, have been very great.

Very wisely the Report does not propose an exhaustive code: it contents itself with our immediate needs and for the most part defines existing practice. In a few instances it deals with matters of long-standing concern such as ecclesiastical courts and lawful authority, where reform is badly needed. But it is a great thing that they should be dealt with not as isolated problems but in the context of a coherent collection of Canon Law, and that a collection which can, once formed, be kept up to date and coherent. But important though the Canons may be, the prospect of outstanding importance which this report opens up to us is that of possessing an authoritative body of Canons to which obedience is

---

[1]   The text of the speech itself may be found in the Fisher Papers 282, fols. 38–9. The printed version is in the *Chronicles of the Convocation of Canterbury*, 20 May 1947, pp. 33–8 (for this extract, see pp. 35–6).

[2]   The report was the work of a commission set up in 1939. It had latterly been chaired by Archbishop Garbett, who had succeeded William Temple at York in 1942.

required. That will restore as nothing else can essential habits of good order and good conscience within the Church.

2. But secondly, if as I trust Convocation undertakes this heavy task, it will be revealing itself to the Church in its true nature as the proper spiritual authority in all matters concerning the formulations of faith, the definition of rites and ceremonies and the ordering of ecclesiastical discipline. It is not the only authority concerned. Convocation itself can make Canons only with the consent of the Crown. Parliament has its authority, and subject to Parliament the Church Assembly is a law-abiding body. The report fully recognises the rights of these other authorities and makes no attempt to go behind them. Some of the proposed Canons would require the consent of Parliament as well as of the Crown: some would require a Church Assembly measure. But at the same time by taking the lead in this matter. Convocation would call attention to a process of readjustment of relations between these various authorities which has been in process for some time and for the well-being of the Church must be wisely continued.

4

Artificial Insemination

A speech in the House of Lords, 16 March 1949[1]

My Lords, difficult and unpleasant though this subject is, I think we should all be grateful to the two noble Lords who have brought it up for discussion this afternoon. The practice of human insemination is far less widespread in this country than it is in the United States, but it is established here, even though at present on a small scale, If left to itself, it will certainly grow. As the noble Marquess, Lord Reading,[2] said, it is the subject of discussions in the Press and of a play now running. It raises matters of such importance that certainly it should not be left to grow merely by inadvertence. It is time that there should be here in this House an open and full discussion of the question.

There are very great difficulties in discussing it, because it touches human and social life at so many points. Moral theology most decidedly is concerned with this matter. It would not be appropriate for me here to develop the arguments which moral theology would put forward, but in my judgment moral theology has a very clear verdict on this matter and I would summarise it in two sentences. First, the practice of artificial insemination by the husband, though it raises certain problems for the moralist, is on the whole justifiable, in that it enables the fulfilment as between husband and wife of one of the chief ends of their marriage and, indeed, of holy matrimony itself – that is, the procreation of children. Secondly, artificial insemination by a donor, is wrong in principle and contrary to Christian standards. That is the finding of the Commission, to which the noble Lord made such generous references.

It was a very representative Commission which I set up, containing doctors, lawyers and theologians. I appointed it in December, 1945 – not, I am sorry to have to tell the noble Lord, because of his Motion in this House – and the report was published in 1948, and is on sale. I shall make frequent reference to it, but first I would affirm as my own profound conviction the finding which I have just quoted. In doing so, I am fairly certain that I am speaking for the vast

---

[1]   H.L. Deb. 16 March 1949, cols. 401–9. A.I.D = Artificial Insemination by Donor; A.I.H. = Artificial Insemination by the Husband. For a full discussion of the subject here, see pp. 122–3.

[2]   Gerald Rufus Isaacs, Second Marquess of Reading (1889–1960).

bulk of opinion in the Church of England, and in other Churches. I do not wish to argue here the matter on the basis of moral theology. We have to consider the sociological, the eugenic, the psychological and the legal implications of this practice. For the rest of my argument I shall be referring only to A.I.D.

My Commission observed, very truly, that as yet there is little evidence available upon which to judge the sociological and the psychological effects of A.I.D. There are too few observed cases, and too few cases observed for a sufficient length of time. If judgments are made about these effects, even though they are highly probable, we cannot claim for them scientific verification. For the moment I wish to postpone those aspects, and to deal, first, with the legal aspect, about which at least we know what is the situation. It is accepted by all those who concern themselves with A.I.D. that it is vitally necessary that the donor should remain absolutely and always unknown to anybody but the doctor concerned; the identity of the real father of the child must not be revealed; the real father must not know what child he has begotten, and the mother and the nominal father must never know who is the real father of their supposed child. But when the child is registered the law requires that the name of the father shall be furnished – and that, surely, is a necessary requirement. The nominal father, contrary to the true fact, registers himself as the real father. That is a criminal offence under the Perjury Act, 1911, for which a sentence of seven years' imprisonment may be imposed. That offence is being deliberately committed whenever A.I.D. is being employed.

This falsity in the declaration of paternity obviously raises other important legal points, connected with titles, estates, interests or funds; quite obviously, it may seriously affect a question of inheritance or succession. I will not elaborate that point; it is fairly clear. The simple fact is that in the eyes of the law of this country the child of A.I.D. is illegitimate, and that fact is deliberately concealed. The whole process rests on a basis of deceit and, indeed, on the committal of an act of perjury. I would submit that the matter cannot be left like that. Either the law must be altered to allow relief from perjury to the nominal father – it is not easy to see how that is to be done without disclosing the fact that A.I.D. has been employed, or without other consequences – or, if not that, then A.I.D. should, as I would submit, be made a criminal offence. It is the recommendation of my Commission that it should be made a criminal offence.

It may be asked: Why make it a criminal offence, since it already involves perjury which is a criminal offence and is, therefore, already illegal? There are three parties concerned in this action – namely, the husband, the wife and the doctor. The husband and wife are directly involved in the act of perjury, but the conditions are such that their perjury cannot be known or detected by any means. They can reckon, therefore, on an absolute impunity, and the law is so far utterly frustrated. But what of the doctor? He assists at an act which, to his knowledge, will involve perjury. I am not clear whether thereby the doctor becomes an accessory to the crime, but he knows that that will follow. It astonishes and perturbs me that the Medical Defence Union should have given advice to medical practitioners concerned in this practice on how to protect themselves professionally against adverse legal consequences to themselves in connection with this practice, when it is known that the doctor is taking part in something which requires the commission of the offence of perjury. If the practice of A.I.D. is made a criminal offence, then no doctor could employ it without losing his professional standing and without himself becoming liable to a charge.

I believe the only effective way to prevent the practice – if that is what is decided – is to forbid the doctor to employ it; and that means to make it a criminal offence. What is intolerable, morally and socially, is to allow a practice which depends upon deceit and perjury to continue without either ending it or making it legitimate. Which it should be depends, of course, upon what is thought of the practice itself ... A year ago, in the case of Baxter v. Baxter in the House of Lords, it was ruled that a marriage had been consummated even though by the use of contraceptives procreation had been prevented. At the time I welcomed the judgment, though not all of the obiter dicta which accompanied it. But, at least, the marriage was taken as having been consummated, although procreation was prevented. More recently, in a case in the Probate and Divorce Division ... a decree of nullity was given – which means that the marriage had not been consummated – although by the use of A.I.H. a child had been born of that marriage. That is to me, with all respect, quite an astonishing decision, and I very much wonder whether it would be upheld if it came to a higher court. A child of the marriage born in wedlock by A.I.H. is thus declared illegitimate, so it was conceived in adultery or in fornication – presumably fornication, since a decree of nullity was given. We then have the absurd position that, although at the time of the marriage it was supposed to be a real marriage, between husband and wife there was fornication. Presumably, any couple who have children born by A.I.H., and a fortiori by A.I.D., if there are no other children, could get a nullity if they came to desire it.

I would ask that we should attach some intelligible meaning to such words as 'consummation of marriage' and 'adultery'. In Baxter v. Baxter, though contraceptives prevented the mutual surrender of the reproductive organs, there was a mutual surrender of the sexual organs. I think the distinction is clear. That is not, in the Christian view, full consummation of the marriage, which requires both. I am sure, however, that the judgment was right which said that, in the eyes of the law, this surrender of the sexual organs, without surrender of the reproductive organs, should be treated as consummation. But in the other case, where A.I.H. was employed, though through the impotence of one party there was not a mutual surrender of the sexual organs there was, by A.I.H., a mutual surrender of the reproductive organs. That, surely, is and must be regarded as consummation of the marriage. Thus, in marriage (if your Lordships can follow this rather complicated argument), mutual surrender either of the sexual organs without procreation, or of the reproductive organs by means of A.I.H., is to be regarded, in my view, as consummation. Equally, adultery must cover all these things. Adultery is the surrender outside the bonds of wedlock, and in violation of it, either of the sexual organs alone, by the use of contraceptives, or of the reproductive organs alone by A.I.D. – or, of course, of both, as in normal intercourse. If that be so, A.I.D. is adultery.

I do not wish thereby to stigmatise A.I.D. as having the same moral turpitude which attaches to the word 'adultery' in ordinary use. A defender of the practice of A.I.D. has said this: Adultery and artificial insemination are the absolute antithesis of each other. One is done clandestinely to enjoy carnal pleasure; the other decently and frankly to beget offspring without the emotional and physical enjoyment. There is certainly a moral difference between adultery in the ordinary sense and A.I.D. – yet in fact A.I.D. is adultery. Lord Dunedin, in Russell v. Russell, said bluntly: '*Fecundation ab extra*' (which I take to mean from another party) 'is, I doubt not, adultery'. Other legal judgments have supported that. It is a mere fact, whether you like to use the word or not, that by the introduction of semen *ab extra* outside wedlock, there is an intrusion into and a breach of the natural marital relations of husband and wife – and that is what adultery means; and the exclusive union set up by marriage between husband and wife is thereby violated – and that is what adultery means.

It may be said that by the use of A.I.D. the marriage bond is violated voluntarily, for a good reason, by the consent and wish of the husband and wife concerned. So we come to the case for A.I.D., which has not yet been stated this afternoon. Seen from one single point of view, there is a case, and even a strong case for it. We of the male sex cannot easily appreciate how much childbearing means to the spiritual and the psychological life of a woman. We know that there are many women who are never married and are thus frustrated in childbearing. We know how splendidly many of them sublimate their maternal instincts and express them gloriously in spacious works of charity and maternal care for others. If some unmarried women feel frustration, they are outnumbered by those who make a splendid life of service out of their childlessness. I would say that society owes an immense debt to the maiden aunt and to the unmarried woman in works of charity, religious service and in countless family circles.

Let me say here – for it is relevant to this discussion – that the suggestion that A.I.D. should be employed to enable unmarried women to bear children is on all grounds to be altogether rejected – even though I am told that there is a movement on foot to found a society to encourage this very thing. It is directly opposed to universal social instincts, to Christian principles of morality and to the meaning and dignity of marriage. It is directly opposed to the interests of the child, who is thus deliberately deprived of its normal right to know both its parents and to be brought up in a home in which each takes its share. There are only two countries in recent times which have encouraged this practice. One was Nazi Germany and the other Soviet Russia, and I do not think that in such matters they are examples which we should wish to follow. Unmarried women, then, must bear the deprivation of childlessness.

It is obviously much harder for a woman who has married in the full expectation that thereby she shall bear children to find in her marriage that that wish is frustrated. It is, indeed, a grievous burden in many cases. It often causes severe psychological disturbances; it often brings strain and stress, and even rupture, into a marriage. Surely, if there is a legitimate way of putting this right it should be taken. As I have said, I think A.I.H. is a legitimate way. But what if it cannot be employed because of the husband's sterility, or because he suffers from a transmissible disease? Here is, so far, a strong case to be considered for the practice. There is evidence that where A.I.D. has been employed it has often had the most beneficial results to the wife and to the marriage, with happiness increased beyond expectation. Let me say at once that I believe that those who have been concerned in it, doctors, husbands and wives, have acted in the utmost sincerity and in the belief that they were doing a thing good in itself.

We recall that the evidence on which A.I.D. is based is not yet very extensive, but some who have a good deal of experience are convinced of the beneficial results. Is the remedy, therefore, still to be refused to them, or taken from them? In passing, I would observe that a husband often has a great longing to have children, and sometimes his longing is frustrated by the sterility of his wife. No one has yet suggested that he should relieve his frustrations by introducing into his family a child whom he has fathered by A.I.D. or otherwise by another woman. He has to bear his frustration, and so can a wife. There are many examples of its being accepted and becoming spiritually valuable and creative in the married life. But is the remedy to be refused?

As soon as one begins to look at it, not merely from the point of view of the husband and wife concerned, but from the general view of society, it becomes, as I think, necessary to reject altogether the practice of A.I.D. This cannot be merely the concern of the husband and wife in their personal and private relations. If there is a handicap to be borne, that is a common and perhaps a salutary part of human life. We all have to bear many deep hardships, for the good of others and for the good of society. Consider, then, very briefly, what the practice will mean if it grows and continues. Consider first what it will mean as between husband and wife themselves.

If difficulties and jealousies arise in their married life these will surely be complicated and aggravated by the father's knowledge that the child of the marriage is not his at all. It is not to be supposed that every marriage will be delivered from all frictions from the fact that A.I.D. has been employed, and the intruded child may easily become a source of recrimination. Secondly, difficulties may arise as the child grows and develops. Suppose, for instance, he shows characteristics markedly other than those of his supposed father or his real mother: it may disturb the home. In some cases, if the characteristics are of one kind or another, it may easily give rise to speculation outside the home as to the parentage of the child. Thirdly, difficulties will arise for the child, and for every child, since the fact that the practice is in use will be known to everybody, young and old. The days have long since disappeared in which things can be kept from the young that are known to the old. The child, as he grows up, knowing of this practice, may begin to suspect his parentage and to ask questions which cannot be avoided and which must be answered and the answer, if he be a child of A.I.D., may profoundly disturb his own psychological and emotional set-up.

But it is worse than that. Even now the sensitive and imaginative child is sometimes seriously affected by utterly unfounded fears and terrors that he is not the child of his own parents. I have known such cases, and I have no doubt others have also. If this practice grows, that kind of fear may occur to anybody. Any child may say, and with some reason, 'I cannot be sure that I am the child of my father and mother'; and the agonies of the sensitive child over a fear like this are probably worse than anything, that adults experience in their grown-up life. Next, family stability equally is gravely threatened. Perhaps I may be allowed to read a sentence from the report of the Commission to which reference has been made: it would chance the whole basis of society if a man could not safely regard his brother's child as of the proper stock of his and his brother's parents and could not feel assured that it was not the product of an anonymous donor. We can imagine few suspicions more fatal to family confidence than that of the intrusion of supposititious offspring into a family. Family pride and family tradition are qualities by no means confined to the propertied or monied classes. They would suffer a grievous blow if trickery and deception in regard to family relationships were to be encouraged or permitted'. In the interests of society, of the family, and of the child – indeed, on a long-term view, since obedience to Christian principles is the only firm basis for happiness, in the interests of those who are drawn to this practice for their own relief – I think it should be neither encouraged nor permitted.

May I put the matter finally in two ways, one negative and one positive? Negatively, it is based on concealment, it is rooted in perjury, it deprives the child of its right to know for certain who its parents are and it deprives relations and society of that same right. If the law were altered so as to make it legitimate, that would merely extend by so much this range of insecurity. For that reason it should be forbidden. If it be said that this would drive it underground, the answer is that it is underground already, for by its very nature it is secret and concealed. Positively, there is at stake here, I believe, a deep spiritual principle and I would put it in words borrowed from an article in the February number of the *Fortnightly*: it is the fundamental principle of Christian belief that God is Love and our common Father, from which belief springs the dignity of human personality. This requires its correlative principle that children should be born of the love of their parents. In A.I.D. the purely material and mechanical element in procreation is separated, and not temporarily but absolutely separated, from the organic and personal lives of the two persons involved. And A.I.D. itself protests that this is wrong by what is regarded as essential in its practice, namely, that the inseminated wife and the donor of seed, shall remain ignorant of each other's identity. In A.I.D. human life is initiated as the result of a momentary mechanical process entirely divorced from the spiritual, mental, emotional and physical lives of its parents. If extensively practised it would inevitably degrade the whole conception of personality and intensify that tendency towards the reduction of life to mechanism which is one of the most sinister features of our time. And, I would add, if all that be true when the semen is derived from a single donor, it becomes yet more true, yet more sinister, yet more destructive of personality and yet more degrading when the semen is derived – and this practice exists – from what the Medical Defence Union describe as a 'Bureau' or 'Bank' in which the semen from many donors is intermingled before use.

So, my Lords, I submit that since the practice of A.I.D. involves criminal perjury, since it is based upon a continuing deception, since it endangers the moral security of child, family and society, since it is contrary to Christian principles and standards, it should not be allowed either to grow or to continue. I agree with my Commission that the evils necessarily involved in A.I.D. are so great that early consideration should be given to the framing of legislation to make the practice a criminal offence. I would therefore support the noble Marquess's proposal that, if nothing else be done, there should be a full official investigation into the matter.

5

Church and State

From a sermon preached in St. Andrew's Cathedral, Sydney,

on 19 November 1950[1]

I ask you to think of that community prayer, the prayer for the Church militant, as you find it in the Book of Common Prayer. It still offers today just those prayers and petitions to Almighty God which are most necessary for the maintaining or the creating of a civilised Christian community. It is to only a few of the many sections to that prayer that I would call your attention on this occasion.

The first object of our prayer is to be the Universal Church. That is to come before the secular authorities to which the prayer goes on, and before the people of God who follow. That was the original order – 'Church and State'; that is still the proper order, 'Church and State'.

You would be surprised if anybody in public used the phrase 'State and Church', and yet, in the minds of ordinary men, that reversal has in fact taken place. They regard the State as omni-competent, and the Church as a body, an organisation, a society, within and under the direction of the secular powers and authorities, less important, less fundamental.

This prayer calls you straight back to the true order, Church comes first before State. Why? Because, to the Church, Christ has entrusted those saving facts of His life, His mission, His redemption, apart from which there can be no sound State, no true community, no peace, no deliverance for mankind; and the Church is the guardian and trustee of the truths of God, revealed in Christ.

Abolish the Church, and there is no other body in the world which would maintain and present to the minds and consciences of man those truths declared in Christ. That is the primary duty of the Church, to bear witness to what God has spoken. I think men are beginning to realise that if you do, in fact, abolish those primary facts of God revealed in Christ, the result is to diminish and finally to abolish the significance of man himself. It is a fact that books are written now, bearing such titles as 'The Abolition of Man'. The abolition of man! And there are vast forces which are tending in that direction, to abolish any vital,

---

[1]   Reprinted in Carpenter, *The Archbishop Speaks*, pp. 95–100.

moral significance in man. That is only the inevitable conclusion once you have broken the link which upholds man as the creature of God, the child of God, and therefore able to know his duty by which he alone is saved. For you will not forget that it is only by doing our duties that men are saved.

No man is ever the better merely for having got his rights. He may deserve his rights, they may be just, but he is no better for having got them. No man is ever made better in any significant sense, more noble, more true-hearted, less selfish and egoistic, except in proportion as he gives himself to his duty – that is, of course, the significance of the one supreme spiritual law which Christ declared, and exemplified, which is this: anybody who hoards his life to himself shall lose it, anyone who gives his life, spends it, casts it away for My sake and the Gospel's, shall keep it unto life eternal. All those truths, embedded in Christ, are, as I say, the heritage of the Church, and the Church stands as their trustee, and because they are so vital to the human problem, Church comes before the State.

Of course the Church has obscured these truths by division, by untruth, and by unlove, and still so obscures them. The Church has used unworthy weapons, it has often conformed to the world which it is here to transform. It has often missed its opportunities or misused them. It has often been blind, often been impotent, and sometimes been tyrannous: and yet, when that has been said, it is still true that it is the depository for men of those divine truths by which alone they can be saved, and it is still the truth that as you look through history it is, in fact, the Church which has brought the salt to preserve man's life, the leaven to permeate the lump, the light by which men have sought to guide their steps upwards and not downwards.

Certainly we cannot think of our tradition in the British Commonwealth without knowing how deeply into that has entered the formative principle of the Christian faith, making us in fact that which we are. For it is from the genius of the Christian faith, as we have received it in England and the Church of England, that has sprung, more than we ever recognise, the good character of our inheritance; and I believe that as man now is feeling uncertain about himself, as men are uncertain about their significance, as they are confronted with strange forces pressing upon them, materialist in profession or in fact, at such a time men are beginning to come back to the Church, to look to the Church for the truth, not made by man but given by God, through which man may be saved. That is the responsibility that rests upon the Church of Christ.

That is why, before anything else, as we look at the Christian community, we pray for the truth, for the unity and for the concord of the Church of Christ. And then, in this great prayer, we go on to pray for secular authorities, kings, princes, and governors, and in particular, of course, for our own sovereign, and for all who are set in authority under him.

And the secular authority always owes its obedience to God just as much as the Church does. Secular authority is sacramental just as the Church is sacramental. All things are meant to express the will, the purpose, the love and the glory of God, and the secular authority, whoever he may be, or whatever it may be, has a responsibility direct to God, direct from God. The powers that be are put there by God. The secular authority is not responsible to the Church (that was an old error out of which fortunately mankind has grown) any more than the Church is responsible to the secular authority.

The Church could not do the work of the secular authorities any more than the secular authority could do the work of the Church. Each has its own functions and purpose in the light of the divine truths declared by Christ. The Church in its practical affairs is by no means infallible: secular authority in its practical affairs is by no means infallible: but both equally look to those truths which the Church possesses and which the Church is to preach, the truths declared to us by Christ.

For a hundred years or more there has been growing a divorce between the religious and the secular, between the Church and all that it stands for, and the secular and what it stands for. In the course of the last century the secular authority has more and more supposed itself competent, without any reference to God or to the laws of God, to order men's lives satisfactorily, to advance from one era of prosperity to another, and to fashion a man-devised and man-made Utopia. That dream has been shattered in the last thirty years. I do not think there is any secular authority now (in the free world) which is not aware of its own incompetence on purely temporal and secular premises to make a happy, true community.

How things have changed in the last hundred years and more! Inevitably, the State now concerns itself with matters which, a hundred years ago, it regarded as outside its concern. In order to direct our complex social life, the secular authority now has to enter into the intimate habits of the men and the women and the children who make up the State and the community, not merely providing physical necessities – drains, and sanitation and all the rest – but providing housing which so intimately concerns the kind of life that people lead, providing creative services such as education: for education means not bricks and mortar for schools, but a person who is delivering through his or her teaching a philosophy of life to children who are there to absorb it.

Almost without knowing it, the secular authority passed from the governmental to the parental and to the pastoral, and by its actions it is affecting not merely the external habits, but the inner way of thinking of its citizens. Now this is a great responsibility – a great peril. Quite easily a state so concerned may start to teach a religion of its own, and that is idolatry. We see the thing visible in the Communist State where there is an official creed, an atheistic creed, which is taught and imposed by every means upon the citizens by the State.

How is the State to be delivered from that terror of inventing its own religion and way of life for its citizens? Only if it recognises that it has its responsibility from God, and that God is found in Jesus Christ.

At this point the secular authority may say: 'But really, religion does not help me to settle this or that practical problem'. It does indeed, in the only way that it can be settled. God is too good an educator to give us all the answers to all our problems without any effort on our part. Like a good schoolmaster he says – 'Here is the principle. Work it out by trial and by error, always looking for the truth, and I am with you to guide you and help you in your thinking and in your actions'.

A Christian will administer drains, let alone education, better than a non-Christian because, even in administering drains, he knows he is working for men and women of the community and that he is working with the people who have got to lay the drains; so he is making it a human problem, and not merely a matter of things to be dealt with. For the moment we come to think about other people and their concerns and even the ordinary matters of life as things at our own disposal, we have committed the ultimate sin; for the ultimate truth is that always in everything we handle, we are dealing with the things of God and the people of God and the children of God and have to seek the spirit of God in which to handle them faithfully.

And so you pray, secondly – after the Church – for your secular authorities, and they do indeed need our prayers that they shall not attempt to build their handiwork on false premises, on the idea that by greed or covetousness or pride or mere planning, still less on atheism, you can build a human community: for that they must go to the principles revealed in Christ. And then the prayer goes on at once to the ministers of the Church and the people of God. Let me say a word on the people of God.

The secular authority cannot operate unless it is in the closest touch with the people – that is a great tradition of the British Commonwealth: there is our security against tyranny that our secular authorities are part and parcel of ourselves. And therefore if the secular authority is truly to do this task there must be behind it a great body of Christian people, of citizens who know what they are about, who can support, correct, guide, the secular authority, because they know themselves to be the people of God, which is just what the word laity means.

6

The Welfare State

From an address delivered at Brisbane, Australia,

19 November 1950[1]

I want to speak of a feature of our modern experience, and see what plain Christianity has to say to us about it. I mean what is now called 'The Welfare State' with which here and at home we have been experimenting for some time.

Go back for a moment to the times in which England took the first great step from a feudal to an industrial order of society. The industrial revolution meant many things – a vast increase in population, great towns springing up in a day with their long rows of bleak and dismal houses, great wealth in comparatively few hands, a very prosperous middle class, and much unrelieved ignorance and poverty for the many. Disraeli spoke of the 'two nations' in England. The cleavage was not of course total: men could and did pass from one end of the scale to the other: the middle classes were in touch with both, and the English are a kindly race. There were many mitigations: but the grave disorder was there.

The Church with its slender means was a leaven, bringing as far as it could, hospitals, schools, teachers and many other forms of social service. But in the main, the vast extent of the revolution in industrial and social life was too much for men to keep pace with in mind and spirit – and social 'welfare' limped along far behind. There were many signs that the Christian conscience was actively at work – Lord Shaftesbury with the Factory Acts, blazed a trail. The Christian Socialists, Kingsley, Maurice and others,[2] forerunners of Scott Holland and Temple,[3] were at work. Most of the first leaders of the trade union movement from Keir Hardie to Lansbury[4] were Christians, taught by their Christian faith

---

[1]   Reprinted in ibid., pp. 122–6.

[2]   Charles Kingsley (1819–75), Christian priest, writer, polemicist, and historian; Frederick Denison Maurice (1805–72), priest, theologian, and Christian Socialist writer.

[3]   Henry Scott Holland (1847–1918), priest, Regius Professor of Divinity at Oxford, and founding member of the Christian Social Union; William Temple (1881–1944), archbishop of York 192842 and archbishop of Canterbury 1942–44.

[4]   Keir Hardie (1856–1915), socialist and first Independent Labour Member of Parliament; George Lansbury (1859–1940), Labour Party leader 1932–35.

to work for a truer social order. Political thought and action through the latter part of the last century moved cautiously in the right direction.

The Welfare State of today is the outcome of this long process; but it operates now on such a scale as to mark a new epoch. The last war accelerated the pace very greatly in England. All parties there, as I expect here, accept the modern idea of the Welfare State, that it is the duty of the State not only to defend the liberties of the nation and the individual, but to see that opportunities of a full life are available to every one of its citizens; and as a means to this end, to exercise such a control of economic and other communal activities as may be necessary to ensure that they shall not impede or endanger the general good of the community but promote it.

There is, of course, room for great political differences when it comes to applying this general conception in detail. Mistakes, and bad mistakes may easily be made. The best plans may suffer from ignorance, lack of foresight, errors of judgment or confusion of motive. But it is accepted that the State should do its best to keep its citizens in health, in work, in a happy community life, and should educate them in all things which make for good citizenship. The Christian says 'yes, indeed'. He rejoices that the State with its great resources should thus take up a task which, on its small resources, the Church has for long been trying to do. Here is a great expansion of work essentially Christian. Christ declared all the principles of the Welfare State when He said 'love your neighbour as yourself', and St. Paul declared its method when he said almost in one breath – 'every man must bear his own burden' and 'bear ye one another's burdens and so fulfil the law of Christ'.

The Welfare State is still in the experimental stage: it is far from perfect. Let me mention one or two dangers involved in this great experiment.

The Welfare State inevitably means much central control, and that means a large machinery of control. There is the danger that the machine will operate clumsily and slowly: but more serious by far is the fact that the power to control the machine passes to a few hands. Even sincere men may by their use of power do as much harm as good.

Or again, the Welfare State has to deal with men's material needs, in bulk. It may come to think that is all a man is – a mouth, a body, an end in himself – unless somebody is going to keep another idea alive, that man has a greater end to serve than himself and a higher law to live by and deeper needs to be fostered and fed.

Or again, the Welfare State finds itself, almost against its will, pushed on into dealing with the spiritual environment of its citizens, with the minds and souls of its people. The Welfare Officer in a factory often has to advise men about their domestic affairs. Political leaders are constantly dealing with ethical questions.

The machine has to teach and encourage civic virtues, to shape to some degree the thoughts, and habits and ideals of its citizens.

What then about education? How are the children to be taught, beyond the subjects of their curriculum, to discipline themselves, to direct their lives; what are they to be taught to believe about life and themselves? The State is in this intimate way dealing with all its citizens, young and old. It is pastoral work. By what faith is it to be done? The Welfare State dare not (this side of Communism) invent its own religion. But it needs for the proper working of the Welfare State, that which in fact only religion can provide – a true sense of vocation, in all its citizens and servants, a true spirit of dedicated service, a true faith, not made by the State, but serving it and leavening it.

In fact, the Welfare State calls at every point for a far higher level of citizenship from all of us than ever before. It requires citizens who put what they do for others before what they get for themselves; who are keen to put more into the common pool than they take out of it. This higher level of citizenship is essential if the Welfare State is to work: and if it does not, the successor State will almost certainly be some sort of tyranny. In this field of citizenship, the plain Christian has his plain Christian duties. For instance, we as Christians, know how to work not merely for reward, but because it is our duty to God and to our neighbour, to work honestly and give our best. The Christian's work is part of what he offers to God and therefore he cannot be content with a second rate – and he finds of course that good work is its own reward and brings its own happiness and satisfaction.

Then the Christian knows how to be humble – how to do the humble job and hold the humble position without envying others or coveting things for himself. His ambition is to do his best where he is; if that brings promotion and advancement, he will see in that a call to greater responsibility and a fuller use of his abilities. He will see it as a vocation or call from God. But he will not seek self-advancement as an end in itself. All this is important. Men have had to fight for their proper rights in the past and may have to again. But to fight for one's rights is always a dangerous thing to do: it may let loose the covetous and acquisitive instincts – just those selfish instincts which have no place in a Welfare State.

The Christian works on a different principle, the principle which in fact governs every family. There is no mathematical equality in a family between different children: only the equality of love which is a very different thing. Each member of society has his gifts, his chances, his abilities, and they are not the same as anyone else's. We are all unequal, meant for different jobs and needs and rewards and expressions of life. The Christian will never be led by covetousness, jealously or greed. He will hope for some useful work in which he can fully use his powers to a good and godly end – he will know how to be content with a decent place in which to serve God and man, and he will know that he and his neighbour are equal in God's love and care.

Lastly, the Christian knows how to face the difficult question of loyalties. We are all bound by many loyalties – to a school, a family, a town, a trade union, a club, a church. All these loyalties are strong and are potentially very good. Loyalty breeds some of the finest and most lovely qualities in men and women. But it is not safe to trust *absolutely* to any human group – it may quite easily get led off into narrowness, prejudice, partisanship, fanaticism, pride, and pharisaism. Sometimes good loyalties conflict – loyalty to two groups, both of which justly claim one. The tension is sometimes very painful. That is what our Lord meant, I think, by saying that He came to send 'not peace, but a sword'. We have got to scrutinise even our loyalty to the Church.

The Christian is ultimately responsible to Christ alone and directly to Him. I read these words lately: 'Only men and women unpurchasable by any human pressure or human loyalty can make a wholesome society; and only religion can breed unpurchasable men and women'. Note that word 'unpurchasable'. That we Christians must be, if we are to contribute the strength of Christian conviction, and ethics, and Christian living and thinking to the Welfare State; and the Welfare State must have that Christian element of vocation, witness, duty, reliance upon God brought to it, if it is in fact to fare well and be a blessing for men. Unpurchasable we are called to be and can be – because Christ has purchased us to Himself; and in prayer and worship and sacrament and the living body of the Church, we are kept true to Him – by His grace bearing each one of us his own burden and yet each bearing his neighbour's burden too.

7

The Festival of Britain

From an address given in St. Paul's Cathedral on 3 May 1951[1]

The only heresy, Pelagianism, which officially bears the name of an Englishman, is the heresy that man can work out his own salvation by his own endeavours and without the aid of God.

To that heresy the British people have always been prone. But at their best, in their best leaders, in their best works, in their best moments they have always rejected it; and have rejoiced to confess their dependence upon God.

> Not unto us, not unto us, O Lord;
> but unto thy name be the praise.
> Still stands God's ancient sacrifice,
> An humble and a contrite heart.

This people has always been ill-at-ease when it has been unable to square its actions, its policy, its desires, its way of life with the just and merciful laws of God. Often enough indeed its perception has been clouded and its conscience has accepted what if it had been more sensitive to the mind of Christ it would have rejected or amended. But there has always been active among us a governing sense of duty to God and of the need for His aid: and often in great moments of our national history our people have had a deep and mystical experience of the good hand of God upon us. The Christian faith is full of contrasting, even contradictory truths, which are nevertheless true and necessary for our health. 'Work out your own salvation', says St. Paul, and in the next breath, 'For it is God which worketh in you both to will and to do of His good pleasure'.

This Festival, like its predecessor one hundred years ago, is a festival to celebrate our achievements as a nation in every kind of art and industry. Here is the record of our brains and of our hands, stamped with the hallmark of our people's character and enterprise arid perseverance and labour. The purest joy comes in the creating of things which, quite apart from any use they may have, come near to a perfect expression of that at which they aim and which reflect

---

[1]   Ibid., pp. 208–10.

the truth and beauty of perfection – designs expressed in music, in words, in pictures, in machines, in material forms, which are just right, things of beauty, touched with immortality.

But mostly things have to be judged also by their use: it is no crime to be utilitarian – but the joy of creativeness is alloyed by other factors and not least by the fact that what may be used for good ends may also be so used as to complicate, confuse or destroy the spiritual fabric of society and of the souls of men. To control what man creates by submitting it always to the laws of man's Creator – that is the first duty of man, his health and his reward.

The greatest creation of our nation has been a way of life, a tradition of how men and women and children may live together in the freedom of mutual respect and trust, free to be themselves, free to be generous to others – with a grand sense of proportion and of patience and a grand power of laughing at ourselves. Our way of life never has been anywhere near perfect by the standard of God's righteousness and love. But we have known in our hearts, that the principles of our tradition were true and life giving and godly, saving truths, more to be valued than life itself: and at terrible cost we have made our sacrifices to keep them.

For this period of festival, even amid the pressing labours which these times impose upon us, and their austerities and their alarms, we snatch brief moments to remind ourselves, and to show to others, what we of these much tried and much blessed islands have done in working out our own salvation, and to be joyful for a season and to renew our strength and spirit.

Such a festival might be a spiritual disaster, a self-indulgence, an exhibition of pride, the sin by which the angels fell. Neither our own character nor the harsh circumstances of our times would encourage such a misuse of this occasion. But even so the festival might be celebrated in a kind of spiritual emptiness, devoid of aspiration or inspiration. And that would be hardly less disastrous. For it would be to deny the past and frustrate the future. It would ignore ruinously the contrasting truth: 'It is God who worketh in you to will and to do of His good pleasure'.

We must not deny the grandeur of our own past: for in very truth the Christian faith, the truths of God therein declared to man, have cradled this nation, nurtured it, encouraged its best qualities, tempered its worst, and Christian people have been always the soul of the nation. We must not frustrate the future, for it becomes daily more evident that civilisations not built on God become vain or violent or vile. If we are to be worthy of our heritage, to preserve it and to add to it, we must keep to the same sure foundations on which our fathers built. If we as a people are to be stablished, strengthened, settled, through all sufferings it must be by our faithfulness to God 'Who hath called us unto

His eternal glory by Christ Jesus'. Our achievements are only achievements to be proud of in so far as they are done by a godly people by the grace of God and to His glory. That is the grand message and challenge of the Festival. This we have wrought: Nay, this God has wrought in us: Praise be to God.

8

The Coronation Service

From a broadcast on the Home Service of the B.B.C.,

Friday, 5 December 1952[1]

The Coronation Service in almost all its parts goes back to the earliest days of our national history. Then and now it is a solemn act of the Church by which the Sovereign enters into a new relation with his people and with God and therefore becomes himself in some sense a new person. You may think of the Coronation as a tremendously impressive and magnificent ceremony; so it is; and the magnificence of its presentation, the music and the multitudes all deepen its dramatic emotion. But read the Service and you will see how deeply personal it is throughout: the Queen herself is the centre of it all, being brought in her own person by the actions and prayers of the Church into this new relation to her peoples, to God and so to herself. God is acting in and through the outward words spoken and things done: the Queen is deeply engaged in every moment of it: and all her peoples, those present in the Abbey directly, and all others by an exercise of sympathy and imagination, must share in the action of the Service with her.

In the first stages attention is fixed specially upon the relation between the Queen and her peoples. They must accept her as their Queen. In old days it was the Peers who gave their consent, since they held all the political and military power. In the Recognition, the Queen will still be presented to the Peers as their 'undoubted Queen' and they will accept her as such. But the wording has been widened so that all those in the Abbey who represent the Queen's realms and territories at home or overseas will be asked whether they give their fealty or fidelity and service to her: and will answer the question by their acclamations. But there is another requirement: there must be assurance that the Queen will respect the laws and customs of all her peoples, that she will maintain justice and equity, that she will observe the laws of God and of the Gospel and will uphold the Protestant Reformed Religion of England and Scotland, and that she will preserve the settlement of the Church of England with its Catholic

---

[1]   Ibid., pp. 227–31.

doctrine, worship, and discipline. So she takes her Oath upon the Holy Bible which is then presented to her. The Recognition, the Oath, and the Holy Bible are the foundations of consent between Queen, People, and God upon which the whole act of Coronation rests. Only when they have been securely laid can the rest follow.

The Coronation rite falls wholly within the service of Holy Communion, and its three central acts are the Anointing, the Crowning, and the Communion. After the Epistle, Gospel, and Creed, the Queen, stripped of her crimson robe and clad in a plain white garment, comes before the Altar to take her seat in St. Edward's Chair. So she offers herself to God for the service of His people: and (as I remember from the last Coronation) the sight of the Sovereign standing thus so simply adorned, so unprotected against all the surrounding magnificence, is profoundly moving. Then comes the sacrament of the anointing with holy oil on head and breast and hands: all through the ages kings and priests have by this act been consecrated, and so God consecrates our Queen to be His anointed servant and sets her apart that in every thought and will and act she may be at the true service of her people. Then she is invested with all the outward signs of her estate. The first garments of anointed majesty are put upon her – the Colobium Sindonis or linen alb and the Supertunica or close fitting coat of cloth of gold.

Then she receives one by one the emblems of majesty, the spiritual meaning of each being revealed in the prayers which accompany them. The Spurs glance back to days of chivalry. So does the Sword but now stands for a Sword of the Spirit wherewith to do justice, destroy evil, reform what is amiss, and confirm what is in good order. The Armill and the Royal Robe are other accepted symbols of Sovereignty. Then the Orb is delivered with these grand words: 'When you see this Orb thus set under the Cross, remember that the whole world is subject to the power and empire of Christ our Redeemer'. The Ring, sometimes called the wedding ring of England, is given as 'the Ring of Kingly Dignity and the seal of the Catholic Faith' of the Church of England. The Sceptre with the Cross (perhaps originally having the same meaning as the Orb) is the ensign of Kingly Power and Justice; the Rod with the Dove is the emblem of Equity and Mercy.

You will see how all through the Queen is being invested with emblems of an authority which she receives from God and is to use in the service of her peoples according to His laws. So finally the Crown is laid on the Altar and, after prayer, is brought to the Archbishop who places it as the concluding and conclusive emblem of Sovereignty upon the Queen's head. So is she consecrated and crowned by God for her people. And now her people in the only outward way possible offer themselves and all their loyalty and service to her as their Queen and as God's anointed servant. It is a glorious moment when, as the Crown is placed on the Queen's head, a sea of arms rises as Peers and Peeresses place their coronets on their heads, and the trumpets sound, and all cry, 'God save the Queen', and far off by a signal given the great guns at the Tower are shot off. Consecration and Coronation, the inward and the outward setting apart of the Sovereign, are over. After a final solemn Benediction of Queen and Peoples, the Queen is 'lifted up into her throne' and the Peers spiritual and temporal do their fealty and homage.

After the solemnity of the Anointing and the magnificence of the Crowning and Homage, comes finally the quiet simplicity of the Communion in which all is carried up to the highest reach of Christian worship. The Queen now will be joined by her husband and just before the prayer for the whole Church, a special prayer will be said for him and a blessing given that in his high dignity he may faithfully help Her Majesty and her people: so on through the majesty of the Sanctus and the mystery of the Consecration Prayer, to the moment when the Queen, as Queen, as wife, as woman, comes to receive with her husband at the hands of Christ the Bread of Life and the Cup of Salvation: and there before the Altar they kneel till the Post Communion prayers are over.

Then the Queen resumes her Crown and returning to her throne takes her place in full outward Majesty with Sceptre and Rod for the Gloria. The solemnity of the Coronation is ended. There remains the joyful Te Deum and the great procession from St. Edward's Chapel the whole length of the Abbey to the West Door.

What has the great ceremony accomplished? It has, as I suggested at the beginning, created a new relation of the Queen to her people, to God and to herself. To herself – she goes out committed by every solemn act and word to be no longer her own but in everything the servant of her peoples. Her private life she must preserve and we must help her to preserve it – but even so, it is not for her own ends but always that she may the better serve her people. That is her sacrifice and with such a sacrifice God is well pleased. So the Queen is in a new relation of confidence and trust towards God. Her best service to her people is to maintain the laws of God and the true profession of Christ's religion among her people: she must move among them all with the authority and grace which come from and only come from the power of a Christian character: she must give it all the dignity, the strength and the human kindness of a disciple of Christ. For so great a task she has received the direct consecration and commission and authority of God who will daily renew in her the grace and guidance of His indwelling spirit.

There remains the new relation between Queen and Peoples: her sacrifice calls for a like sacrifice and offering from them. Her loyalty to them demands a no less exacting loyalty from them to her. Together they are committed to purge her realms of bitter things, to be a people at unity in itself because they all unite under their Queen to serve the common good; to rely on God's grace and by that grace to mark our national life with the dignity, the strength, the human kindness of Christian men and women and Christian homes. Her peoples by this solemn rite are drawn into a new relation to their Queen and to God.

All this and more is to be found in the Coronation Service. It gathers together in one surpassing moment, the continuity through all change of our national life, our blessings, our heritage, our character, our trust, as a Christian nation, our sense of purpose, duty, and aspiration; and it links us all to one lovely, gracious figure dedicated to God's service and to ours who is to stand for us and go before us through the years.

God grant to her many years to reign over us, faithful people to serve her, wisdom and knowledge to be the stability of her times: the fear of the Lord her treasure.

9

The New World of the Church Commissioners

Memorandum, 12 February 1953[1]

Malcolm Eve came and had a long talk with me about the Church Commissioners. He himself greatly enjoys the work and is keenly interested in it. But he said to me that he was frankly a little alarmed: he told me, which I had not realised before, that the Church Commissioners are the second largest holders of investments in the country, only being exceeded by the Prudential; but the Commissioners come in advance of the Pearl and other such Insurance Companies. Further than that, they are the biggest single land holders in the country. All this means an immense responsibility, and he is frankly just a little anxious as to whether, admirable though the management has been, it stands up to such a very heavy responsibility.

We talked first about the investment policy. Here is this immense amount of money. I told him I had had Butler's letter[2] and there was the suggestion of an Advisory panel, he thinks this is first class and hopes that I will go forward with it and invite the proposed people ... Apart from this Advisory panel he is perfectly certain that there must be inside the Church Commissioners somebody of real financial competence able to keep daily touch with the affairs and to advise the panel and to take the advice of the panel. The Government brokers only come into the picture in their way: they do not advise as to what stocks should be held, but merely are the experts to know precisely when a given stock should be bought or sold. But they must be told what stocks are to be bought and sold and then be given an instruction to choose the right minute. As Eve says there must be in the Commissioners themselves a man with financial experience and judgement who can be the chief executive. I said that if my memory was right once upon a time the Secretary was not also financial adviser but there were two

---

[1] Fishers Papers, Memorandum by Fisher, 12 February 1953, vol. 121, fols. 186–90.

[2] On 30 January 1953 the Chancellor of the Exchequer, 'Rab' Butler, had written to Fisher to report on a conversation which Fisher himself had proposed should take place between him and Eve on the matter of how best to devise a panel of experts to oversee the investment policies of the Church Commissioners. See Fisher Papers, vol. 121, fols. 181–2.

separate offices. Eve said that he thought this was so, and he clearly had it in mind that we ought to go back to a system in which the Secretary is one person and the chief financial adviser is his immediate second-in-command above anybody else in the office.

... he is not perfectly satisfied about the management of the Estates. It is committed to two well-known firms in the north and the south, Cluttons and Smith Gore but they are independent and go their own way ... He thinks that on the whole opinion among surveyors is that the Commissioners are hard land lords and open to criticism and he thinks that tenants are not particularly fond of them ... here too there is need inside the office for somebody whose whole time is given to considering the Estates ... Both of us felt inclined to say that the thing will not get really right until the agents' control is decentralised ... there ought to be devolution here. If you think of Derbyshire with German and Co., or Kent with Gearing and Collier, it is these local firms who know everybody, know the farmers and are local men themselves and are trusted throughout who make the working of the thing easy. And if the Commissioners had somebody in sole charge in the centre of this department of their concerns they might then devolve in each diocese or county the direct dealings with the tenants to some local firm who would gladly do it and who would have far more personal touch with the farmers ...

We talked frankly of the future ... quite frankly I said I hope that Trustram Eve will become First Estates Commissioners and he recognises that that is my wish and I think he would be willing to do it.

10

Premium Bonds:
The Small Lotteries and Gaming Bill

The House of Lords, 26 April 1956[1]

My Lords, this Bill concerns a subject upon which probably our personal experiences are quite different, and most of us have prejudices of one kind or another which make an objective judgement difficult. It is also one in regard to which moral theologians find many perplexities. However, I shall not concern myself with their questions. I shall not discuss whether gambling is wrong in itself; indeed, I find it difficult to know what that means, since you can never find gambling by itself. It always requires the participation in it of at least two people; in other words, it is a social activity, and the Bill is meant in a small way to affect our social life. It is tine effect which it may have which we, as reasonable people, have to try to estimate and evaluate.

There is almost universal agreement that while some manifestations of the gambling instinct are widely regarded as allowable or even desirable, yet, as the noble Lord, Lord Chorley,[2] has said, this instinct is, or is easily liable to become, a disturbing factor in social life; and that almost all its organised operations involve elements or possibilities of real social evil. Often, there is disagreement among the churches as to the quality or extent of the social evil involved. Generally speaking, the Church of England and the Free Churches, and the Lambeth Conferences which represent the whole Anglican Communion throughout the world, consider the degree of social evil involved to be so high that they resist any legislative encouragement of gambling and seek to extrude, it altogether from church activities.

The Roman Catholic Church, on the other hand, employs the gambling instinct for its own church purposes very freely, and I think approves of large-scale national lotteries and sweepstakes, such as the Irish Sweepstake. But the Roman Catholic Church is, of course, just as aware as we are that a degree of

---

[1]   H.L. Deb., 26 April 1956, cols. 1298–1309. The Bill sought to permit small lotteries held for charitable purposes.

[2]   Robert Samuel Theodore Chorley, 1st Baron Chorley (1895–1978), Labour peer and legal authority.

social evil is involved and that it may become serious. Thus a Roman Catholic Archbishop, not long ago, in a pastoral letter called for an end to all games of chance for the raising of funds for church purposes, urging that they should be free from the taint – note the words 'from the taint' – of gaming for chance. Everyone would agree that there is little positively right about gambling, and, if not wrong in itself, it presents undesirable and sometimes disastrous social features.

It is, my Lords, against that background that this Bill must be considered; and we must be as clear as we can about what kind of contribution this Bill will make to the health and happiness of our social order. We shall not forget that, as the noble Lord, Lord Chorley, has said, gambling does in fact often bring real family degradation and spiritual ruin to many individuals and to their families; no social worker could ever be forgetful of that fact. But no doubt your Lordships will be thinking, rather as I think the noble Lord, Lord Chorley, was, of the ordinary citizen well able to look after himself, who is very well content to buy a bit of amusement in this way with the chance of a little unearned increment thrown in to make it more amusing. The usual question is: 'What is the harm in it?' Indeed, the noble Lord said that it does no harm. But the prime question is: 'What is there to be harmed?' Let me in a few sentences say what it is that is liable to be harmed. A nation depends for its health upon the constructive spirit of its people. A constructive spirit is occupied positively with the good to be achieved, and the spirit of a people is to be found in the nature of their ordinary activities and their constant ways of thinking; it is to be found also in the incentives to which they most readily respond. Anything which to a serious degree debases what I will call this spiritual coinage of a people is dangerous and debilitating.

This Bill about small lotteries certainly does not add anything very significant to the value of the nation's spiritual coinage, nor does it attempt to do anything to check its spiritual devaluation – it does not pretend to. These small lotteries are designed to win support for purposes which people otherwise will not take the trouble to support in sufficient numbers – charitable purposes, athletic sports, cultural activities presumed to be good (but how is anybody to tell that?) and apparently any other purposes of any kind whatsoever, good or bad, which do not involve private gain or commercial undertakings. May I say in passing that there seems something a little odd about carefully excluding purposes of private gain from this Bill, when a lottery by its nature exists only by offering to its supporters chances of private gain. It is strange that there seems nothing in this Bill to exclude purposes of dubious social value or purposes socially undesirable. I do not discover any means of checking the value of these 'other purposes'.

But, of course, the intention of the Bill is to encourage people to support desirable causes which they would not be so easily induced to support otherwise.

A speaker in another place said, very movingly – and the noble Lord no doubt had this in mind: In my own constituency, many small village clubs, sporting clubs, garden clubs, horticultural clubs and all those causes which are so important in village life and which are a good moral influence have found their finances knocked endwise when such lotteries as these were found to be illegal. No doubt this Bill is one answer. But it does in fact make use of and put into circulation what is in some degree a debased coinage, as will be obvious when it is contrasted with what I would call the gold standard by which those who care for admirable causes such as these take trouble to interest others to care for and support them too; or, if not to care for them, at least to give a subscription as an exercise of social duty discharged without thought of reward or gain.

As I read this Bill I wonder whether it has not been chiefly inspired by the managerial class, if I may so call it; by organisers of clubs and enterprises who find the task of money-raising very difficult and who are trying to take a short cut to solvency by the risky methods of inflation. I wonder whether it is not a Bill devised chiefly by the middle-aged, too young to dream dreams and too old any longer to see visions. There has been no demand or support for this Bill from youth organisations or those who speak for young people. Young people can, and still do, respond to the simple idea that if things are worth doing, they are worth doing for their own sakes. All education tries to teach them that simple truth. It seems a pity to encourage them – as this Bill does – always to look for a prize, and one awarded not on merit but by pure chance, for well-doing.

The Bill seems, rather appropriately, to trust to luck that no one will attempt to exploit its provisions in any undesirable way. The noble Lord, Lord Chorley, spoke if its 'stringent conditions'. I cannot find them. It imposes singularly few restraints. Any purpose which is not for private gain or of a commercial nature is allowed. Any 'society' not thus excluded can apply for registration. The local authority does not appear to have any discretion about registering a society, and if the application is in due form and £1 is paid, then, so far as I can see, the local authority must register the society. The society fixes the opening and closing date of each lottery which it runs, and, I suppose, can start a new one as soon as the old one closes and thus run a perpetual lottery. For the purpose of the Bill a society includes: an association of persons, by whatever name called. How many make 'an association'? I find in the Bill that there must be a promoter and also two members to certify the required return. Will two other members suffice, making five in all? Can fifty like-minded enthusiasts register themselves as ten different societies, each promoting its own lottery? The Bill provides that no tickets may be sold by a person under sixteen years of age; but, so far as I can see, tickets may be sold to any member of the public. Does that mean that children of school age may, along with the rest of us, be invited at any time, by any enthusiast over the age of sixteen, to buy a ticket? No wonder the Youth Department of the British Council of Churches and the Council itself has asked that no children or young persons under the age of eighteen shall be in any way concerned in the organisation, sale, purchase or possession of tickets under this Bill!

It is to be noted that local authorities, apparently, will have no knowledge of what lotteries are actually in operation at any given time. They will not know that until they receive a return from each lottery promoter, and that need not be until three months after the lottery has ended; so that at any given moment the local authority will not know how many lotteries are actually in progress in its area, each trying, or being able to try, to sell up to 15,000 tickets – the maximum fixed by the Bill. There may be quite a lot, all competing to secure shillings from as many people as possible. There is an arrangement by which local authorities control flag days for charitable purposes so that they do not clash with one another or become a nuisance to the public. If promoters of these small lotteries are to be encouraged to do what is now illegal and will become legal – to seek to sell their tickets to the general public – ought not the local authority to have power to control them as it controls flag days, to protect the general public from being unduly exploited by endless small lotteries, or even to protect ordinary citizens from ardent aldermen wishing to organise lotteries in relief of rates?

My Lords, this title of 'Small Lotteries' is very misleading. The noble Lord has said that they are small and therefore quite harmless. Each may be small, although already they are not so small as they were when the Bill first appeared; but if one is to judge their total social effect one must aggregate them, and I believe the Bill should require local authorities to make an annual return of the number and proceeds of all lotteries in their area. Thus aggregated they are certainly not small. A chief constable stated in *The Times* two years ago that: taken in the aggregate small lotteries probably amount to the equivalent of running one Irish Sweepstake each week in this country. If the true standard is to do things for their own sakes because they are worth doing, and without bribery, if the general spiritual currency of the community is to some extent debased by taking this line of least resistance, it is no answer to say that each person has only a few of these debased coins in his pocket at any one time. The whole coinage has been debased.

On such grounds I should maintain that, in the general interest, this Bill should be rejected. But there is a wider reason which makes it in my view mote important that the Bill should not proceed. This Bill might, perhaps, have crept through as a small, even if a rather small-minded, Bill; but, as we have been reminded, the Chancellor of the Exchequer has now raised the same general principle on a far larger scale. I know that the Chancellor says that his premium bonds are not a gamble, but there will be all the paraphernalia of a national lottery – the sale of what are the equivalent of tickets, quarterly drawings (which already some would make monthly drawings), publication of winning numbers, the recurrent excitement to see whether one has a winning ticket and all the rest of it. How long will the general public (or, shall I say, future Chancellors of the Exchequer) be aware of some tenuous argument about when is a gamble not a gamble, or remember that because they are only gambling with the interest, they are not really gambling at all?

The Financial Secretary to the Treasury is reported as saying this – and with the first half of it I entirely agree: ... it is utterly in the national interest that the sort of people who are spending money without a thought of saving should get the idea that they are doing a service to the nation and to themselves and have a flutter at the same time. And Mr. Davies, who first promoted this Bill, said of it in another place: if a person can combine a flutter with charity, he gives more generously and regularly. So whether it is the duty of supporting good causes or the duty of saving for one's own benefit and for the nation's good, there must be a 'flutter' attached to make duty palatable.

The Chancellor has compelled us to consider the matter on a national scale. We all agree that we are engaged in a great struggle to preserve, to restore, to re-create, the economic stability and the spiritual capital of this people. The Government know, as well as all the rest of us, that we can regain stability and strength only by unremitting exercise all through the nation of the old-fashioned but essential virtues: integrity of character, strict honesty, the duty of honest work honestly rewarded, thrift, saving and the like. We all know that, at present, calls to such virtues fall on barren soil – not enough people listen when they are told that it is their duty to work or their duty to save. So what? The Government's duty, surely, is by every means in their power to restore the true coinage without which we cannot endure as a great people. They have chosen instead not a dazzling but a rather second-rate expedient, which may attract savings but which adds nothing to the spiritual capital of the nation, and which insinuates on a large scale this, as I should say, undignified and unedifying adulteration of public duty by motives of private gain.

And it comes, my Lords – if I may keep you for a few moments longer – at a peculiarly inappropriate time. We live in a Welfare State. The whole basis of it is responsible citizenship, and particularly responsibility in the use of money. To make this Welfare State viable spiritually and economically every citizen must develop a sense of responsibility superior, as I would say, to that required under any other order of society that has ever existed. Chance, in the sense of the unforeseeable or the uncontrollable, does, of course, enter into every occupation and often decides whether a State, a society, or a company pays its way and whether individuals are in prosperity or adversity. But the whole endeavour of our society is that each in his own place shall earn and contribute and control his share by the exercise of his own reasoned responsibility. Private gain divorced from responsibility, whether in management or workers or anywhere else, is anti-social. The Government's great concern must be that money gained shall be truly earned and that money earned shall be used reasonably, thoughtfully and for the general good.

The Chancellor's action and this Bill both contradict that social principle, and do so now of all times, when our existence and influence as a nation depend upon it. The Bill might be regarded as a small and, therefore, unimportant thing; but it is now caught up into this far wider context of concern. The Chancellor of the Exchequer, too, talks of his premium bonds as being 'too small to corrupt'. Once more there is this misleading emphasis on smallness. It is as though an athlete in training said that a chocolate was too small a thing to injure his training, and then proceeded to eat chocolates the whole day long. When everybody is making seductive offers all round, fresh offers of the same kind, from the Government of premium bonds, or from this Parliament in this Bill, become of serious concern for the training and disciplined spirit of the nation. Bad currency always drives out good. A long succession of small gambles, always tending to grow larger or more numerous, added on to the commercial gambles as a whole, cannot make a nation great. They can only make it flabby or, shall I say, fluttering in spirit.

The Chancellor of the Exchequer will no doubt go his own way. But the Government have now undertaken to deal by legislation with the recommendations of the Royal Commission on Betting and Gambling, and your Lordships know that the Royal Commission did not recommend any change in the Lottery Laws. Surely, on every ground, this Bill must now await the general review which the Government have promised, in which the undoubted anomalies to which the noble Lord referred will be dealt with, and any necessary relaxation from an over-Puritanical spirit will no doubt be deliberately made.

If the Chancellor of the Exchequer can claim to prejudge the issue for his own purposes, this Bill cannot claim the same right. It is no longer a small one. It must now be considered along with all other similar matters. The Bill utters this coinage – what I have called this slightly debased coinage – in maximum denominations of £100, the Chancellor of £1,000 and the football pools of £75,000, But it is all the same spiritual currency, and its value for the public health should be considered by the Government and by Parliament as a single problem. No doubt, the general public will require that a place, a substantial place, be left in the national life for the gambling instinct to express itself, and

I should accept the fact. But when the Chancellor of the Exchequer and the promoter of this Bill suggest that their measures are too small to corrupt, they bear witness that large indulgence of the gambling instinct may easily corrupt the life of the nation. But small and large are matters of proportion, and can only be wisely considered when all the elements of the problem are brought together in the general review now promised by the Government. For this reason, also, I suggest that it would be improvident to proceed with this Bill until that general review can take place.

11

The Suez Debate

The House of Lords, 1 November 1956[1]

The Lord Archbishop of Canterbury

For many reasons I want to say very little. The obvious reason is that when matters come to such a perilous pass as this, full of confusion, passion and distress, any attempt to isolate and express a Christian judgment upon them must be full of danger that it may, in fact, only increase the confusion and release all kinds of misunderstandings. Yet it is demanded of me and of my office that I should make an attempt, very briefly, to isolate from all other considerations what may be the peculiar and limited Christian judgment on this matter. What I say, I say with fear and trembling.

The only helpful thing that any one of us can do at this moment is to stick severely to the single point of immediate relevance. Most of the troubles in this world are due to the fact that people will not stick to the one point that has to be dealt with, but bring into consideration, and therefore into confusion, every other conceivable related point. The single point is that Israeli troops are deep in Egyptian territory, and that the British and French Governments, with the sincere desire to limit the struggle, are in process of sending their own troops into Egyptian territory. The only question that we, as a responsible nation have to ask ourselves is: Are we doing the right thing by the highest and wisest standards that we, as a nation, know? [...]

The point to which the Christian conscience must acutely address itself is whether or no we are standing to the spirit of the United Nations Charter. Talk about our vital interests is not the main point, any more than (if I may say so) talk about the vital interests of Israel, on which the noble Viscount spoke, is the main point. It is not. Talk about international interests in general is beside the point, since under the United Nations Charter, we, like every other nation, have bound ourselves in honour not to claim to be judges in our own cause nor to presume to constitute ourselves the sole guardian of the interests of other nations or sole guardians, with France, of international order. It is impossible to

---

[1]   H.L. Deb., 5s, cols. 1293–354.

feel that on this field we are on secure ground – again I speak from such contacts as I have had. Most people seem to me to feel sure that here we are standing on slippery ground and not on secure ground: and even if the Government could prove that we are, in fact, standing on the letter of the United Nations Charter, that would not really satisfy any of the spiritual challenge of this day and hour with which we are confronted.

I do not wish to say more. I trust that I have said enough to show what I know to be the fact: that Christian opinion in the country, Christian opinion of those whose duty it is to concentrate on that one aspect, is terribly uneasy and unhappy. I suggest that even those most convinced that the Government have taken the right action would be wise to give heed not only to this uneasiness in the country but to the hostile reactions which the Government's action has evoked in all parts of the world. It is said that nothing succeeds like success, and I saw in one paper the view that, if this comes off, all will be well. But in this case, even if the Government's action does succeed, in separating the combatants, it will leave a legacy all over the world which temporary success can never obliterate, a legacy which will cause us to be regarded for years to come as all that our worst enemies have been saying about us for many years past.

Is there nothing, my Lords, that can be done? I look at the bare situation, and I speak as a fool, knowing none of the details of these things. Our call was to Israel and to Egypt to withdraw ten miles from the Canal, and the request was declared to be for the sole purpose of protecting the Canal. The simplest, the most obvious, the most imperative way of securing the safety of the Canal is that Israel should withdraw within its own borders. Then the temporary situation is saved and the Canal is no longer under threat.

Can we now, as a nation, led by the Government, make a new proposal? Objectively regarded, Egypt is at present within her own borders. Israel is out of bounds, and the British and French Governments propose to be out of bounds also. The immediate task is to bring everybody back within his own rightful place, so that nobody is trespassing. Can we say to Israel that, if they will withdraw their forces within their own bounds, France and ourselves will not intrude ourselves into Egypt? And can we say to Israel that the whole world is demanding that, both of Israel and ourselves, and that therefore we are willing to do it? With that standstill arrangement we can securely say, taught by this terrible experience, that all the statesmen of the world will see to it that Israel shall not suffer for its obedience or longer have to live under continuous threats. [...]

Viscount de Lisle[2]

... Are the United Nations to be used, to be manipulated, by small Powers, to gain their objects, and is lawlessness not to be visited by retribution or those confusions remedied? Nothing has more degraded the currency of international affairs in recent times than the fact that Colonel Nasser was able to seize the Canal illegally and so far no remedy for the seizure has been offered. It is not a question of preserving the prestige of the United Nations because, alas! I fear that a great deal of its prestige is already lost. Surely our duty is to look at the underlying situation, which is that if no Power intervenes in the Middle East, the course is set for a general conflagration and a third world war.

When the Charter of the United Nations was drawn up, did any of the nations then contemplate that its terms laying down international relations would become the plaything of American internal politics? if that is the case, then nobody can doubt that nothing has given Colonel Nasser more encouragement than the Republican Party's slogan, 'Peace with prosperity'. Colonel Nasser was a shrewd judge and took his opportunity. Therefore I say that, whether or not the general opinion of other nations is with us – and I cannot follow the most reverend Primate's argument that that, so to speak, is an equation with Christianity –

The Lord Archbishop of Canterbury

My Lords, I never said any such thing. I said that any wise people, judging themselves, would take account of what their friends and other people thought of them. That is just a piece of common sense, not Christianity.

Viscount de Lisle

My Lords, I do not want to misinterpret the most reverend Primate, but he started off by saying that he was evaluating the situation from a Christian point of view.

The Lord Archbishop of Canterbury

Your Lordships will remember that I came to a point when I said that what the Christian conscience must seize upon was our relation to the United Nations

---

[2] William Sidney, Viscount de Lisle (1909–91). Fifteenth (and final) British Governor-General of Australia.

Charter and how we stand with regard to that. That was the point which I specially said the Christian must consider. There are several answers to that, but at least I put forward one.

Viscount de Lisle

My Lords, the impression that the most reverend Primate gave is that world opinion is in some way connected with Christian opinion. I listened to the most reverend Primate's speech and he must allow me to debate it. I cannot accept that the Charter of the United Nations is in itself a part of the Christian credo.

The Lord Archbishop of Canterbury

My Lords, I am sorry to rise again, but I never said that the United Nations Charter was part of the Christian Faith. I said that we had pledged our word and our honour to stand by the United Nations Charter. I thought we had.

Viscount de Lisle

My Lords, we are talking here about the Christian credo and about political affairs and what is right in political affairs. There are certain connections between the two, but I think that the most reverend Primate, speaking with all his authority as leader of the Church of England, ought to be particularly careful not to confuse the Christian ethic with the to and fro of political life.

The Lord Archbishop of Canterbury

My Lords, if the noble Viscount will read the debate, he will see that I was extremely careful to do just that one thing.

Viscount de Lisle

My Lords, I hope that the most reverend Primate will re-read the debate and he will see, in all fairness, how easily he would give the impression, speaking with all the authority of the leader of a Christian Church, that the Government are guilty of some unchristian act, and I deny that absolutely. I believe that one of the virtues of the Christian religion is courage, and courage very often means doing things that are unpopular. The fact that what we are doing now is unpopular – I admit it – does not deter me in the slightest, and I am afraid that I cannot accept the implied rebuke from the most reverend Primate.

The Lord Archbishop of Canterbury

My Lords, I am afraid we are going to keep this going for a long time. What I said was that it was my business to isolate the particular Christian point, apart from all other questions – that is, leaving aside political conditions or self-interest or anything else. I froze on the point that we are committed by our own words to the United Nations Charter. That is a perfectly right thing for me to say as a Christian, and, as one with a Christian conscience, I ask how far we are sticking to our pledged word.

Viscount de Lisle

My Lords, I am grateful for the intervention of the most reverend Primate. Perhaps he has redefined his point, but I still maintain that in his speech he said that there was a grave danger that the Government would be condemned from a Christian standpoint because they were doing things that were unpopular. The Charter of the United Nations is a man-made affair and is admitted by all to be imperfect. If it has been manipulated in the interests of lawbreakers, the Charter suffers and international relations and the whole currency of international conduct suffer. If we waited until the full procedure of the United Nations was carried out. can anybody say, using his ordinary common sense, that the conflagration would not have spread? I believe that it is our duty, first to the United Nations and then to the whole community of nations, to see that this terrible difficulty in the Middle East, this struggle of interests and races, is brought to rest as soon as possible. For that reason, I commend the action of Her Majesty's Government. [...]

Lord Wilmot of Selmeston[3]

My Lords, it is difficult to follow the argument of the noble and learned Viscount about preserving the right of free passage through the Canal in the light of the news that the first material effect of our intervention is to block the Canal by bombing and sinking a ship in the Canal.

---

[3]   John Charles Wilmot, 1st Baron Wilmot of Selveston (1893–1964), Labour peer.

The Lord Chancellor[4]

My Lords, I can only say that I have not received confirmation that that is the position. As your Lordships will have seen, I have been on the Woolsack the whole afternoon, except for the minimum periods necessary for human sustenance, so I have not been able to make full inquiries; but I have made inquiries and I have no confirmation that that is the effect of the sinking of the ship.

The Lord Archbishop of Canterbury

My Lords, the noble and learned Viscount referred to the attacking Power against which we have to exercise self-defence. Who is the attacking Power?

The Lord Chancellor

My Lords, I said that self-defence extended to the protection of nationals on someone else's territory. In that case, we have the right to intervene and use force in that territory to protect our nationals. Then the second point arises – I hope I made this clear; I intended to put it entirely fairly – first, we make a peaceful landing; then, if the Power into whose territory we are going says that they will resist with all their force, the force which we have the right to use is automatically extended to that sufficient to repulse the force threatened.

The Lord Archbishop of Canterbury

Which is the attacking Power in this case?

The Lord Chancellor

In the case that I have mentioned, the person who threatens to use force in answer to a proffered peaceful intervention.

The Lord Archbishop of Canterbury

Here is the Canal; here are our nationals; here is our property. There is an attack upon them which you have to resist. Who is making the attack?

---

4   David Maxwell Fyfe, 1st Earl of Kilmuir (1900–1967), Conservative peer and lawyer.

The Lord Chancellor

I see it now. The most reverend Primate is asking me a question of fact.

The Lord Archbishop of Canterbury

Yes.

The Lord Chancellor

Then I will deal with that. The threat of force is made by the person who refuses to stop the hostile operations that are threatening the people and the installations. I really must be allowed to continue – perhaps after just one more interruption.

The Lord Archbishop of Canterbury

Who is this attacking Power in this case?

The Lord Chancellor

I should have thought the most reverend Primate might have guessed that for himself. It is obviously Egypt, who has refused to stop.

The Lord Archbishop of Canterbury

This is terribly important, and perhaps I might ask the Lord Chancellor this. Where does the operational force originate? I should have thought that the attacking force, whether you like it or not, was Israel. Is that not so?

The Lord Chancellor

Yes. I explained the law, and I was going to proceed to the facts. But in applying that to this case, our nationals, our ships and the Canal itself are in danger from the conflict between Israel and Egypt. We then, with, I believe, complete moral propriety and rightness, ask them both to stop the conflict which is threatening our nationals, our ships and the Canal. The most reverend Primate really must not interrupt again.

Several Noble Lords

Order, Order!

The Lord Chancellor

The Israelis agreed to stop hostilities and to retire, but Egypt refused, and indicated that they would use force to prevent the steps which we proposed for a peaceful stoppage of the fighting. That is the sense in which I used it. Perhaps now the most reverend Primate will allow me to continue my speech.

The Lord Archbishop of Canterbury

May I say this? I entirely accept everything that the Lord Chancellor has said. I was not criticising it nor attacking it. I was merely asking a question: where did the force originate? That, he says, is Israel; and that is all I wanted to establish.

A Noble Lord

No; he did not say that.

The Lord Chancellor

The most reverend Primate has, I am sure entirely unintentionally, sought to confuse two situations. There is the first situation, which attracted our peace-making intention, which was started when Israel crossed the border. Then there is the second situation, which I have been at some pains to explain, when the Egyptians refused our peaceful measures. I hope that I have now made that clear.

The Lord Archbishop of Canterbury

I merely said that there are two states, one and two. You omitted to mention the first. I have now inserted it.

12

Death Penalty (Abolition) Bill

A speech in the House of Lords, 10 July 1956[1]

My Lords, I think I shall best serve the interests of this debate if I state, as briefly as I can and with as little argument as I can, the final and conclusive considerations which will direct my vote to-night. And in doing so I take some account of the moving and weighty speech, based on vast experience, to which we have just listened. First, I accept the doctrine of the Church that the State has the right, in the name of God and of society, to impose the death penalty. There are those who regard the death penalty for murder as the last surviving relic of a particular kind of barbarism. Indeed it has been ill-used and barbarously used in the past. Churches have used it to punish heresy. States have used it to protect the trivialities of property.

But in our day the death penalty is used in the one legitimate way open to it. Society may use it in defence of society itself. A murderer contradicts and violates the fundamental first principle on which society rests: that every member of it will respect the life of every other member and will at least allow him to live. Where murder exists, it is the first duty of society – I particularly put it in this way – to repair the damage done by murder to its own integrity, and to bear witness to the majesty of its own first principles. That, I would say, is its sole duty in this matter. That is Christian doctrine, and, like my fellow Primate, I disagree profoundly with those sincere but mistaken people who regard the death penalty as a thing altogether and always un-Christian and wrong. The progress of this Bill owes not a little to those who hold these mistaken views. If I vote for it, it may seem that I agree with them when, in fact, I totally disagree with them. If I vote for the Bill, it will be in spite of them and for quite different reasons.

Next I ask myself this question: if society may legitimately employ this penalty, ought it to continue to do so? And I find my answer to be: Yes, but not without certain changes in its application. I say 'Yes' for one sufficient reason – that with which the noble and learned Lord the Lord Chief Justice concluded his speech. The death penalty is a witness to the sacredness of human life and of

---

[1]   H.L. Deb., 5s., cols. 746–52.

social order, which no society, perhaps, should ever altogether dispense with, and which our society to-day certainly cannot afford to dispense with altogether. I say, 'a witness to the sacredness of human life'. For, in fact, to require a man to surrender his life (as in defence of his country), or to take it from him because of his evil use of it, may be the greatest possible tribute to its intrinsic value. And there is evidence that the imminence of death has a very great power in opening the eyes of a condemned man to that truth and so to God.

I say we cannot afford to dispense with it. It is always difficult to assess public opinion, but I think, as many others do, that general opinion requires that in some form the terrible, irrevocable and cleansing witness which this penalty gives against the crime of murder should continue. I agree, and I think it would be dangerous and wrong to frustrate that requirement. But while I am not an abolitionist, I find it very difficult to give a vote which would appear to support the continuance of the present system unchanged. For I believe that it is too clumsy to continue as it is in an age where scientific accuracy is a primary requirement, where everyone is more sensitive than he used to be to the chance of cruelty and error in punishment, where there has been revealed to us most embarrassing knowledge about the way in which the human mind works, and where, I would add, sensationalism can and does exploit this topic in unwholesome and repulsive ways.

May I explain what I mean by calling this method too clumsy to continue as it is? It is certainly clumsy as a deterrent. No one can tell for certain how much deterrent effect it has. And this very uncertainty leads to endless argument and makes any conclusion based upon it doubtful. In certain societies – and the noble Viscount, Lord Malvern, had this properly very much in mind – its deterrent effect could be quite obvious and its retention justified on that ground alone. But the evidence does not make me think that the abolition of the death penalty here would in fact increase the number of murders. Certainly, there is no scientific basis of ascertained fact here upon which we can rely, and as I listened to the Lord Chief Justice referring to the dreadful rise in crimes of violence I could not but say that in one sense that is an argument in itself against the ineffectiveness of the death penalty as a deterrent. But I cannot rest myself on deterrence.

Then the argument of retribution is brought in. That is not only clumsy, too, but a very dangerous argument. To defend society against murder is one thing. To repay the murderer for what he has done, which is the strict meaning of retribution, is a far more perplexing and dangerous undertaking. In fact, it cannot be done at all. Nothing equivalent to the evil the murderer has done can ever be inflicted on him. And the attempt to do it, the desire to do it, even the lust to do it, attacks us all on our weakest side. The more repulsive the crime, the more violent is our desire that the murderer should hang. But that is, or may easily be, nothing more than a surrender on our part to emotionalism and an indulgence by us in a vengeful passion. Scripture was right when it said: Vengeance is mine, I will repay, saith the Lord. For man cannot repay. In fact we cannot balance evil done with punishment endured and we should not attempt to build our system on that. We must, I think, frankly recognise, that some who are less evil than others may yet have to hang, and some who have shown themselves far more evil may yet escape with their lives. This system as it is now cannot rest itself on deterrence, except in some particulars I shall come to in a moment, or on retribution, but only on its general accuracy in defending society and in defending the moral law.

Here comes another great evidence of its clumsiness. Something like 50 per cent of those who are condemned to death are reprieved. The noble and learned Lord the Lord Chief Justice has referred to this. The death sentence is passed, and most rightly it is invested with all the solemnity that the occasion demands. The judge, in the name of the whole community and before God, sentences the murderer to death by hanging, and in the most solemn and searching words sends him to face the judgment seat of God. And almost as often as not a reprieve follows, and the solemn form has become an empty form. As the noble and learned Lord the Lord Chief Justice said, in delivering it a judge may know that in the very words he uses he is using an empty form. That seems to me a most dreadful situation.

The Home Secretary is brought in, very properly, to correct the errors of the present system. He does it with immense care; but should it be required of him? A 50 per cent margin of error in the operation of the system is certainly evidence of clumsiness, and that at a point where it can least be tolerated in the quiet mind. I may say that the noble and learned Lord the Lord Chief Justice immensely increased my uneasiness on this point by a passing remark he made just now, that a reprieve could be granted in spite of the fact that there was no medical or legal evidence calling for it.

So, by this system, uncertainty is introduced where, above all, finality should be final. The way is opened for all the doubts and hesitations of which the noble Viscount, Lord Templewood,[2] and all of us are acutely aware. The death penalty is no longer left as it should be, clearly and decisively the voice of the community, bearing its witness purposefully, deliberately and prayerfully to solemn laws of society and of God. It becomes instead a matter of controversy and thereby loses its power to speak as it should speak. Whatever we may do to-day, that power

---

[2]   Samuel John Gurney Hoare, from 1944 Viscount Templewood (1880–1959), Conservative peer.

has already been largely lost, and neither a change of majority in another place nor an overruling of the other place by your Lordships' House can restore to this penalty the moral value that it should have. Only a general agreement amongst us all or a reasonable adjustment in the system can do that. And if all I have said were not enough, those organs of publicity which drown murder and hanging in a flood of emotional and sensational exploitation have robbed the system as it stands, as they have robbed so much else in our lives and social order, of all its proper dignity and sense of eternal worth.

What then, since I cannot happily altogether abolish or altogether retain the present system? There seems to be afforded to us in this House at this moment a real opportunity of retaining the true place for the death penalty in the moral order of our society, while removing some of its features which seem clumsy or dangerous or specially open to criticism. We are told on the highest legal authority that it is impossible to introduce 'degrees of murder'. It may be so: I am not sure. But I am sure that it is possible to introduce categories of murder for which the death penalty shall remain, categories so clearly and conclusively defined that all uncertainties in this field are removed and the need for reprieve almost totally abolished. By this means, many of the fears to which the noble and learned Lord the Lord Chief Justice[3] rightly directed our attention would be at least alleviated and largely abolished. There are murders committed against society itself in the person of its appointed guardians – the murder of a policeman on duty, the murder of a warder. There are murders which show deliberation and premeditation and some preparatory action, certainly when the murderer is carrying arms or a lethal weapon, possibly when the murderer employs poison, perhaps when it can be shown that over a period of time the murderer has planned and plotted. Any category which is capable of an exact definition could be included as liable to the death sentence.

Within these given categories the deterrent power of the death penalty obviously would have its maximum possible effect, for a murderer would have to put himself into the reach of the death penalty by deliberate act. He would have openly declared war on society, and that not in a moment of passion but of choice. In such cases there would be no room for self-delusion, for uncertainty or for reprieves. The death sentence would be passed with all its solemnity and there would be a final and decisive proclamation of the moral truth of society. I must make one observation. It is true that some murders, some of the most abominable murders, would fall outside the categories and would escape the death penalty. They would be murders chiefly of a specially beastly and passionate kind. I think that if any are to be excepted from the death penalty,

---

3   Lord Goddard (1877–1971), Lord Chief Justice, 1946–58.

it had better be these. Society already repudiates them sufficiently by its own reaction of horror. There is nothing attractive about them and it is just in them that the temptation to indulge in this dangerous passion of 'making him pay' or of 'making her pay' is at its strongest and its indulgence most likely to be harmful to our own moral sense. Their exclusion from the death penalty will make them less valuable for exploitation by sensational journalism.

I believe that there is an opportunity before us so to amend this Bill as to make it of real service to the common good, and that we ought to take it. Thereby we should lift this matter, as it should be lifted and, I would say, must be lifted, above the issues of majority voting in one House or another and above clashes between Lords and Commons, on to a firm basis of reasoned action and of respect for the majesty of the law and the true voice of the community. I do not call this a compromise, for it will be abhorrent to the root and branch abolitionists. I do call it a course of wisdom. Most other people, apart from the abolitionists, could come to a common mind. I believe that if we were to take this line, the Commons very likely would agree with us on it, and so we should avoid the confusion of conflict between our two Houses. If they did not agree, at least we should stand then on much firmer ground than we should by simply rejecting this Bill, and on ground which, having taken, we could properly refuse to abandon.

I cannot simply vote to retain the present system; I cannot simply vote for its abolition, though I may find myself in the uneasy position of appearing to do so. I shall vote for the Second Reading of the Bill, hoping earnestly, and believing that, if it is given a Second Reading, it will certainly be amended in Committee – the function which this House exists specially to perform. I believe that by amendment this may be made a wise measure on the merits of the case; one that would bring relief of conscience and judgment to many who are unhappy with the present system. And by bringing the two Houses into agreement it will refound the death penalty on its only secure and legitimate foundation as an act expressing the general will of the community for the defence of society and for the solemn vindication of the laws of God.

13

Partnership in Industry

From a sermon preached at a Service of Dedication for the

Trades Union Congress at Brighton,

Sunday, 2 September 1956[1]

Yet show I unto you a more excellent way.

I Corinthians 12.31

With these words St. Paul introduces the famous chapter which he ends with the words: 'And now abideth faith, hope, charity, these three: but the greatest of these is charity'.

For the increase of faith, hope, and charity we have just prayed. But remember what St. Paul and the Christian faith mean by charity.

Without it knowledge of economics or anything else is nothing. Without it faith in a cause, however righteous, is nothing. Without it sacrifice brings no profit. 'Charity is patient and generous; is not jealous or boastful; is not arrogant or rude; does not insist on its own way; is not irritable or resentful; bears all things, believes all things, hopes all things, endures all things'. Charity can be seen at its best in Jesus Christ: and whosoever sees him, hath seen the truth of God. In the light of this tremendous and terrifying truth about charity as the law of God's being and His law for ours, I shall try to speak to you as leaders in the world of industry.

I

At the Duke of Edinburgh's Oxford Conference of Industrialists[2] it was said that the final purpose of industry is to produce happy communities and satisfied

---

[1] Fisher Papers 283, fols. 181–97. But see, too, Carpenter, *The Archbishop Speaks*, pp. 181–4.

[2] In 1956 the Duke of Edinburgh had chaired a Study Conference on the Human Problems of Industrial Communities within the Commonwealth and Empire at Oxford. This conspicuous

individuals. That is a good point to start from. How far does industry make those engaged in it happy in their community life and contented in themselves?

The industrial machine is the result of man's God-given instinct to explore, to understand, to control nature, and having gained the mastery over it, to turn it to the service of man. But what the mind and hand of man creates will destroy him unless he retains his mastery over it, and keeps the whole industrial process subject to the moral power of his creative spirit.

Industry itself is a kind of atom bomb tending to disrupt society, as you can see if you watch its introduction into Central and East Africa. If man is to control industry, he must remain industrious, with his heart in it to keep it morally and spiritually wholesome. Only so can men attain and keep their personal and social integrity and their self-respect.

We all know that from our own experience. It is among those who work at some worth-while task, and work together at it as a team, and put the demands of the work above their own interests, and face hazards hopefully that we find in the highest degree integrity of character, loyalty to one another and to their common enterprise, and real satisfaction.

That is what industry ought to be doing for all engaged in it. But in fact the conditions of modern industry make it harder than ever before for this to happen. Efficiency demands that more and more the doing of things shall be transferred from the limited and erratic powers of man to the much more potent and sustained energies of the machine. But each such transfer takes away something of personal effort and application from the man and absorbs it into the machine, leaving a real part of himself no longer fully integrated into his work. The real danger of automation is that it limits still more the range in which a man can exercise his own initiative and craftsmanship and personal effort, which are what really give men satisfaction and happiness.

At the same time the complexity of modern industry and the scale of its operations combine to diminish yet more men's sense of their own personal worth. It is hard to think in terms of loyalty about the vast enterprises in which men are engaged: it is hard to believe that they matter to the individual or the individual matters to them. Everything is too big for a true interplay of human interests and understanding and fellowship to keep it wholesome. The goal of every industrial operation is that it should be done as well as it can be done: and this should be the proper ambition and pride of everyone engaged in the industry. But such conditions as I have mentioned encourage not pride of performance but impoverishment of personality, and breed, if not irresponsibility and

---

occasion brought together a number of leading, ethically minded industrialists including the Jamaican Clarence McWhinnie and Sir Ivan Ewart, from Northern Ireland.

impatience, at least a kind of moral inertia. And these things reflect themselves in a general restlessness and discontent.

These dangers are real in our society. They are inherent in the whole nature of mass industrialism. Unless resisted and overcome, they must lead to a destruction of all real happiness and satisfaction in the life of the community and nation far worse than any vagaries of the economic machine. Are we to accept this result as inevitable?

II

There is a remedy, a more excellent way. Since the industrial machine must from its own nature become more and more inhuman, and impersonal, men must increase their moral stature in the field of personal expression. They must increase the humble and creative sense of pride in their work, for itself and for what it does for others. And as management and the machine and automation increase their impersonal functions, all engaged in industry must achieve new heights of personal trust in one another, partnership with one another, team work, and that charity without which neither a team nor the Body of Christ itself can function efficiently. There and nowhere else man's victory over the machine, over himself, must be won or lost: there and nowhere else is the way to happiness and satisfaction.

There must be in industry a great deal of this spirit of pride, team work and charity, or the thing would not work as well as it does. But we shall all agree that there is a vast amount which contradicts it: no doubt the blame for it is to be shared out among all concerned. Nothing but bitterness can be got by asking which is the more to blame: and there is never any final answer.

Charity does not bother about that at all. The moral challenge is to abolish all that impairs the efficiency, the partnership and the integrity of those engaged in industry, that, as St. Paul says of the Church, there should be no schism in industry but all the members should have the same care one for another.

That is the demand which God makes on all of us. He is, as I think, compelling men in this and other fields to make now a fateful choice between life and death. Consider for a moment the nature of this choice.

III

Modern industry came to life under a system of imperialism. Owners held the power, did the thinking, and gave orders to labour which got for its service such rewards as society in general then thought suitable. That system like other forms of imperialism and colonialism produced much sincere goodness, much true fellowship, much honest loyalty, much real happiness among all classes, along with the injustices and miseries and cruelties which are now so obvious to us. But imperialism, good or bad, always invites rebellion: sooner or later its power is challenged: rights conflict: strife is engendered and the appeal to force is made. As Englishmen, we know both ends of that story. We have through the centuries fought again and again to preserve our freedom against foreign imperialism: we have ourselves in our turn been the imperialists holding other people subject to our power. In both, our strength has always been in our loyalty to one another and to true ends.

Against industrial imperialism, the Trade Unions made in due course the inevitable rebellion and, using the traditional weapons of human struggle, embarked on industrial wars. Until recently there was a truly great and gallant element to be found in national wars. There was certainly much that was great and gallant about earlier strikes, in which were displayed loyalties, suffering, sacrifices and idealism such as have often been displayed in national wars. But the judgment of God is that all war and all violence is devil's work and in the long run brings only evil upon mankind: and history is one of God's means of teaching men this lesson. In the field of international politics everyone knows that war is no longer compatible with civilisation; that when nations dispute with one another the appeal should always be no longer to force against force but to reason against reason. But to change from the one to the other is as we know terribly difficult and risks disaster. Right-minded statesmen whose desire and purpose is to abolish war between nations but who must not forget that they are guardians of a nation's freedom and responsible for the well-being of their people and of the world, know the fierceness of the dilemma. How far dare they go in abandoning the appeal to force when reason may find itself powerless before the unreason of those who through stupidity or passion or greed for power or impudence or some kind of idealism seek to obtain what they regard as their rights in defiance of others? If the answer to unreason must not be found in force, then it must look to the co-operation and partnership of all the reasonable and right-minded. But even so, reason is of itself an insufficient weapon with which to work a partnership successfully. Reason involves argument and as we see every day there is no end to argument. Good reasons may get good answers; more often they get bad answers made to appear good by cleverness, or partial answers which ignore what is to be said against them: or they get swamped in the kind of verbal fireworks which St. Paul calls sounding brass and clanging cymbals. Even among the right-minded reason must be subject to the law of Christian charity which, seeking not its own, is ready to abandon empty argument and to put up with less than reason may justify and to think better of other people than they deserve and this as the only way in the long run to keep faith with God and justify hope in mankind. That is St. Paul's more excellent way. If we are seeking that more excellent way in international affairs, must it not prevail even more clearly at home? Is not God pressing us in this nation and in the industrial world to follow courageously the same difficult, risky but creative way, from reliance on force to reliance on reason: and that reason may function helpfully, from reliance on reason to the spirit of charity expressed in frank and generous partnership?

We shall all agree that in industrial affairs the language is too much the language of war, the appeal too readily to drastic action. Whereas in international affairs those who are quick to 'rattle the sabre' and talk of forceful action are regarded as public enemies, in industry that is much less so. There are too many spoiling for a fight or speaking in terms of militant assertiveness about their rights and wrongs, and on the other side, no doubt, too many upholders of an outworn imperialist or colonialist attitude. In such an atmosphere partnership finds it hard to flourish, efficiency and pride in the work suffers, and charity finds few friends.

Every responsible person knows that the change over from force to reason, from distrust to partnership, must for everybody's sake be made and made quickly, if the challenge which the whole industrial system makes to the human spirit is to be met, if all sharers in industry are to possess their integrity of purpose and of pride in their work, and if they are to render to the community a service honourable to themselves and useful to others. And yet the change over, here as in the international field, is full of immense difficulties and dangers. There are all the old fears and suspicions, the old loyalties and idealism, the old obstinacies of past habit and experience, and many new antagonisms, social, economic and political. And the way of reason is still unsure and untried. It may so easily be over-run by unreason on one side or on both. It may mean submitting to the judgment of others, accepting an adverse or even an unjust decision. How can impatient men endure that or how can responsible leaders ask that of them?

Only be when the whole operation is seen as a great challenge to go forward and become part of that more excellent way which puts charity before rights or demands, and subordinates every faith and every hope to the way of true fellowship. The challenge before us is that this spirit of co-operation should possess all parties and be evident throughout industry. It is a severe challenge.

It cannot fully be met until individual workers on every side of industry capture the idea and the spirit. But it can only come at all through leaders who can see the risks and face them, and can lead the general will to follow the more excellent way. God places upon everyone in his own degree the responsibility to choose rightly before God.

IV

Some of you may think that the Church has done too little in the past to help you in your battles and has little right to advise you now. That the Church has helped you too little, in spite of some outstanding exceptions, I would agree. But we have the best of reasons for offering you now this advice to follow the more excellent way. For the churches themselves have in the past fifty years rediscovered this way for themselves and have found it good and God-given.

The divisions and clashes of interest within the industrial world are no more bitter than those which fifty years ago divided the churches. In either case the causes of difference were and are substantial and real and bear witness in some way or another to truth. But Christ Jesus has led the Church to re-find the better way which does not abolish differences but robs them of their hatefulness and turns them all to the increase of truth and unity. The churches have largely – not all, not quite, but largely – laid aside the rancour and hostility of denominational rights and rivalries and self-interest by rediscovering their fellowship in Christ, the common purpose which He calls them all to serve, and the humility which Christian charity confers. And, of course, thus recovering charity, we find faith made more clear and comprehensive and hope more confident and constructive.

What Christ has done and is doing for the churches He can do for industry, making out of all its sections one body whereof if one member suffers all the members suffer with it, wherein all seek to give of their best and to have the best to give, where faith is deepened to embrace every man and nation in the loving purpose of God, and hope is strengthened to overcome all the separatist and selfish evils of mankind. But if we are to pursue these necessary human and social and personal ends in true faith and in a realistic hope, then we must have our feet firmly on the more excellent way of Christian charity – a hard way, hard for everyone, specially hard for those who bear the strains of responsibility and leadership. But it is the way of Christ and experience as well as Christian devotion declare it to be the way of wisdom and of our salvation, making communities happy and persons satisfied as no temporal things can ever do. It is not St Paul but Christ Himself who calls us to follow it.

14

Homosexual Offences and Prostitution

A speech in the House of Lords, 4 December 1957[1]

My Lords, after that interval of comparatively light relief may I return to a matter which is of even more profound significance. I do not intend to speak from any particular Christian grounds: I assume only the generally accepted beliefs of theists, and, indeed, of every reasonable and responsible citizen. This Report[2] has already accomplished two great things, one deliberately and one by accident. It has compelled people to think about and compare the sphere of crime and the sphere of sin, in the sense of an offence against the general moral standards of the community, and that is all I ask for in using the word 'sin'. Of course the two spheres overlap, but they are not coterminous, and it is of real importance for the national well-being that the difference between the two should be clearly understood, both as to the moral grounds they respectively cover and as to the sanctions on which the two spheres respectively rest.

One of my correspondents boldly writes to me: 'So far as possible, every sin should be declared a crime' – which is precisely the belief of the totalitarian State, which defines its own sense of sin and then makes it a crime. I am afraid that there is a very common belief that only crimes are sins and that the not illegal is therefore lawful and right. That such a belief should continue is a very dangerous thing. There is a phrase, *Pro saluti animæ et pro reformatione morum.* The State and the Law are not concerned directly, as the Church is, with saving the souls of men from their own destruction. The right to decide one's own moral code and obey it, even to a man's own hurt, is a fundamental right of man, given him by God and to be strictly respected by society and the criminal code.

I believe that it is of vital importance to maintain this principle against the law and against society. Indeed, it may at any time feel compelled to invoke the law against some organ of publicity which in one way or another so intrudes a moral code of its own, and so employs the powers of publicity and suggestion, as almost to impose that code upon society; and at least the private rights of a

---

[1]   H.L. Deb., 4 December 1957, vol. 206, cols. 753–60.

[2]   The Report of the Departmental Committee on Homosexual offences and Prostitution, chaired by Lord Wolfenden, September 1957, had recommended the decriminalisation of homosexuality.

citizen so to choose his own moralities and protect his own privacies against some forms of publicity must not be allowed to be outraged. The State becomes concerned only when for the general good, for the protection of those who need protection, or for the promotion of a healthy community life – *pro reformation morum* – it ought to act. Of course in this sphere there will always be special and borderline cases. As an example of a special case there is the protection of the young, or (a subject to which the noble Lord, Lord Pakenham, has referred), the need to discourage suicide and suicide pacts. Such cases create especial problems and justify interference with private rights. And there are also the borderline cases, and homosexual offences may come under this category.

In general, however, a sin is not made a crime until it becomes a cause of public offence, although it remains a sin whether or not it be a crime. That is obvious enough but great numbers of people, having lost the sense of sin, have lost sight of this distinction, and it is most valuable that this Report should cast the limelight once more upon it. Secondly, although the Report refuses to consider it, it must make people think about the difference between what is natural and what is unnatural. There is a great general moral indignation against homosexual sins because they are unnatural. There is a queer lack of general moral indignation against heterosexual sins, fornication and adultery, because they are supposed to be natural, and therefore, in some sense, less wrong.

There is here a serious and now very dangerous confusion of thought. Nature makes both heterosexuals and homosexuals alike – there is no doubt about that. Nature makes more heterosexuals than homosexuals, thank God!, but we are told with authority that, in varied proportions, both tendencies are present in every one of us. What is thus unnatural is bad and must be disciplined; but much of what is natural, if left to itself, is equally bad and must no less be disciplined. Both homosexual and heterosexual sins or vices may become something more than private; then they raise questions of public morality, though I would say that they do not necessarily raise them equally. For in my judgment the threat to general public moral standards from homosexual offences done in private is far less, and far less widespread, than the damage openly done to public morality and domestic health by fornication and adultery. The principle here is that what man is made of in his instincts by nature is less important than what he is made for, and can be shaped to by the influence of the community, by training and, if necessary, by the processes of law.

My Lords, it is in the light of these principles that I wish to make a few observations on the recommendations of the Report. Here I would briefly report that the Church Assembly had a most admirable talk upon this whole Report, and its results are not without significance. For the principles of the Report there was a majority so large that no division was necessary. On the question of the immediate application of the recommendations about homosexuality there was a vote which resulted in a small majority of 17 in favour of the Committee's recommendation of at once applying this principle. The vote was, in fact, 155 to 138. I believe that that is significant, for it means that quite a number of people who accepted the principle were yet so disturbed that they did not think it was expedient or wise to apply it forthwith; and there are many people who, very naturally, hold that view.

First, a word as to homosexual offences. I believe that the Report is right in recommending that, while all existing laws shall remain in force to protect and control those under 21, and to protect the unwilling over that age, homosexual acts between consenting adults in private should not come within the ambit of the law. That seems to me right in principle. There will be misunderstanding and talk of 'legalising homosexuality and unnatural vice', but at least it is not a bad thing to start from the right principle. There appears to me to be one great immediate benefit from obeying this principle. I have reason to believe that great pressure is often put upon a consenting adult, once he has consented, to continue this practice when, left to himself, he would like to get free of it.

I have known a young man wishing to get free pursued by his partner from Australia to this country and so brought back into the practice. I have known another young man in the provinces though wishing to get free, leaving the provinces and being recommended on to fresh friends and partners, first from the provinces to London and later, when he left London for a country overseas, to partners in that country. There are, I believe groups or clubs of homosexuals with an organisation of their own, with a language of their own and a kind of freemasonry from which it is not at all easy to escape. So long as homosexual offences between consenting adults are criminal and punishable by law, the pressure of this kind of freemasonry will remain and will operate powerfully, for it gains strength from the fact that it must remain a secret society to avoid the law. It has all the glamour and romance of chosen and select rebels against the conventions of society and the forces of the law.

At the heart of this kind of freemasonry are men of passionate sincerity who are made strongly homosexual by nature; who believe that what is wrong for others is right for them, and that society is not merely hostile but unjust and cruel. Into this kind of nightmare world – for it is a nightmare world – there can be no entrance for the forces of righteousness until the offences are made not criminal, so that there is no question any longer of betraying companions for committing criminal offences. At once, I am quite certain, the fresh air of normal morality will begin to circulate amongst them far more easily. Those who are involved in it will be set free to talk to others outside without giving anybody away to the law. They will seek advice openly – indeed, they will be free, if they like, to seek protection by the police from molestation by their former companions without bringing in the question of prosecution for illegal offences. It will be all the more easy, I think, to convince them of the restraints of common sense and Christian morality when they are delivered from the fears, the glamour and even the crusading spirit of the rebel against law and convention who can claim to be made a martyr by persecution.

I know many people have grave hesitation about this recommendation. They think it will lead to an increase in offences. Their information may be different from mine, and it is not at all easy to be dogmatic; but, like the Church Assembly itself, I feel that if there is a doubt the risk should be taken. I would add only this one further reflection: that if it proved legally possible – I do not know whether it is – to separate what the noble Lord, Lord Pakenham, called the extreme offence, and to leave that still a crime, I should wish to leave it a crime still. The Report goes so far as to say this: We believe that there is some case for retaining sodomy as a separate offence. I believe that if that could be done, it would relieve the anxieties, fears and indignation of a great number of people; and, more than that, I believe that this crime does stand in a class by itself and is almost different in kind from other homosexual offences.

I believe personally that that opinion can be upheld on moral grounds. Unlike the Report, I believe also that many active homosexuals really feel that in that extreme offence there is a degree of depravity to which they are thankful not to have fallen or in which they are especially reluctant to be partners. And I believe it would help them and public opinion and public morals if that extreme offence remained, as now, a crime. That would, in fact, only revert to what was the law up to 1885. I believe a study of Appendix I of the Report will show that there is a reason for retaining this offence as a crime, since this particular offence has increased in a far higher proportion than any other of the homosexual offences.

On the other part of the Report, I wish to confine myself to one main argument only. The argument of the Report comes to this: prostitution is not an offence; it is a private affair between two consenting adults and no concern of the law; but so far as possible (the argument goes on) it must be kept private and, therefore, we will drive prostitutes off the streets so that there may be no visible offence to public morals. The Report recognises that there are some consequences of this private traffic which obtrude themselves and must be dealt with, such as exploitation of the private traffic for gain, living on the earnings of prostitutes, causing houses or a neighbourhood to become a public nuisance, and the like.

But, my Lords, there are other obtrusive consequences of the utmost gravity for the social well-being of our people which the Report leaves completely untouched and for which it has no remedy at all. One is what I am told is called 'kerb crawling'. The Report says: 'While we appreciate the reality of the problem ... we do not feel able to make any positive recommendation. The Committee can make no recommendation on how to deal with the problem'. That weak conclusion makes me very uneasy. The Report recognises that if the streets are cleared 'there will doubtless be consequences' and various other ways of arranging the trade 'under the counter' are anticipated. But the Committee conclude: 'We feel that the possible consequences of clearing the streets are less harmful than what now exists'. Main, I feel uneasy at this conclusion and at this impotence to deal with the problem. To drive a thing underground is sometimes the worst way of dealing with it and not the best.

Attention has been drawn, in public, to one particular paragraph which refers to the use by prostitutes of cafes and clubs and even licensed premises, and it says: In two large cities ... certain public houses, cafes and coffee stalls are known to be frequented by prostitutes ... but in neither of these cities is there any significant street problem. That is according to the Report, not according to public morality. The Report suggests that in such cases too rigorous an enforcement of the law might have the result of driving inoffensive prostitutes on to the streets where their presence would offend. Again, I am terribly uneasy if all we can do is turn a blind eye to the problem. The argument is that we must drive prostitutes off the streets; if then they congregate in clubs, cafés, at coffee stalls or elsewhere, these must be treated as private places and, therefore (unless the neighbourhood is offended), as privileged places, for if we do otherwise we shall drive the prostitutes back to the streets just when we have succeeded in driving them off the streets. This is no solution. There seems something 'phoney' about all this.

I wholly accept the principle that consenting adults in private, whether the offences be homosexual or heterosexual, should not come under the law. I said there were special cases, borderline cases. The Report gets really into trouble when trying to decide in this context what is private and what is public. The root of the confusion, my Lords – it may be that I shall not carry you with me in saying this – seems to lie here: prostitution is not a private occupation; it is a trade and nothing else, and if it is a trade then it has to be dealt with as any other trade. It is a trading transaction between two persons engaged in what is a very long-established trade.

The Wolfenden Report says that driving prostitutes off the streets is not 'mere hypocrisy'. It says it would be if we were avowedly trying to extinguish prostitution, for in that case the less open, carrying on of the trade would be as objectionable as the open carrying on of the trade. Yes, my Lords, but if you are looking at public morality and the general concern of the community – that this particular evil thing should not be allowed to flourish – whether it flourishes openly or in secret, it is equally against the public interest; and I would repeat that it is not a private affair and cannot be – it is a trade of buying and selling. The Report wants to make it more 'under the counter' than it was before. But public morality wants, I submit, to curb the whole trade.

It is not, I imagine, possible to abolish it – it has gone on for 2,000 years and will go on – but I do not want it to go on without a good many impediments for it to overcome. We should curb the trade, believing that the fewer prostitutes, the fewer fornicators, and the fewer adulterers there are in the community the better equipped the nation will be to get on with its own communal life. Once the trade is recognised as a trade akin, shall we say, to traffic in drugs or the like, the whole approach is altered.

I should become not less but more anxious to secure fair and just treatment for the prostitutes, just for the reason that hitherto they have been made to bear the whole brunt of legal actions against this trade. I believe that Society in general has been of a split mind on the matter. It has been agreed that prostitution is undesirable as a profession, and it is accepted that prostitutes must be kept out of sight. It has been taken for granted that their customers, men, have every right to a reasonable supply of prostitutes, and should not in any way be restrained from resorting to them. I venture to say that that is an old-fashioned view – it certainly goes back 2,000 years, dating from the time when women had no rights, and men, in the sexual field, claimed and possessed almost unlimited rights. If, in fact, this is a trade, with women the sellers and men the buyers, and if the trade is against the public interest and public morals, then it is a fact that the women have borne the whole brunt of their own and their customers' complicity in this trade. And they are still to do so – according to this Report. They and they alone can be arrested in the streets for being traders on the look out for business. The customers, even if they are kerb crawlers, are innocent and untouchable.

I do not think that this kind of arrangement holds in the traffic in illegal drugs. It is the possession which is illegal, without distinction between buyer and seller. The Report says that there are limits to the degree of discouragement which the criminal law can properly exercise towards a woman who chooses this way of life. That is perfectly true. But are there no methods by which restraint by the criminal law can be brought to bear upon the customer in the case of prostitution? The preliminaries must take place in public where they meet, or by means of some public service, like public telephone boxes and the rest of it. It is a trade and nothing else. The safeguard of 'in private' is quite irrelevant. So far in our history the prostitute can in various ways be got at and restrained. There has been little serious attempt to get at, to restrain or to punish, the customer – the man.

I would submit that it is time that a serious attempt was made to do just that one thing. It is far the quickest way to restrain the trade. Very many men would be strongly restrained if there was a fear that they would find themselves the next day in the police court and their names then made public. I do not believe that the lawyers would be utterly unable to find some way of getting the men there along with the prostitutes if the community said that they were to find a way.

15

Apartheid and the Church in South Africa

A private letter to Miss Joy D. Cartwright,

SPG Sister in Charge, the Healing House of Africa, Natal,

23 December 1959[1]

Dear Miss Cartwright,

I write to acknowledge receipt of your letter of December 14th, which I have read with great distress. It is another example of the suffering caused by the heartless application of a senseless policy of Apartheid. We do indeed constantly pray for all of you, African and European, as you wrestle with this almost intolerable situation. But when you ask for advice from me, or spiritual comfort, there is little that I can do. In the Church of England, we have made plain again and again that we totally disapprove of the policy of Apartheid, and regard it as unChristian in principle. More than that, it is very difficult for us to do. As you know, any interference from England, merely angers the South African Government, and makes their actions even more uncontrollable. And I am sorry to say that some people in England expressing their righteous indignation, do have the effect of deterring some South Africans who ought to agree with them, into supporting the Government out of a kind of resentment of advice from this country.

There is the great difficulty of the situation. I can assure you that in every possible way, we are showing our complete support of the Church of the Province, and of all others who are resisting Apartheid, but we cannot take any direct action. Action *must* be taken by the people on the spot, and by the Church in the Province. I will gladly send down your letter to the Bishop of Natal if you wished me to, but I have no doubt you have other means of making him completely aware of the situation; and I have no doubt that he, like all the other Bishops, is doing all that can be done. You must remember I think, our Lord's teaching and example that sometimes in the face of militant evil, the Christian

---

[1]   Fisher Papers 256, fols. 8–9.

has to be content to bear all things after the example of Our Lord, with long-suffering. But indeed it is a terrible cross to bear, and we do sympathise with you.

There are some rays of light in South Africa. There is a sign of a change of heart in the Dutch Reformed Church, and the beginning of a common mind between the Dutch Reformed and the other Christian bodies. That is the one hope – and if that can grow and spread, then indeed the future may become more bright. We pray for you, and we long for some relief of your burdens. May God keep and comfort you.

Yours sincerely,
Geoffrey Cantuar

16

The Visit to Rome, 2 December 1960

An account dictated to John Satterthwaite immediately after the meeting with Pope John XXIII[1]

The Pope came to the Library door to meet the Archbp. and the two shook each other warmly by the hand. The Archbp. Said, 'We are making history Your Holiness', to which the Pope agreed. The Pope pointed to the big globe and began talking quickly about Eisenhower's visit, and explained how he had been able to send a message through him to the Turkish Prime Minister. He mentioned the necessity of keeping in touch, especially where difficulties occurred.

The Archbp. Then said that he had just come from Istanbul and spoke of his great admiration for the Oecumenical Patriarch. He gave the Pope the Patriarchal message, viz that His All H. wished to do everything in his power to better relations between the Churches and that he would welcome an opportunity of meeting the Pope (on neutral ground).

At the first mention of the Orthodox Patriarch the Pope beamed and shook his own imaginary whiskers and laughed. The Pope mentioned that he had known and liked the Anglican Chaplain during his time in Istanbul, but could not remember his name.

The Archbp. said that whilst he had been in Istanbul he had been received most warmly by the inter-Nuncio – Mgr. Francesco Lordani – who lived in the same house which the Pope shared when Apostolic Delegate in Istanbul. The Archbp. Passed on Mgr. Lordani's message that he preferred being a simple Parish Priest and did not care for the life of diplomacy.

Jerusalem was next discussed and the Archbp. said how moved he had been by the warmth of his reception from every section of the Church. He confessed to being particularly moved by the friendship of the Franciscan – who were obviously hoping for some result from the Archbishop's visit.

This led to the Pope expressing his great yearning for the unity of all Xtian brethren. The Pope said that he desired unity quite simply in the words of St.

---

[1]   Reproduced in Carpenter, *Archbishop Fisher*, pp. 734–6.

John's Gospel – chapter 17 'That they may be one, even as we are one, I in them and thou in me, that they may be made perfect in me'.

At this point the Holy Father gave the Archbp. a folder containing copies of his Addresses last Aug[ust] to the Directors of Catholic Action. Monsignor Samori then read a paragraph from page 3.

The Archbp. spoke afterwards about the need for friendship and understanding between Christians of every denomination and said that in England there was a great lack of contact between R.C.s and Anglicans. The Pope never followed this up directly but referred to Cardinal Bea and outlined his hopes of better understanding now that the Secretariat for Unity had been established. The Archbp. congratulated the Pope on this machinery and said that he himself looked upon it as one of the best actions of the Pope since he took office as a regular means of communications ... The Pope accepted the Archbp's praise of Cardinal Bea and said that he knew he was the right man for the post. The Holy Father went on to say that he had in fact arranged for the Archbp. to meet Cardinal Bea that afternoon. The forthcoming Vatican Council was then discussed at some length and the Pope emphasised that it would be concerned with the R.C. Church first and foremost as R.C.s must order their own affairs first. He said too that there were many things which would benefit by reform. The Archbp. said that he appreciated that the Vatican Council intended to have the R.C. Church as its prime concern, but he went on to remind the Pope that non-R.C.s were already interested in what was being done. The Pope said that in due course he expected that they would be able to take up matters regarding other Churches and [he] read an extract (from page 5) of his special Address to the Council.

At this point, when the Pope spoke of his concern for the Separated Eastern Churches and for the Protestant Churches, the Archbp. inserted a plea for Anglicans too as falling in neither of these categories and the Pope readily accepted the distinction of Anglicans having a different position from Protestant bodies generally.

The Pope then went on to speak of our distant forebears and said what joy it was that he as successor of St. Peter should be brought into contact with the Church of St. Augustine. The thought of this alone had given him great happiness. The Archbp. said he was profoundly thankful that such a visit and contacts were possible. He pointed out that no-one could return to the past and that it is useless merely looking backwards. What is necessary is that we all advance – that in going forward *together* we will never remain quite the same as we were before. The Archbp. said that this was why he was so thankful to hear of the existence of Cardinal Bea's Council.

The Pope then mentioned the Malines Conversations[2] and said that he had been interested in Anglicanism from that time. The Archbp. said that, because of the times, the conversations then were surrounded by secrecy and suspicion – made even more difficult by the antagonism of Roman Catholics in England. He pointed out that no direct contact between Archbishop Davidson and the Pope was possible at the time of Malines. Had it been possible the result might have been more fruitful.

Looking to the future the Holy Fr. Stressed the importance of the spiritual in this field and he then launched into a long history of his own spiritual development. He said that he was most happy as a Pastor and that he disliked ambition. He told the Archbp. that from his Ordination as a Priest he had tried to have three guides for his own spiritual life (a) a love and desire to serve others always; (b) to accept cheerfully whatever was sent; (c) to wish for less more and more. He said (with a twinkle) that those who never asked for anything were never disappointed.

A long account followed by the Holy Fr. of how he became Pope much to his own surprise. [This was not dictated by the Archbp. as it bore no relevance to anything else]. In return the Archbp. himself felt called upon to speak of the foundations upon which his own spiritual life had been based. He said that from his own experience he knew that no-one could really command unless he really understood how to obey himself. [...]

The Archbp. repeated that this would remain a great event in his life and that he would like to leave a small reminder of his visit. He asked the Pope whether he would accept a copy of the Coronation Service – as it had a special significance. It follows the ancient Catholic Consecration Rite – Queen Elizabeth herself ... had been crowned by the Archbp. according to the Rite. The Pope said he would be delighted to receive it – and the book together with a large illustrated copy of English cathedrals was given to the Archbp. by the Chaplains who carried them in.

The Pope himself after thanking the Archbp. said that he had some small presents; and as they were rather heavy he would arrange to have them sent to His Grace before we left.

Before saying our farewells the Holy Fr. Repeated how grateful he was for the visit ... He said that in his meditations earlier that morning he had again thought of the two Disciples on the road to Emmaus in the presence of their Risen Saviour.

---

2   The Malines Conversations took place between a number of Anglicans and Roman Catholics in Belgium, 1921–25. Hosted by Cardinal Mercier, they were permitted, and even quietly encouraged, by the Vatican and the archbishops of Canterbury and York.

As we took our leave, the Pope himself came to the Library door and waved to us until we disappeared through the outer door of the South Throne Room.

Bibliography

Primary Sources

Manuscripts

Church of England Record Centre, London
    Papers of the Church Commissioners
Fisher Papers
Fulham Papers: Fisher
Lambeth Palace Library, London
Lang Papers
National Archives, Kew
    Atomic Energy (FO 371/123119)

Printed Sources

Barnes, Ernest William. *The Rise of Christianity*. London: Longmans, Green & Co., 1947.

Bea, Augustin Cardinal. *The Unity of Christians*. Edited by J. Bernard and S.J. Leeming. London: Geoffrey Chapman, 1963.

Bell, George. *The Church and Humanity*. New York: Longmans, Green, 1946.

The Canons of the Church of England: Canons Ecclesiastical Promulgated by the Convocations of Canterbury and York in 1964 and 1969. London: SPCK, 1969.

The Chronicle of Convocation: Being a Record of the Proceedings of the Convocation of Canterbury.

Dawley, Powel Mills (ed.). *Report of the Anglican Congress, 1954*. London: SPCK, 1955.

Evanston Speaks: Reports from the Second Assembly of the World Council of Churches August 15–31, 1954. London, 1954.

Fisher, Geoffrey. *I Here Present Unto You: Addresses Interpreting the Coronation of Her Majesty Queen Elizabeth II, Given on Various Occasions by His Grace the Lord Archbishop of Canterbury, Primate of All England*. London: SPCK, 1953.

———. 'A Remarkable Campaign'. In Charles T. Cook, *London Hears Billy Graham: The Greater London Crusade*, vii–ix. London: Marshall, Morgan & Scott, 1954.

————. *The Archbishop Speaks: Addresses and Speeches by the Archbishop of Canterbury the Most Reverend Geoffrey Francis Fisher, PC, GCVO, DD.* Edited by Edward Carpenter. London: Evans Brothers, 1958.

————. 'Church and Nation'. In *The Church and the Nation: Six Studies in the Anglican Tradition*, edited by Charles Smyth, 13–17. London: Hodder & Stoughton, 1962.

————. *Standards of Morality: Christian and Humanist*. London: Mowbray, 1967.

————. *Covenant and Reconciliation: A Critical Examination of the First Report of the English Standing Conference on 'Covenanting for Union' and of the Interim Statement of the Anglican-Methodist Unity Commission Entitled 'Towards Reconciliation'.* London: Mowbray, 1967.

————. *Touching on Christian Truth: The Kingdom of God, the Christian Church and the World*. London: Mowbray, 1971.

————. 'A Step Forward in Church Relations'. In *The Church of England, 1815–1948: A Documentary History*, edited by R.P. Flindall, 434–41. London: SPCK, 1972.

Flindall, R.P. (ed.). *The Church of England, 1815–1948: A Documentary History*. London: SPCK, 1972.

Gollancz, Victor. *More for Timothy: Being the Second Installment of an Autobiographical Letter to His Grandson*. London: n.p., 1953.

Gollancz, Victor, and David Somervell. *Political Education at a Public School*. London: Collins, 1918.

————. *The School and the World*. London: Chapman & Hall, 1919.

Graham, Billy. *Just as I Am: The Autobiography of Billy Graham*. San Francisco: Zondervan, 1997.

Harris, Kenneth. 'Dr. Geoffrey Fisher, 1959 [interview]'. In *Conversations*, 70–87. London: Hodder & Stoughton, 1967.

Lambeth Conference 1948. London: SPCK, 1948.

Lambeth Conference 1958. London: SPCK, 1958.

Macaulay, Rose. *The World My Wilderness*. 1950. Reprint, London: Virago, 1983.

————. *The Towers of Trebizond*. 1956. Reprint, New York: New York Review Books, 2003.

————. *Letters to a Friend, 1950–1952*, edited by Constance Babington-Smith. New York: Atheneum, 1962.

Macmillan, Harold. *The Macmillan Diaries: The Cabinet Years, 1950–1957*, edited by Peter Catterall. London: Macmillan, 2003.

————. *The Macmillan Diaries: Prime Minister and After, 1957–1966*, edited by Peter Catterall. London: Macmillan, 2011.

Matthews, W.R. *Memories and Meanings*. London: Hodder & Stoughton, 1969.

Mayfield, Guy. *The Church of England: Its Members and Its Business*. Oxford: Oxford University Press, 1958.

Men for the Ministry, 1963. London: Church Information Board for the Central Advisory Council of Training for the Ministry, n.d. [One in a series of annuals; these booklets are available in LPL.]

The Parliamentary Debates (Hansard): House of Lords Official Report.

Ratcliff, Edward C. *The Coronation Service of Her Majesty Queen Elizabeth II*. London: SPCK; Cambridge: Cambridge University Press, 1953.

Report of the Anglican-Methodist Union Commission. London: SPCK, 1968.

Robinson, John A.T. *Christian Freedom in a Permissive Society*. London: SCM Press, 1970.

Sherrill, *Henry Knox. Among Friends*. Boston: Little, Brown, 1962.

Temple, William. Foreword to *Standing Orders of the Church of England: An Attempt to State What Canon Law Is Now in Force*, edited by J.V. Bullard. London: Faith Press, 1934.

Time, 1 September 1952, 53.

Secondary Sources

Adair, John. *The Becoming Church*. London: SPCK, 1977.

Aikman, David. *Billy Graham: His Life and Influence*. Nashville: Thomas Nelson, 2007.

Andrew, John G.B. 'Michael Ramsey–Archbishop Extraordinary and Contemporary Prophet: Personal Recollections by his Chaplain'. *The Anglican: A Journal of Anglican Identity*, 39/1 (Winter 2010), 10–17.

Arblaster, Ted. '"All the world's a stage … "'. *St. Mark's Review*, No. 152 (Summer 1993), 45–6.

Bailey, Simon. *A Tactful God*. Leominster: Gracewing, 1995.

Barnes, John. *Ahead of His Age: Bishop Barnes of Birmingham*. London: Collins, 1979.

Barry, F.R. *Mervyn Haigh*. London: SPCK, 1964.

Beeson, Trevor. *The Church of England in Crisis*. London: Davis-Poynter, 1973.

———. *The Bishops*. London: SCM Press, 2002.

Bliss, Frederick. *Anglicans in Rome: A History*, 37. Norwich: Canterbury Press, 2006.

Booty, John. *An American Apostle: The Life of Stephen Fielding Bayne Jr*. Valley Forge, Pa.: Trinity Press International, 1997.

Brown, Callum G. *The Death of Christian Britain: Understanding Secularisation, 1800–2000*. New York: Routledge, 2001.

———. *Religion and Society in Twentieth-century Britain*. Harlow, U.K.: Pearson, 2006.

Brown, David. *God and Enchantment of Place: Reclaiming Human Experience*. Oxford: Oxford University Press, 2004.

Brown, William Francis. 'Cardinal Hinsley'. In *Through Windows of Memory*, 96–101. London: Sands & Co., 1946.

Butler, R.A. *The Art of the Possible*. London: Hamilton, 1971.

Carpenter, Edward. *Cantuar: The Archbishops in Their Office*. London: Cassell, 1971.

———. *Archbishop Fisher: His Life and Times*. Norwich: Canterbury Press, 1991.

Carpenter, S.C. *Winnington-Ingram: The Biography of Arthur Foley Winnington-Ingram: Bishop of London, 1901–1939*. London: Hodder & Stoughton, 1949.

Chadwick, Owen. *Michael Ramsey: A Life*. Oxford: Clarendon Press, 1990.

Chandler, Andrew. 'Faith in the Nation? The Church of England in the 20th Century'. *History Today* 47 (May 1997), 9–15.

———. *The Church of England in the Twentieth Century: The Church Commissioners and the Politics of Reform, 1948–1998*. Woodbridge, U.K.: Boydell, 2006.

Clements, Keith W. *Lovers of Discord: Twentieth-century Theological Controversies in England*. London: SPCK, 1988.

Conradi, Peter J. *Iris Murdoch: A Life*. New York: Norton, 2001.

Cornwall, Peter. *The Church and the Nation: The Case for Disestablishment*. London: Blackwell, 1983.

Cox, Jeffrey. *The English Churches in a Secular Society: Lambeth, 1870–1930*. New York, 1982.

Dahl, Roald. *Boy: Tales of Childhood*. New York: Farrar, Straus & Giroux, 1984.

Davie, Grace. *Religion in Britain since 1945: Believing without Belonging*. Oxford: Blackwell, 1994.

Davies, Christie. *Permissive Britain: Social Change in the Sixties and Seventies*. London: Pitman, 1975.

———. 'Religion, Politics, and "Permissive" Legislation'. In *Religion, State, and Society in Modern Britain*, edited by Paul Badham, 319–40. Texts and Studies in Religion 43. Lewiston, N.Y.: Edwin Mellen Press, 1989.

———. 'The British State and the Power of Life and Death'. In *The Boundaries of the State in Modern Britain*, edited by S.J.D. Green and R.C. Whiting, 341–74. Cambridge: Cambridge University Press, 1996.

————. *The Strange Death of Moral Britain*. New Brunswick, N.J.: Transaction, 2004.

De-la-Noy, Michael. *Michael Ramsey: A Portrait*. London: Collins, 1990.

————. *The Church of England: A Portrait*. London: Simon & Schuster, 1993.

————. *Mervyn Stockwood: A Lonely Life*. London: Hodder & Stoughton, 1996.

Driver, Christopher. *The Disarmers: A Study in Protest*. London: Hodder & Stoughton, 1964.

Dudley-Smith, Timothy. *John Stott: The Making of a Leader*. Downers Grove, Ill.: Inter-Varsity Press, 1999.

Edwards, David L. *Leaders of the Church of England, 1828–1978*. London: Hodder & Stoughton, 1978.

Edwards, Jill. 'The President, the Archbishop and the Envoy: Religion and Diplomacy in the Cold War'. *Diplomacy and Statecraft* 6 (1995), 490–511.

Edwards, Ruth Dudley. *Victor Gollancz: A Biography*. London: Victor Gollancz, 1987.

Elmer, Paul. 'Anglican Morality'. In *The Study of Anglicanism*, edited by Stephen Sykes and John Booty, 325–38. London: SPCK; Philadelphia: Fortress, 1988.

Frame, Tom. *Anglicans in Australia*. Sydney: UNSW Press, 2007.

Garbett, Cyril. *The Claims of the Church of England*. London: Hodder & Stoughton, 1947.

————. *Church and State in England*. London: Hodder & Stoughton, 1950.

————. *The Church of England Today*. London: Hodder & Stoughton, 1953.

Green, S.J.D. 'The Revenge of the Periphery? Conservative Religion and the Dilemma of Liberal Society in Contemporary Britain'. In *Modernity and Religion*, edited by Ralph McInerny, 89–115. South Bend, Ind.: University of Notre Dame Press, 1994.

————. *The Passing of Protestant England: Secularization and Social Change, c. 1920–1960*. Cambridge: Cambridge University Press, 2011.

Grimley, Matthew. *Citizenship, Community, and the Church of England: Liberal Anglican Theories of the State between the Wars*. Oxford: Clarendon Press, 2004.

Gronn, Peter C. 'An Experiment in Political Education: "V.G.", "Slimy", and the Repton Sixth, 1916–1918'. *History of Education* 19 (1990), 1–21.

Habgood, John. *Church and Nation in a Secular Age*. London: Darton, Longman and Todd, 1983.

Hart, A. Tindall. *The Country Priest in English History*. London: Phoenix House, 1959.

Hastings, Adrian. *A History of English Christianity, 1920–2000*. London: SCM Press, 2001.

Hebblethwaite, Peter. *John XXIII: Pope of the Council*. London: Chapman, 1984.

Heenan, John C. *Cardinal Hinsley*. London: Burns, Oates & Washbourne, 1944.

———. *A Crown of Thorns: An Autobiography, 1951–1963*. London: Hodder & Stoughton, 1974.

Hein, David. 'George Bell, Bishop of Chichester, on the Morality of War'. *Anglican and Episcopal History* 58 (1989), 498–509.

———. 'The Episcopal Church and the Ecumenical Movement, 1937–1997: Presbyterians, Lutherans, and the Future'. *Anglican and Episcopal History* 66 (1997), 4–29.

———. *Noble Powell and the Episcopal Establishment in the Twentieth Century*. Studies in Anglican History. Urbana: University of Illinois Press, 2001.

———. 'Faith and Doubt in Rose Macaulay's *The Towers of Trebizond*'. *Anglican Theological Review* 88 (2006), 47–68.

———. 'Rose Macaulay: A Voice from the Edge'. In *C.S. Lewis and Friends*, edited by David Hein and Edward Hugh Henderson, 93–115. London: SPCK, 2011.

Hein, David, and Edward Hugh Henderson (eds). *Captured by the Crucified: The Practical Theology of Austin Farrer*. New York and London: T & T Clark / Continuum, 2004.

Hein, David, and Gardiner H. Shattuck Jr. *The Episcopalians*. Denominations in America. Westport, Conn.: Praeger, 2004.

Hempton, David. 'Established Churches and the Growth of Religious Pluralism: A Case Study of Christianisation and Secularisation in England since 1970'. In *The Decline of Christendom in Western Europe, 1750–2000*, edited by Hugh McLeod and Werner Ustorf, 81–98. Cambridge: Cambridge University Press, 2003.

Hennessy, Peter. *Never Again: Britain, 1945–1951*. New York: Pantheon, 1994.

———. *Having It So Good: Britain in the Fifties*. London: Allen Lane / Penguin, 2006.

Heppell, Muriel. *George Bell and Nikolai Velimirovic: The Story of a Friendship*. Birmingham: Lazarica Press, 2001.

Herklots, H.G.G. *Frontiers of the Church: The Making of the Anglican Communion*. London: Ernest Benn, 1961.

Hinchcliff, Peter. 'Church–State Relations'. In *The Study of Anglicanism*, edited by Stephen Sykes and John Booty, 351–63. London: SPCK; Philadelphia: Fortress, 1988.

Holtby, Robert T. *Robert Wright Stopford, 1901–1976*. London: The National Society for Promoting Religious Education, 1988.

Horne, Alistair. *Harold Macmillan: 1957–1986*, 611. London: Macmillan, 1989.

Iremonger, F.A. *William Temple, Archbishop of Canterbury: His Life and Letters*. London: Oxford University Press, 1948.

Jacob, W.M. *The Making of the Anglican Church Worldwide*. London: SPCK, 1997.

Jacobson, Dan. "'If England Was What England Seems": Safety in Spelling Things Out: The Changes of the Last Fifty Years'. In *Times Literary Supplement*, 11 March 2005, 11.

James, E.O. *A History of Christianity in England*. London: Hutchinson's University Library, 1949.

James, Eric. *A Life of Bishop John A.T. Robinson: Scholar, Pastor, Prophet*. Grand Rapids, Mich.: Eerdmans, 1988.

Jasper, R.C.D. *George Bell: Bishop of Chichester*. London: Oxford University Press, 1967.

Jefferys, Kevin. *Retreat from New Jerusalem: British Politics, 1951–64*. New York: St. Martin's Press, 1997.

Judt, Tony. *Postwar: A History of Europe since 1945*. New York: Penguin Press, 2005.

Kemp, Eric W. *The Life and Letters of Kenneth Escott Kirk: Bishop of Oxford, 1937–1954*. London: Hodder & Stoughton, 1959.

———. 'Chairmanly Cantuar'. *Times Literary Supplement*, 10 April 1992, 23–4.

———. *Shy But Not Retiring: The Memoirs of the Right Reverend Eric Waldram Kemp*, edited by Jeremy Matthew Haselock. London: Continuum, 2006.

Kent, John. *William Temple: Church, State, and Society in Britain, 1880–1950*. Cambridge: Cambridge University Press, 1993.

Kirby, Dianne. 'The Church of England and the Cold War Nuclear Debate'. *Twentieth Century British History* 4 (1993), 250–83.

———. 'Responses within the Anglican Church to Nuclear Weapons, 1945–1961'. *Journal of Church and State* 37 (1995), 599–622.

———. 'Christianity and Freemasonry: The Compatibility Debate within the Church of England'. In the *Journal of Religious History* 29/1 (February 2005), 43–66.

Kirby, Dianne (ed.). *Religion and the Cold War*. New York: Palgrave Macmillan, 2003.

Kirk, Peter. *One Army Strong?* London: Faith Press, 1958.

Kunter, Katharina, and Jens Holger Schjørring. *Changing Relations between Churches in Europe and Africa: The Internationalization of Christianity and Politics in the 20th Century.* Wiesbaden: Harrassowitz, 2008.

Kyle, Keith. *Suez.* New York: St. Martin's Press, 1991.

Kynaston, David. *Austerity Britain, 1945–51.* New York: Walker & Co, 2008.

Leslie, Paul. *A Church by Daylight: A Reappraisement of the Church of England and Its Future.* London: Geoffrey Chapman, 1973.

Lloyd, Roger. *The Church of England, 1900–1965.* London: SCM Press, 1966.

Loades, Ann. 'The Vitality of Tradition: Austin Farrer and Friends'. In *Captured by the Crucified: The Practical Theology of Austin Farrer*, edited by David Hein and Edward Hugh Henderson, 15–46. New York and London: T & T Clark / Continuum, 2001.

'Lord Fisher of Lambeth: Former Archbishop of Canterbury'. [Obituary.] *The Times*, 16 September 1972.

Machin, G.I.T. *Churches and Social Issues in Twentieth-Century Britain.* Oxford: Clarendon Press, 1998.

MacKinnon, Donald M. 'Justice'. *Theology* 66 (1963), 97–104.

———. *Themes in Theology: The Three-Fold Cord.* Edinburgh: T & T Clark, 1987.

Mantle, Jonathan. *Archbishop: The Life and Times of Robert Runcie.* London: Sinclair-Stevenson, 1991.

Manwaring, Randle. *From Controversy to Co-existence: Evangelicals in the Church of England 1914–1980.* Cambridge: Cambridge University Press, 1985.

Mascall, E.L. *Saraband: The Memoirs of E.L. Mascall.* Leominster: Gracewing, 1992.

McLeod, Hugh. *Religion and Society in England, 1850–1914.* Basingstoke: Macmillan, 1996.

Mews, Stuart. "The Sword of the Spirit: A Catholic Cultural Crusade of 1940." In *The Church and War*, edited by W.J. Sheils, 409–30. *Studies in Church History* 20. Oxford: Blackwell, 1983.

Moore, Charles, A.N. Wilson, and Gavin Stamp. *The Church in Crisis.* London: Hodder & Stoughton, 1986.

Moorman, John R.H. *A History of the Church in England.* 3rd edn. Harrisburg, Pa: Morehouse, 1994.

Murray, Geoffrey. 'He Is the Great Reconciler'. *News Chronicle*, 21 January 1958, 4–5.

Mutharaj, Joseph. 'An Indian Perspective on Bishop George Bell'. In Chandler, Andrew (ed.), *The Church and Humanity: The Life and Work of George Bell, 1883–1958.* Farnham: Ashgate, 2012.

Neill, Stephen. *The Christian Society*. London: Nisbet, 1952.

Nichols, Peter. *The Politics of the Vatican*. New York: Praeger, 1968.

Norman, Edward R. *Church and Society in England, 1770–1970: A Historical Study*. Oxford: Clarendon Press, 1976.

———. *Christianity and the World Order*. Oxford: Oxford University Press, 1979.

———. 'Church and State since 1800'. In *A History of Religion in Britain: Practice and Belief from Pre-Roman Times to the Present*, edited by Sheridan Gilley and W.J. Sheils, 277–91. Oxford: Blackwell, 1994.

Page, Robert J. *New Directions in Anglican Theology: A Survey from Temple to Robinson*. New York: Seabury, 1965.

Palmer, Bernard. *High and Mitred: A Study of Prime Ministers as Bishop-Makers, 1837–1977*. London: SPCK, 1992.

———. *A Class of Their Own: Six Public School Headmasters Who Became Archbishop of Canterbury*. Lewes: Book Guild, 1997.

Pattinson, Derek. 'Archbishop Fisher: His Life and Times'. *Theology* 95 (1992), 388–90.

Paul, Leslie. *A Church by Daylight: A Reappraisement of the Church of England and Its Future*. London: Geoffrey Chapman, 1973.

Pawley, Margaret. *Donald Coggan: Servant of Christ*. London: SPCK, 1987.

Peart-Binns, John S. *Ambrose Reeves*. London: Victor Gollancz, 1973.

———. *Wand of London*. London: Mowbray, 1987.

Pimlott, Ben. *The Queen: A Biography of Elizabeth II*. London: HarperCollins, 1996.

Porter, Muriel. *The New Puritans: The Rise of Fundamentalism in the Anglican Church* Melbourne University Press, Victoria, 2006.

Potter, Harry. *Hanging in Judgment: Religion and the Death Penalty in England from the Bloody Code to Abolition*. London: SCM Press, 1993.

Prochaska, Frank. *Royal Bounty: The Making of a Welfare Monarchy*. New Haven and London: Yale University Press, 1995.

Purcell, William. *Fisher of Lambeth: A Portrait from Life*. London: Hodder & Stoughton, 1969.

Raven, C.E. 'E.W.B.—The Man for the Moment'. *The Modern Churchman* 45 (1955), 11–24.

Reid, Duncan. Review of *Beyond Colonial Anglicanism: The Anglican Communion in the Twenty-first Century*, edited by Ian T. Douglas and Kwok Pui-lan. *Journal of Anglican Studies* 3 (2005), 126–7.

Richards, Jeffrey. 'The Coronation of Queen Elizabeth II and Film'. *Court Historian* 9 (2004), 67–79.

Robbins, Keith. *England, Ireland, Scotland, Wales: The Christian Church, 1900–2000*. Oxford: Oxford University Press, 2008.

Robinson, John A.T. *Christian Freedom in a Permissive Society*. London: SCM Press, 1970.

Rodd, Cyril S. 'A Great and Godly Man [Geoffrey Francis Fisher]'. *Expository Times* 103 (1992), 288.

Sachs, William L. *The Transformation of Anglicanism: From State Church to Global Communion*. Cambridge: Cambridge University Press, 1993.

Sampson, Anthony. *Anatomy of Britain Today*. New York: Harper & Row, 1965.

Sandbrook, Dominic. *Never Had It So Good: A History of Britain from Suez to the Beatles*. London: Little, Brown, 2005.

Schleiermacher, Friedrich. *On Religion: Speeches to Its Cultured Despisers*. Translated by John Oman. New York: Harper & Row, 1958.

Sisson, C.H. *Is There a Church of England?* Manchester: Carcanet, 1993.

Smyth, Charles. *Cyril Forster Garbett: Archbishop of York*. London: Hodder & Stoughton, 1959.

———. *The Church and the Nation: Six Studies in the Anglican Tradition*. London: Hodder & Stoughton, 1962.

———. 'In Duty's Path: Fisher of Lambeth'. *Theology* 73 (1970), 64–73.

Snape, Henry Currie. 'A Dean and an Archbishop'. *The Modern Churchman*, n.s., 14 (1971), 286–90.

Spinks, G. Stephens. 'World War II and Aftermath'. In *Religion in Britain since 1900*, edited by G. Stephens Spinks, 215–30. London: Andrew Dakers, 1952.

Stanley, Brian and Low, Alaine. *Missions, Nationalism and the End of Empire*. Grand Rapids, Mich.: William B. Eerdmans, 2003.

Staples, Peter. 'Archbishop Geoffrey Francis Fisher: An Appraisal'. *Nederlands Theologisch Tijdschrift* 28 (1974), 239–63.

Sykes, Stephen. *The Integrity of Anglicanism*. London: Mowbray, 1977.

———. 'The Genius of Anglicanism'. In *The English Religious Tradition and the Genius of Anglicanism*, edited by Geoffrey Rowell, 227–41. Wantage: Ikon, 1992.

Taylor, Vincent. 'Living Issues in Biblical Scholarship: The Church and the Ministry'. *Expository Times* 62 (1951), 269–74.

Thomas, Bernard (ed.). *Repton, 1557–1957*. London: Batsford, 1957.

Thompson, David M. 'Theological and Sociological Approaches to the Motivation of the Ecumenical Movement'. In *Religious Motivation: Biographical and Sociological Problems for the Church Historian*, edited by Derek Baker, 467–79. Studies in Church History 15. Oxford: Blackwell, 1978.

Thompson, Kenneth A. *Bureaucracy and Church Reform: The Organizational Response of the Church of England to Social Change, 1800–1965*. Oxford: Clarendon Press, 1970.

Thorpe, D.R. *Eden: The Life and Times of Anthony Eden, First Earl of Avon, 1897–1977*. London: Chatto & Windus, 2003.

Treglown, Jeremy. *Roald Dahl: A Biography*. New York: Farrar, Straus & Giroux, 1994.

Waller, Maureen. *London 1945: Life in the Debris of War*. New York: St. Martin's Press, 2004.

Walsh, Michael J. 'Ecumenism in War-time Britain: The Sword of the Spirit and Religion and Life, 1940–1945 (1)'. *Heythrop Journal* 23 (1982), 243–58.

———. 'Ecumenism in War-Time Britain: The Sword of the Spirit and Religion and Life, 1940–1945 (2)'. *Heythrop Journal* 23 (1982), 377–94.

Wand, J.W.C. *Anglicanism in History and Today*. New York: Thomas Nelson and Sons, 1962.

Ward, Garry. 'Austerity Britain: Jewish–Christian relations in post-World War II Britain between the Church of England and the Jewish Community during the Primacy of Archbishop Fisher 1945–1961'. A Dissertation in partial fulfillment of the requirements of Anglia Ruskin University for the degree of Master of Arts in Jewish-Christian Relations in association with the Cambridge Theological Federation of Theological Colleges. Submitted April 2009.

Warren, Heather A. *Theologians of a New World Order: Reinhold Niebuhr and the Christian Realists, 1920–1948*. New York: Oxford University Press, 1997.

Webster, Alan. 'Fisher, Geoffrey Francis, Baron Fisher of Lambeth (1887–1972)'. In the *Oxford Dictionary of National Biography*, 671–6. Oxford: Oxford University Press, 2004.

Webster, Harvey Curtis. *After the Trauma: Representative British Novelists since 1920*. Lexington: University Press of Kentucky, 1970.

Wedderspoon, Alexander. *Grow or Die: Essays on Church Growth to Mark the 900th Anniversary of Winchester Cathedral*. London: SPCK, 1981.

Weight, Richard. *Patriots: National Identity in Britain, 1940–2000*. London: Macmillan, 2002.

Welsby, Paul A. *A History of the Church of England, 1945–1980*. Oxford: Oxford University Press, 1986.

White, Gavin. '"No-one is Free from Parliament": The Worship and Doctrine Measure in Parliament, 1974'. In *Religion and National Identity*, edited by Stuart Mews, 557–65. Studies in Church History 18. Oxford: Blackwell, 1982.

White-Thomson, Ian H. 'Fisher, Geoffrey Francis, Baron Fisher of Lambeth'. In *DNB, 1971–1980*, 316–18. Oxford: Oxford University Press, 1986.

Williams, A.T.P. 'Religion'. In *The Character of England*, edited by Ernest Barker, 56–84. Oxford: Clarendon Press, 1947.

Wilson, A.N. *After the Victorians: The Decline of Britain in the World*. New York: Farrar, Straus & Giroux, 2005.

Wolffe, John. *God and Greater Britain: Religion and National Life in Britain and Ireland, 1843–1945*. London: Routledge, 1994.

Yates, Nigel. *Anglican Ritualism in Victorian Britain, 1830–1910*. Oxford: Oxford University Press, 1999.

Index

Page numbers in *italic* refer to notes at the bottom of the page.